Growing Up In California

Growing Up In California

Life In The Golden State In The 40's & 50's

Michael B. Barker

Authors Choice Press

San Jose New York Lincoln Shanghai

Growing Up In California
Life In The Golden State In The 40's & 50's

Authors Choice Press
an imprint of iUniverse.com, Inc.

For information address:
iUniverse.com, Inc.
5220 S 16th, Ste. 200
Lincoln, NE 68512
www.iuniverse.com

ISBN: 0-595-19567-9

Printed in the United States of America

For my sons:
The Barker Brothers of Los Angeles

CONTENTS

LIST OF PHOTOGRAPHS

1. Cecil Barker's 1927 Franklin touring car—Vacation snapshot—California Hot Springs (1946)

2. "Mr. & Mrs. Of Radio Fame" restaurant—Publicity photo by unknown photographer—Author on hood of race car, father by radiator with two restaurant cooks—Bakersfield, California (1939)

3. Cecil Barker at home—Family snapshot—Bakersfield, California (1940)

4. Author with mother—Photograph by Bear Studio—Bakersfield, California (1938)

5. Uncle Saint, "Uncle Jack" (holding Helen, author's sister), and Cecil Barker, author's father—Family snapshot—Garden of "Mr. & Mrs. Of Radio Fame" restaurant—Bakersfield California (1940)

6. Marion and Saint Claire Barker—Unknown photographer—Author's Aunt and Uncle—San Rafael, California (1938)

7. Author, mother, and sister Helen—Family snapshot—Backyard of grandparent's (Hobrecht) house—San Francisco, California (1943)

8. Uncle Ed and author after big Christmas dinner—Family snapshot—Hobrecht house, San Francisco, California (1944)

9. Cecil B. Barker, author's father, at age 27—Photograph by Fisher Studio—Los Angeles, California (1927)

10. Author's mother and father, author sitting on piano—Photograph by CCC Studio—Bakersfield, California (1939)

FORWORD

In 1982 I read Russell Baker's best selling book, "Growing Up". It recorded Baker's experiences growing up in Baltimore in the 1930's during the Great American Depression. Baker's book convinced me that I must eventually write about my growing up, not to tell my personal story, but to write about the people, places, and events shaping my generation that would otherwise be unrecorded and unexamined. My journey started 10 years later than Baker's on the opposite coast. Our experiences are as different as Maryland is from California, as hard times are from global war. The Great American Depression is Baker's backdrop. Mine, while culturally influenced by The Great American Depression, is total immersion in World War II. Looking west from Baltimore at our country is a remarkably different perspective than looking east from San Francisco. Further, depression and war have profoundly different social, economic, and technical dynamics; and when viewed from the Pacific Rim the western mind-set adds yet another unique dimension to these American experiences. Western adults imprinted the next generation according to how they saw life, many of their Eastern and European roots pulled out in the move west. These western people unshackled from the old world and the eastern establishment made growing up in California as wide open as the Great Plains they crossed. My hope is that this narrative will reveal something interesting about these times, people, and places. I further hope that many readers will find a transcendental thread of enjoyable common experience.

Each Chapter is a self contained essay about unique individuals and places. This means the chronology of events overlaps among Chapters to some extent. Chapters can be read out of sequence. However, time generally flows from chapter one to chapter ten, from the beginning to the end. Getting to know the characters in earlier chapters will enhance the reader's understanding of subsequent chapters, and if my wishes were to be indulged, also the reader's pleasure.

Friends and relatives still on this journey with me will notice that I have on the rare occasion overcome my normal slavish devotion to fact for the sake of a good story. Accordingly, here and there, I have enlightened reality to produce a clearer sense of the time, the place, and the people; and to offer anonymity to a few saints and sinners, living and dead. Digressions and interpretations are included only to improve the way the narrative captures how it was, growing up in California.

Michael Barker
Warren Vermont
September 2001

PART I—INFLUENCES

CHAPTER I

THE W.C. FIELDS CUPS

LIBATIONS

A stinging September rain ripped across the tops of the Adirondacks on the New York shore, accelerated over the 12 miles of white capped Lake Champlain, and slashed onto the rocky Vermont shore. Four of us cowered in the cockpit. Dressed in yellow slickers looking like miserable drowned canaries, we huddled while WINGDAM'S throbbing engine provided the bass line to the quivering alto line of the wailing northwest wind. We surfed down the face of white rollers, not sure whether the engine or the wind in the rigging propelled us forward at hull speed. Moments earlier, as we got the gun at the finish, WINGDAM broached leaving her on her side with crew clinging to the comings. I asked the crew to get all of the 650 square feet of thrashing sail down, pronto. The sea was so rough all that could be managed was to drop all the canvas on the deck and secure it temporarily with lashings. At least the boat was upright again. Twenty minutes later we ducked behind the lee of Vermont's Shelburne Point and headed for the historic Shelburne Shipyard dock where during World War II wooden-hulled mine sweepers were built. Usually tying up to the dock was accomplished with alacrity, today high wind and rain made the task more challenging. After five hours of racing our hands were puckered and raw; our bodies stiff and fatigued. With energy stimulated by the prospect of shelter and a good drink the crew soon had the bow, stern, and spring lines secure, and the sails neatly furled and covered. WINGDAM settled against the dock, squeezing the big white fenders like giant marshmallows. The protection of Shelburne Point did little to abate the shrieking wind in the rigging. Frequent gusts heeled the 13,000 pound boat, arcing the mast like a giant metronome. The sky turned an ugly purple as the frontal system rolled over us.

Like eager hobbits we plunged down below into the cozy teak paneled cabin of WINGDAM, my Tartan 34 sloop. Struggling and bumping into each other in the confined space, we stripped off our wet weather gear and gathered around the big table in the saloon. I put a leather case containing drinking cups and a bottle of Jack Daniels on the table. The silver cups sparkled as I removed them from their fitted leather case and ceremoniously handed one to each of the three men. I filled each cup. Raising my cup so the light from the oil lamp blazed off the cup I offered a toast to our victory. We all drank, more to drive out the chill than celebrate, at least at first. I refilled the sparkling cups. We toasted our good fortune—no injuries to crew or damage to boat, all the more heartfelt remembering that two boats had tragically lost their masts in the race. Camaraderie and good cheer, founded on a sense of shared survival, permeated each denizen of WINGDAM that afternoon.

Topside the rain drummed on the deck. The wind continued to wail like a banshee in the rigging. Down below we were dry and close, inhaling damp air laced with the smell of wet wool and good whiskey. It was the first time in five hours that we felt safe. Our voices made horse from the necessity of shouting over the roar of wind now returned to normal as we recounted the most exciting moments of the race. We, and I say we, because I was as guilty as the rest, shamelessly concluding that it was our superior tactics and daring boat handling that earned us a 30 second win over our closest rival. Not to offend the weather gods, we offered a proper libation in their honor for our good luck to be on the favored side of the course when the storm front hit. The silver cups so employed were succeeding in driving out all the evil spirits in mind and body, serving the exact purpose for which they were designed. It was then that I noticed a new crew member holding his cup up so it caught the light from the swinging brass oil lamp overhead. He turned it slowly, studying it. "Captain, were did you get these neat drinking cups?" he asked.

"W.C. Fields gave them to my father", I said; as a flash memory of my father's big smile crossed my mind. Maybe it was intentional, maybe not, but I smugly believed that I had crafted an answer that demanded a fuller account. My show business father would have been proud. To him life was show business, only the size and nature of the audience varied. The old saw, "Always leave them begging for more" was his motto. In this case would the bait be taken? While I anxiously waited I topped off each cup held out in front of a smiling wind burned face. The crew obliged. Even the old hands who heard parts of the story before fell into my clutches. The whiskey warmed their bodies, opened their minds, and loosened my tongue. The occasion simply demanded nothing less than a full account. I laid on some junk food, adjusted the wick on the lamp, and began.

W.C. Fields himself, gave my father the cups in 1937 on the condition that they be kept in the glove compartment of his car, a bright yellow, 1927 super-charged Franklin. (see photo #1) The car was my dad's most cherished possession and the only remaining legacy of his days in booming Los Angeles real estate. He had the car custom built. The coach work was done in Italy; the mechanical systems built in the US. A massive six cylinder aviation type air-cooled engine provided more than ample power to the flashy spoke wheels. Lowly exhaust gas was elevated to art, exiting through graceful chromed pipes in the hood to an exposed muffler under the right running board. Sumptuous Italian leather bucket seats overlooked airplane type gauges and switches set in burled walnut. Protruding from the center of the dash was a large lever that controlled a Cyclops spot light mounted between the sweeping fenders. The steering wheel was crafted from American walnut and brass in the same motif as the grips for the floor mounted gear shifter and emergency brake. My father told me he had designed the massive laminated wood and brass controls himself. Flower vases and window shades provided additional comfort for the passengers in the rear seats. Unfortunately, all of these seductive amenities did little to distract Mr. Fields from quickly discovering the vehicle's most distressing shortcoming.

Photo 1—Cecil Barker's 1927 Franklin Touring Car—California Hot Springs (1946)

The occasion was W.C.'s first visit to my father's new residence in Bakersfield. It was a short drive from the train station to my father's house, perhaps 15 minutes. When my father pulled up to the station W.C. recognized the car immediately. He got in greeting my father warmly. He knew my father to be a very fine host, which meant in part that a man could get a good drink whenever he needed one. As they pulled away from the station W.C. was ready for hospitality. My dad opened the glove compartment and pulled out a bottle of gin, Mr. Field's favorite brand. What my dad didn't realize was that W.C. felt that drinking directly from a bottle could lead a man astray. He remained dry the whole trip home for lack of proper drinking cups. When they reached my father's studio and residence where W.C. was to be a frequent guest, W.C. dug into his leather valise and found the ideal present, the very drinking cups that were today gleaming in WINGDAM'S cabin and bringing solace to her crew.

"How did your father come to know W.C. Fields?" asked the same new crew member. "Why did they meet in Bakersfield?" he demanded, aware that I spent much of my professional life in Washington, D.C. , but not knowing that I grew up in California. "It had to do with war, grave illness, and show business", I said feeling a bit like a rapture about to descend on trapped prey. However, scanning the faces glowing in good cheer in front of me and hearing no objections I poured another round, opened two tins of smoked oysters, topped off the bowl of peanuts, and began the rest of the story about the characters and historical events that brought my father and Mr. Fields to Bakersfield that day of the cups; these very cups.

BAKERSFIELD, CALIFORNIA

"Cecil, if you don't leave the cold dampness of San Francisco and the stress of the radio business you'll be dead in 12 months of pneumonia or a heart attack". This harsh prognosis was laid on my father by his doctor in pre-penicillin 1937. He was just 37 years old! At the time my father was the producer and the MC of a popular radio show in San Francisco called "Barker Frivolities", starring among others my future mother. His work schedule was extreme, producing five live shows a week. My father had always worked and played very hard. Before going into show business he made and lost a fortune in rough and tumble Los Angeles real estate. Stressful as that life was, his health problems actually started when he was a very young soldier. At age 17 he enlisted in the United States Marines for adventure and the lack of better opportunities in San Francisco, his hometown. He fought the Bolsheviks through two bitter Siberian winters in America's least remembered, but no less miserable war.

President Woodrow Wilson sent 7,000 US Marines to Vladivostok in the summer of 1918 while World War I was raging in Europe. The US joined the forces of France, Great Britain, and Japan to capture military supplies that had been stockpiled by the Allies for Russian use against the Germans. The Allies suspected the Bolsheviks might use some of the stockpiled weapons, those weapons in excess of what they needed against their own population to secure the revolution, in a swap for German support for their cause, thereby prolonging the "War to End All Wars". The Japanese, on the other hand, had territorial ambitions in Siberia and were happy to have the help of the Western Powers to add to their 72,000 troops already probing for territorial expansion during Russia's political turmoil. The Bolsheviks saw the US Marines as the enemy of the revolution. When World War I ended in November 1919, the Marines in Siberia fought on till April 1920. The youngest and newest Marines, like my father, pulled the most gruesome and loathed duties. My father was assigned the horrible task of picking up the bodies and body parts from the battle field so they could be cold-stored for shipment back to the US. He caught pneumonia twice, once on the battle field in Romonofska on the Siberian plain after spending 48 hours without sleep under fire, and then having to continue on after the engagement picking up seventeen Marine bodies by moon light. His second bout with pneumonia came a short time later back in Vladivostok. He was trapped overnight in a cold storage building for bodies. His sergeant mistakenly locked him inside. Although he was only 18 years old, these sicknesses weakened his heart and made him prone to pneumonia for the rest of his life. Penicillin that could have stopped the pneumonia was not commercially available until 1942.

An honorable discharge from the Marines, a box of medals for bravery, and a weakened constitution summed up Cecil Barker's first 18 years. He decided to study law while living at home in San Francisco. He did well. Two years later he moved to booming Los Angeles to seek his fortune in real estate law. He rose to Vice President of Tatum Realty, one of the largest and best development firms in the LA area. In 10 years he was a paper millionaire. As one of the principal developers of Beverly Hills he became acquainted with many Hollywood celebrities, including W.C. Fields. Then came the crash in 1929. Over the next three years he lost everything, except his car. He was proud of the fact that nobody lost money in his deals, except himself. Broke in 1932, at the depth of the Great Depression, with only the clothes on his back and his cherished Franklin, he headed back home to San Francisco. He had an idea that the Bay Area needed a radio variety show featuring a talent contest for locals. With a stake from show business friends and his own resourceful personality, he sold the idea and went into radio production, one of the few sectors of the economy that had prospects for growth. Mr. Fields may have actually helped my dad with some "walking-around" money in those days, but this is only family rumor. Radio was truly beginning to boom in the Bay Area and throughout the country. The deeper the economy sank into depression, the greater was the need for affordable diversions from the cold hard reality of every day life. Broadcast radio was an emerging technology that needed content. Cecil Barker stepped forward to provide content.

"But how did your father get from San Francisco show business to the backwater of Bakersfield where W.C. gave him these cups?" asked Bob, my old impatient friend and crew who knew something about California geography. I pointed out that Bakersfield wasn't exactly a backwater since I was born there. In the mellow glow of the swaying oil lamp, I opened a large can of mixed nuts, two tins of kippered snacks, poured another round, and continued, while the wind and rain cruelly lashed the deck above our heads creating little incentive for anyone to leave the shelter of the warm cabin and my narrative. Maybe I was exploiting my friends in their relative captivity, but the weather was on my side. The show went on.

While increasingly successful in radio, the damp climate of San Francisco caused my dad to suffer several more bouts of pneumonia and heart seizures. Before long his doctor issued the ultimatum. After a particularly serious case of pneumonia and a related mild heart attack, my newly married father reluctantly decided to leave show business and move to Bakersfield, California, where his sister Burnedette, and her husband, Cal, an oil "wildcatter" lived. My mother had no desire to leave the Bay Area, particularly for Bakersfield, however she urged my father to follow his doctor's orders. She realized Bakersfield had a therapeutic climate. It was also a good stopping place for old friends traveling between LA and San Francisco. It was here that my father built a restaurant, residence, and recording studio.

The steak house restaurant was called Mr. and Mrs. of Radio Fame. (see photo # 2) It was one of the few air conditioned buildings between LA and San Francisco. Each of the booths in the restaurant featured a photo of a star with my dad, usually with a flowery autograph like; "To Cecil, my dear friend, I will visit you often—Bing ". A brass plate bearing the star's name was imbedded in the table. The names read like a "Who's Who" of 1936 show business—the stars of stage, screen, and radio. Bing Crosby, Guy Lombardo, Edgar Bergin, Fred Allen, Jack Benny, Kate Smith, Burns & Allen, Kay Kyser, Don Ameche, Connie

Boswell and of course Mr. W.C. Fields, among many others, had name-sake booths in Mr. & Mrs. of Radio Fame.

Photo 2—"Mr. & Mrs. of Radio Fame" restaurant—Bakersfield California—author on hood of race car, father standing by radiator, with two restaurant cooks (1939)

When old show business friends visited, sometimes in groups, my dad would invite them into his state-of-the-art studio to make a memorial recording. He was very proud of his record collection. (see photo # 3) The recording sessions were strictly private, only for the amusement of the participants. These well lubricated off the record jam sessions often deteriorated into drunken singing, off-color skits, and bad jokes. My record collection still has the recording of a session that featured Guy Lombardo, Bing Crosby, W.C. Fields and my father doing off-color take-offs on popular radio shows of the time. The record sounds quite professional with fade-in and fade-out background music and effects. For authenticity they performed ribald parodies of well known commercials. Field's, a former vaudeville juggler, portrayed drunken, mischievous, and slightly down-at-the-heels characters on the screen and likewise on these home recordings. His private life seemed a close match with his public persona, except he was far from being down-at-the-heels. My father shared some of these endearing qualities with Mr. Fields. Over many years they became good friends.

Photo 3—Cecil Barker at home in Bakersfield, California (1940)

The family living quarters were uncomfortably close to the studio for my abstemious, usually pregnant mother. My mother was often quite upset at the carrying on. W.C.'s well known charming irreverence could not change her opinion that W.C. was a bad influence on my dad—too much booze and off-color humor. The charm part was insufficient to offset the irreverent part.

Whenever she thought she was making real progress at reforming my dad who would show up? None other than W.C. himself to undo all her good work in one night of revelry. I have kept a few of the huge old platters that record the downfall of reform. I eventually gave the rest of my father's collection of these impromptu sessions along with a collection of autographed first presses to the archives of the University of California, my alma mater.

When I was born in 1938, W.C. at least paid some attention. (see photo # 4) I was the untimely first born, and only son of Cecil "Ben" Barker of Bakersfield California. My conception was more than inconvenient! My mother was two months pregnant with me when she was offered the movie part of a singing cowgirl opposite a new comer called Roy Rogers. She knew Rogers from gigs she did on the radio with his old group the "Sons of the Pioneers". This was before he changed his name from Sylvester Sly to the more artful alliteration. Her female show biz friends suggested an immediate abortion. They said that this was a simple and well used procedure. They knew "certain" doctors in Tijuana that could keep her career on track as it had for many other aspiring talents. My mother, a devout practicing Roman Catholic, as anomalous in show business in those days as it is today, reacted in horror and seven months later I arrived! This amused W.C. greatly. Rascally W.C. who normally hated children and animals uncharacteristically accepted me. He was once asked if he liked children. He replied "yes, very much, par boiled". Baby Barker came from naive morality triumphing over ambition, in his eyes. How could that be all bad!

Photo 4—Author with mother—Bakersfield, California (1938)

Mr. Fields, after enjoying a drink with my dad, in a momentary self-delusion of domesticity, offered to assist in my mother in feeding me in my high chair. My mother warned him that he would need to remember his considerable juggling skills. It must have been a trying experience for W.C. His cravat and face got splattered with baby food puree. He used an unkind pornographic characterization of Baby Barker and was summarily and irrevocably banned from feeding duty!

W.C. visited my father in Bakersfield quite often. The problem of getting from the train station to the house was solved by the silver cups. At home my father's hospitality was impeccable. He knew that W.C. placed enormous importance on a good drink—this meant strong and cold. My father kept a coffee can full of ball bearings in his freezer at all times. When W.C. visited the usual ice cubes in W.C's drinks were replaced with frozen ball-bearings to chill the gin without dilution. This greatly delighted W.C. who always knew he could get a good drink, a good meal, and find a kindred spirit in Bakersfield.

The final chapter in the relationship of W.C. with my father concluded when my father had the honor of being cast as W.C. himself in a proposed Warner Brothers movie of the vaudeville life of the great star. Unfortunately, both W.C. and my father died before shooting started; W.C. on Christmas day 1946 at age 66, and my father in the summer of 1948 at the age of 48.

SAVING THE CUPS

I was 10 years old when my father died in 1948. Eavesdropping on the adults I learned that my dad's Franklin was going to be sold to a car collector in Nevada named Harrah. The car was parked in our garage as the estate was being settled. This was my last opportunity to sit in the cool, soft leather seats and play driver. The view from the driver's seat, nothing more than the dark end of the garage, didn't dampen my imagination as I gripped the wheel. Only months before I saw my father's big hairy fore arms vibrating on the great wood and brass steering wheel as we flashed past Bakersfield landmarks. My skinny hairless arms attached to my slight body could barely turn the wheel; I felt quite fatherless. My fantasy drive dejectedly ended with a climb over the brake and gear shifter to the passenger's bucket seat. I peered into the glove compartment and found the drinking cups my father talked about receiving from his friend W.C. Even at 10 years old I knew my dad would not have wanted these to fall into abstemious hands, besides they had great sentimental value, to a Barker who knew the story. The thought of these cups being coldly sold with the car was repugnant—just glove-box junk for the new owner to clean out—or worse, winding up with a relative, not only ignorant of their history, but disapproving of my father and his choice of friends .

I secretly took the cups into protective custody. While I grew up the cups remained in a cardboard box of favorite treasures, like my first Duncan yo-yo, my Diamond Dick gun belt, and my single Joe Dimaggio baseball card. The yo-yo, gun belt, and baseball card are still in the same old shabby box. The cups turned out to be far more useful. They reside in a galley locker on my sailboat for crew refreshment, especially after racing, and to stimulate the occasional opportunity of entertaining new friends with some Barker family lore.

The rain stopped and shards of late afternoon sun streaked through gaps in the fast-moving cumulus clouds. Light flooded into WINDAM's saloon through the cabin ports. I rose stiffly, extinguished the oil lamp, and flung-open the main hatch. The spell was broken. Story time was over. After vigorous hand shakes and back slaps the crew climbed up the companionway ladder and left for their cars to head home. I opened all the hatches to let in the new fresh dry air. As I cleaned up the mess down below I reflected on my father's short 48 year life; all that he was able to cram into it was amazing. With religious ritual I polished the silver cups, placed them back into the leather case, and pleasurably anticipated their next use.

CHAPTER II

A COWBOY REMEMBERED

"UNCLE " JACK

Often I would find the old man reading in his room, slouched in his big oak rocking chair under the halo of an overhanging Mexican wrought iron floor lamp. There was a fit between man and room. The room was honest, spare, natural, orderly, and Western. So was the man.

The room seemed church-like. Not in a religious or monumental sense, but in a tactile and symbolic sense. Like a miniaturized cathedral the light squeezed into the room, not through stained glass, but in strips through natural wood Venetian blinds. The polarized air carried a faint smell of cigar smoke, after shave, and tanned leather, recalling past rituals and pleasures. The altar was on the wall opposite the door, its reredos a river stone fireplace. The smooth stones could have come from any arroyo on any western location where movie cowboys played out their heroic film destiny. The mantel was hand hewn out of an eight-by-twelve craggy oak timber. The craftsman instinctively respected the direction and toughness of the natural grain. It was honest and strong, not beautiful or delicate. The craftsman worked around several prominent knots accepting these imperfections as one would accept imperfections in a man of strength and character. In the traditional place of the cross hung a large framed print of "The Waterhole" by Frederick

Remington depicting four weary cowboys in a little muddy crater holding off a circling band of hostile Indians .

The relics on display said a lot about the man. On one side of the hearth leaned a brass trimmed lever action Winchester model 1873. The rifle that won the West. The blued steel barrel and walnut stock glowed as if just polished. It stood ready for action. On the other side squatted a shiny bulbous brass spittoon, the device making a virtue of something I was told never to do. An Apache rug, its geometric design surprisingly cubist, lay in front of the fireplace on the dark stained pine floor. It was a magic carpet. Over the next several months I would sit at the feet of the old cowboy on that rug listening to fascinating tales of the Old West.

The other furnishings were plain. A large oak chest of drawers crammed against one wall, the top bare except for a small framed photo of two young well-armed cowboys. Astride fine horses, they stared menacingly at the lens, rifles resting across the saddle. Both had drooping mustaches. Their Stetsons were thrown back over their shoulders revealing long dark stringy hair. I learned later from my Aunt Amanda that one of the cowboys was my grandfather, Joe Barker, the other was "Uncle" Jack.

"Uncle" Jack slept in a low single bed, its long side and headboard against the wall. The headboard was made of branches and raw hide. It looked like a primitive giant snow shoe. The bed was covered by a hairy brown and white cowhide displaying the double bar brand. It was easy to imagine the raging howls of the steer and the smell of burning hide as red hot steel pressed on its hind quarter. "Uncle" Jack told me he branded this one himself! Next to the door was a side-alter in the form of an elaborate coat rack, a brace of single-action Colt .45 caliber pistols in tooled leather holsters commanded the most prominent peg. Silver .45 Long Colt bullets sparkled from loops on the belt. A stag handled Bowie knife dangled on a separate peg. Like a cowboy's baldachino, a tan 10 gallon Stetson perched on top of the rack; upside-down to preserve the shape of the brim. To my 7 year old eyes all of the icons for a man of the West were on display and within easy reach.

I didn't get to know "Uncle" Jack until 1944, when I was 7 and he was 82. Some might think that this is a large age difference for one person to become acquainted with another. Surprisingly we seemed to have the most important things in common. He had time. I had time. He knew the Old West. I longed to find out about the Old West. He could comfortably walk about 6 blocks. My permitted range was similar.

Two unrelated circumstances conspired to bring us together, god parenthood and World War II. Uncle Saint, my father's brother, and my Aunt Marion had the uncertain honor of being my Godparents. In this capacity they had two responsibilities. First of all, and most importantly, but of no detectable consequence, they provided backup for my spiritual development. This duty was fulfilled by a greeting card containing a peakaboo money envelope with $5.00 on my birthday and at Christmas. It could be argued that I was living proof that monetary investment alone produced little spiritual results, although I was happy to have Godparents. Later in life my spirituality would be much more costly and ultimately diminished by lack of even greater investment. At least my mother must have been comforted to know that my early spiritual development and my basic goodness could be attained with such a modest amount of cash. The other job of godparents was to fill in for parents should they be out of parental commission. This turned out to be the case due to the war.

My mother, then separated from my father, had to make an emergency train trip to Miami, Florida, where her younger sister, my Aunt Loraine, was having a hard time with her first pregnancy. Jack, her husband, would be no help. He flew a P-51 Mustang over Germany escorting B-17s. He had his hands full just staying alive. Many in the family, understanding the attrition rate for pilots in the European Theater, thought he might never be back, and that starting a family before the war ended was ill advised at best. It was too late for hand wringing. Aunt Loraine would have a baby. My 5 year old sister, Helen, and I temporarily became part of our respective godparents' households; Helen in Oakland with Aunt Anna, and me on the other side of San Francisco Bay, in San Rafael with Uncle Saint, Aunt Marion, and "Uncle" Jack.

Mother knew and liked "Uncle" Jack. (see photo #5) My earliest recollection of any reference mother made to "Uncle" Jack was her calling him a real gentleman. This meant he was respectfully reserved and polite around women, in the cowboy tradition. She was well aware of my youthful delusional interest in the Old West. In a way she was match-making interests, trying to make a virtue out of a necessity. When she told me that I would like "Uncle" Jack it sounded like an order. As it turned out such an order was quite unnecessary.

The word "uncle" is in quotes because the old cowboy really wasn't an uncle to anyone in my family. This was a title of affection bestowed upon him when he moved in with the Barker family in 1915. Not much is known about his past except that he was a cowboy from the late 1880's until 1915 when he left the range and became part of the Barker family. My Aunt Amanda (Auntie) told me that in the old days "Uncle" Jack and my Grandfather Joe Barker rode the range together as fellow soldiers of fortune. She overheard one of their rare conversations about the old days that had to do with gunplay, gambling, and women. Aunt Amanda told me "Uncle" Jack saved my grandfather's life in a gun fight, stimulating my gullible overactive imagination. What happened will never be fully known during those years on the range. We do know that "Uncle" Jack and my grandfather were bonded together for life.

Photo 5—Uncle Saint, "Uncle" Jack (holding author's sister), and Cecil Barker—in "Mr. & Mrs." garden—Bakersfield, California (1940)

THE BARKERS OF SAN FRANCISCO

My grandfather, Joe Barker, left the range for San Francisco just before the turn of the century. He married and became a San Francisco police officer. The Barkers lived in a Victorian house on Clement Street with a cow out back. My grandfather built the pattern book two story house with the help of some carpenter friends. They built well. The house survived the great earthquake and fire of 1906, mainly by being separated from the houses on either side. My Aunt Amanda, who was in the house on the day of the great earthquake, said that the contents flew out of cabinets and off shelves. She said she dove under the kitchen table to escape the airborne dishes only to have to crawl back and forth rapidly to stay under the table as it moved with each shock. Today the house still exists; its gingerbread totally obscured by additions. In the 1930's the front and sides were extended to the property lines. Two shops were built at street level becoming part of the active Clement Street commercial life. Apartments occupied the space over the shops. The house at 438 Clement Street that my grandfather built in 1903 is still there, entombed. Almost a century later, if the encrustation's could be magically removed, Joe Barker and "Uncle "Jack would easily recognize the house where the Barker family lived in 1915.

Before "Uncle" Jack arrived in 1915 , the Barker family consisted of my grandparents, Joe and Clara, my father Cecil, my Uncle Saint Claire, and my Aunts Amanda and Bernadette.

My Grandmother, Clara Calumet Barker had a lot to do with concealing the past of both my grandfather and "Uncle" Jack. She was born into moneyed high society. Nothing was spared on her education and "finishing." She mingled with San Francisco's social establishment. She was expected to marry well. She not only failed to marry "well", but brought disgrace to her class in the process. She abandoned an arranged society marriage at the last minute to elope with a rag-tag, futureless drifter named Joe Barker. Rebelliousness and love conspired to create in later years melancholy speculation and family myth of what might have been. Turn-of-the-century San Francisco high society itself was nouveau riche from the gold rush and held only a precarious grip on a self-conscious respectability. Transgressions were treated harshly. Grandmother Barker spent the remaining years of her life trying to recapture respectability, but ended up redefining it in her terms. She was proud of her working class "officer" husband and four children. Nevertheless she let it be known that it was impolite, if not subversive, to discuss "the past". I knew her in her old age. What impressed me was that she always dressed in a long black Victorian dress with pleated white lace at her throat and wrists. She wore black high button shoes. The first shoes I ever saw without laces. Aunt Amanda had to do-up her shoes each morning with the aid of an ivory handled button hook. She "dressed" everyday no matter how long it took, usually until late morning.

Aunt Amanda, who was 14 years old in 1915, said that no one expected "Uncle" Jack to visit. He just arrived one day with his horse attached to the bumper of a shiny black new Model T Ford. The car turned out to be a present for the family; a gesture she thought consumed the cowboy's last penny. His intention to find permanent accommodation at the Barker house was never questioned. Grandfather told the Barker children that this new member of the family was "Uncle" Jack. He simply moved in. Grandfather built an additional bedroom onto the back of the house for "Uncle" Jack. His horse grudgingly shared the backyard with the family cow.

"Uncle" Jack's handiness with a gun landed him a job as a civilian guard at Alcatraz Military Prison. Each working day he would take the streetcar to the Ferry Building on San Francisco's Embarcadero. From there he caught a launch to "The Rock" in San Francisco Bay. He retired in 1932, 6 years before I was born, and 2 years before Alcatraz became a Federal prison for incorrigible criminals. The Commanding Officer presented him with a fine gold watch. My future father Cecil, who was developing real estate in Los Angeles, took the Southern Pacific night train to attend the retirement festivities.

In 1934 Uncle Saint Claire married and moved to San Rafael in Marin County on the North side of the Golden Gate near San Quentin Prison where he worked. Uncle Saint built a house large enough to accommodate his expected children. He was strong and athletic. He wanted sons. Aunt Marion was petite and considered quite beautiful.

(see photo #6) She wanted a daughter. Unfortunately, they could not have children. Uncle Saint's large house and the warm climate of San Rafael attracted "Uncle" Jack. He move in with Uncle Saint shortly after grandfather Joe Barker unexpectedly died of diabetes in 1939. My grandfather's mysterious early bond to "Uncle" Jack passed onto the next generation when the old cowboy moved to San Rafael. According to my cousin Barbara, "Uncle Jack" contributed to the mortgage payments on the San Rafael house in return for room and board.

Photo 6—Marion and Saint Claire Barker, author's Aunt and Uncle (1938)

My grandmother lived out her remaining years in San Francisco in the family house that Joe built without the presence of a living reminder ("Uncle" Jack) of "the past." Aunt Amanda, who lived with grandmother until she died, said that grandmother was also very happy to get the guns out of the house. On a summer afternoon in 1946 grandmother Barker died peacefully fully dressed in her favorite chair, at 438 Clement Street, ready for her last formal appearance a few days later. At the "viewing" I peered into the open casket. She looked exactly like she did any afternoon, same black dress, white lace, and a sweet contented half-smile on her face. The artful cosmetic smile was a credit to the mortician who lived next door. Before I went up to the alter to view the body, Uncle Saint whispered to me that he thought she was still alive, and that sometimes people were mistakenly buried alive. He asked me how I would feel confined in a small wooden box six feet underground. I knelt down before the casket and watched a long time. She didn't move. During the wake back at the house I overheard Uncle Saint tell my mother as he was pouring himself a second funerary libation, that he was impressed by my long prayer at the casket. He attributed my religious zeal to his influence as my Godfather.

In his youth Uncle Saint was an athlete. He belonged to the Olympic Club marathon swim team. He swam the Golden Gate, timing the tides just right so as not to be swept out sea. On one occasion he misjudged the tide by an hour. Luckily the crew of a salty old Monterey style fishing boat returning late against the tide due to engine trouble, saw him departing the Bay heading for the Onion Patch at six knots on the ebb tide. He was hauled out of the 54 degree water by the incredulous Italian captain who would simply not believe that anyone would willingly swim in the brutally cold water. So repulsive was the sea that no one on the boat could swim or had ever been in the water. Maybe it was because Uncle Saint had such a warm heart that he could tolerate the cold water. He also had a keen sense of humor. He liked kids, and he particularly liked to play jokes on them. For 34 years he was employed as a prison guard at San Quentin, the prison named for a point of land jutting out into San Francisco Bay near San Rafael.

San Quentin Point was an unlikely place for a prison. It was there mostly by accident. During the gold rush one of the many abandoned clipper ships that plagued the San Francisco waterfront was towed to Point San Quentin to temporarily house an overflow of prisoners from the San Francisco jail. Soon the ship became overcrowded; its hull began to rot. Faced with the prospect of sinking the prisoners were not unenthusiastic when pressed to construct a stone cell block on San Quentin Point for their accommodation. By 1944, San Quentin was the largest prison in California. Uncle Saint's guard job was considered "critical" so he was one of the few men in the family not on active military duty. The fact that I would have two professional guards on my case during my stay in San Rafael was not lost on mother! Two weeks after "D Day"(June 7, 1944), mother piloted her 1936 Hudson Terraplane across the Golden Gate bridge, drove 14 more miles to San Rafael, and dropped me off at Uncle Saint's. The next morning she boarded a train in San Francisco bound for Miami, Florida.

The popularity of cowboy film heroes that emerged in the 1930's carried right into the war years. Radio shows for kids on Saturday morning also propagated the genre. It was not only politically correct, but somehow expected, male children would play cowboys and Indians. To some extent adults used the make believe world of cowboys and Indians to shield kids from the real-world horrors of the war raging in Europe and the Pacific, where fathers fought for their lives in conflicts unfathomable to young minds. Cowboy heroism as interpreted by John Wayne, Randolf Scott, and John Ford emblazoned every neighborhood silver screen. The good cowboys always won. Unfortunately, in the real war many fathers and relatives, good and bad, never came back. The tinsel heroes stood for the fantasy of the American Way. There were white hats (good guys) and black hats (bad guys). I childishly adored the simplistic western heroes and role models cranked out by Hollywood. At Christmas and birthdays I received gifts that furthered the delusion with six-shooter cap guns, chaps, and spurs. I pretended to be a cowboy, talked incessantly about cowboy screen heroes, and played cowboys and Indians with friends. No kid wanted to play an Indian due to the inevitable ending of the game. One Christmas I received an Indian warriors feathered headset and a bow that shot rubber tipped arrows that at least temporarily condemned me to the "other" side. Thinking fast, I decided to play the good Indian, Tonto, and kept my cowboy guns on as a supplement to the bow. The Indians won that day!

To get to know a real cowboy, even if he was very old and "retired" from the range, was a real opportunity. The pistols and rifle I saw in his bedroom were all the proof I needed of "Uncle" Jack's authenticity and his vast knowledge of the Old West. While the ancient cowboy's virtuosity with tall tales of the West was well known in the Barker family, his patience with an inquisitive kid had not been tested. It would be! Uncle Saint, wearing his guard uniform, left for work early each morning. So did Aunt Marion. She made parts for hand grenades and land mines in a small defense plant just off Highway 101 a few miles north of San Rafael. It was "Uncle" Jack's lot to be my caretaker those long, hot, Marin summer days.

UNCLE SAINT'S HOUSE

San Rafael was still rural in the 40's. The Golden Gate Bridge opened Marin County to potential commuters to San Francisco in 1937. Before that commuting was by ferry. Towns like Tiburon and Sausalito, directly on the Bay, were suburbanized to some extent. Those some distance from the ferry docks, like San Rafael, San Anselmo, and Navato had little time to suburbanize before the war stopped virtually all housing construction in 1941. Uncle Saint's house was on a corner near the edge of town; the edge being defined by the end of paved roads, sidewalks, and utilities. Apricot orchards abutted the property on the rear boundaries. The house sat on a half acre of a former orchard, as if the farmer split off a piece of land for a family member with minimum damage to the productive orchard in mind. The front yard had a formal lawn, ornamental shrubbery, and two mature tulip trees. I remember the trees only because "Uncle" Jack and I were assigned the chore of raking and burning the fallen leaves in the gutter. In the back yard a spacious flagstone patio served as the outside living space during the hot summer; a necessity in warm weather before affordable air conditioning. Six vestigial apricot trees shaded the patio.

The house was a single story classic 1920's bungalow. Colorful blue, white, and green striped canvas awnings projected over the South and west facing windows to intercept the ubiquitous hot Marin County sun. On the west side, running the full length of the house, was a large screened porch, its last 8 feet enclosed to make a small bedroom. The tiny eight by eight foot porch bedroom was mine for the summer. It was spartanly furnished with a sagging steel framed cot in one corner, a small painted chest under the window, and a battered chrome and plastic kitchen chair near the door. The door to the patio was at the opposite end of the porch from my bedroom. About midway was the door to the kitchen. It was always open. The spacious country kitchen was entered directly from the porch. This was the main family room. All meals except for Sunday dinner were eaten in the kitchen. Most family business transpired at the long checkered oil cloth covered table in the center of the room.

When I arrived the apricots were ripening. As the summer progressed, more and more fruit fell off the trees onto the patio creating a slippery mess of rotten fruit. The fruit was so abundant it was not possible to pick it all for eating or canning. As the sun warmed the flagstones millions of ants surfaced through the joints to feast on the rotting fruit. My first regular household chore was to hose-off the patio each morning. It was more fun than work. I took off my shoes. Too bad the ants were biters. When the larger ones bit a red welt would appear that stung at first, then unmercifully itched. Aunt Marion kept telling me not to scratch, but like the old family dog, Buck, it was instinctive and unavoidable. I attacked the ants blasting them and fallen fruit off the patio with a high pressure stream of water, killing millions I thought. Whatever guilt I had about my ruthless extermination of the ant enemy was forsaken by the itching welts on my ankles and knowing I would confront even more ant divisions the next day.

The center piece of outdoor furniture was a giant, awning covered glider swing. Under its cushy padding and striped canvas lurked an armature of steel. It sported a fully adjustable sofa-like seat suspended on springs for a ride comparable to being in a glider sailing in soft cumulus clouds. The canvas canopy shielded the occupants from the sun, falling apricots, and the very rare rain shower. The mattressed seat was long enough for an adult to stretch out on. Many afternoons "Uncle" Jack would nap in the glider while old Buck did the same in its large shadow. I was instructed to never make noise or otherwise disturb "Uncle" Jack when he was napping, signified by his Stetson tipped over his face. Impatient, I watched him for long periods looking for signs of life, as I did at grandmother's casket, only he eventually moved to my great relief.

Twelve mature apricot trees in two orderly rows occupied most of the rest of the back yard, remnants of the former orchard. The trees if they could speak, would certainly have expressed their displeasure at being cut off from their brethren in the main orchard by an intruding residential board fence. Like their cohorts in the orchard, all the Barker trees had their trunks painted white with an insecticide to discourage ants from climbing up to eat the apricots. The balance of the lot accommodated a large 20X60 foot victory garden, an unpainted garden/wood shed, and a substantial two car garage with a workshop in one end. Growing and preserving food, particularly vegetables, was patriotic, partly necessitated by unintended consequences of wartime Government Policy.

The Japanese American "truck farmers" who grew most of the commercial produce for the San Francisco Bay Area before the war, were rounded up and sent inland to Nevada desert internment camps as security risks. This applied to not only foreign born Japanese, but to the US born second generation nisei as well. Virtually all the fruit and vegetables consumed year round by the Barker household, their neighbors, and everyone else in the Bay Area, had to be grown in their own yards. The abundant apricots were canned and made into preserves. Everyone in the household was expected to labor in the victory garden. I watered and weeded. Perhaps the biggest sacrifice I made for the war effort was eating vast, or what seemed like vast, quantities of victory garden abundance that I heartily disliked, such as rhubarb, egg plant, kale, and squash. Aunt Marion heaped this stuff on my plate without mercy. She said it would make a man of me, put hair on my chest, and keep me regular. Of the three, regularity was the only detectable benefit. We all craved meat. There was very little. What there was, was rationed by the government and Aunt Marion. On Sunday, as a reward for going to church, Aunt Marion celebrated the Sabbath by cooking roast beef or chicken for the main meal to be taken in the luxury of the dining room. "Uncle " Jack slept-in on Sundays, didn't go to church, and celebrated just the meal part of the Sabbath. Seemed unfair. Unfortunately, respect for the Sabbath, the holiest day of the week, could not prevent some form of apricots sneaking onto the Sunday menu, such as chopped, stewed apricots in cream for desert.

The cool dry basement of the house was entered from an exterior stair. A few light wells admitted feeble illumination to the otherwise dark, cavernous space. Two big black commercial gas stoves, a pair of large sinks, a refrigerator, and two 8 foot long preparation tables left little doubt that this was a place for work. Shelves lined all available wall space displaying glass Mason jars of preserved food. The place had an eerie feeling, like a deserted canned fruit museum. On canning days the basement turned into a fiery factory production line. Neighbors brought fruits and produce from their victory gardens for communal canning. There were as many as 5 or 6 people working on the production line at one time. The smell of cooking apricots, berries, tomatoes, and rhubarb overwhelmed the nose and stayed in clothes for weeks. One time Aunt Marion asked me to fetch a Mason jar of apricot preserves before breakfast. I surprised a red-eyed black rat when I opened the door. We both froze for a second before scampering in opposite directions, non the worse for the encounter. No doubt the encounter was more memorable for me than the rat. Uncle Saint said he regretted hearing that I let fresh meat get away so easily.

There were two cars in the garage, a gray 1934 Ford coupe, "her's", and a blue 1940 Hudson four door sedan, "his". Most families had one car, used by the husband to get to work. However with Aunt Marion working, and no public transportation available she needed a car. Combined, their war-time gas rationing allotment was twelve gallons per week. If they were careful this would be enough to get to work using some car-pooling and leave them with gas for a weekend drive and possibly a camping trip to Yosemite. The ubiquitous automobile was a basic transportation necessity; but more than that, a symbol of the reality of American spatial and economic freedom. The Hollywood film based on John Steinbeck's 1939 Pulitzer prize winning book, "The Grapes of Wrath", was selected by the Russian Communists Party propagandists to show American poverty and capitalistic decadence. Instead, the Russian peasants who saw the film were astounded that the Okies and Arkies had cars, decrepit as they were, and could drive wherever they pleased. The social unjustness portrayed in the film did not seem out of the ordinary to them. Eventually the film was banned as pressures to immigrate to the US increased! To the Barkers, their cars were an integral part of their "American Dream."

The Hudson was the car I rode in the most. I clearly remember sitting on the itchy mohair seats scratching my bare legs staring at the eye level (for me) simulated wood dashboard. Uncle Saint was very proud of his streamlined Hudson. It had the latest technology, including headlights recessed in the fenders, a radio in the dash, and a gear shift on the steering column. He serviced the cars himself. It was not unusual on a weekend to find him leaning over a fender tinkering with the "super six" engine. Once he let me "help" him change the oil. I got so much oil and grease on my shirt (I only had two) that Aunt Marion forbid me any further mechanical work, a slight burden since the workshop part of the garage was far more intriguing.

There were many interesting tools, all serviceable. Broken tools and any scrap metal was collected monthly by neighborhood volunteers for the war effort. There were a few shiny new tools, but not many, due to the high cost and shortage of steel. Plumber's wrenches, mechanic's sockets, carpenter's planes, saws, hand drills, and an array of clamps and jacks invited experimentation, particularly in a kid with little exposure to real tools. An ancient hand cranked stone grinder with a three foot wheel was a special delight. When it was at top speed the exposed square cut gears whined like the siren on a fire truck. I found an old rusty horse shoe near the woodshed, obviously overlooked by the collectors. It was nailed over the rickety door upside-down to hold good luck, but it fell off and into my hands. I pressed it against the spinning stone. My reward was five seconds of showering sparks in the dim light—a valuable lesson in inertia and metallurgy that literally sparked my later interest in things mechanical.

ENTERTAINMENT

Today the average kid watches TV five hours a day. Not having a TV was a blessing in disguise in 1944. Those five hours were available to do other more important things. Many enjoyable hours were filled with getting to know an old cowboy and listening to his stories. If TV were available, both "Uncle" Jack and I would have been shortchanged; me because I would have gullibly watched five hours of forgettable programming and missed a great opportunity to get to know a truly remarkable old man; and "Uncle" Jack, because without an audience, he would not have had the pleasure of reliving his stories by the retelling. Of course there was commercial entertainment in Uncle Saint's house in the form of radio and records. Most evenings the lack of evening programming of interest to kids, and the adults only control of the knobs, sent me to bed early without protest. There I read five cent "Batman" and "Superman" comics till I fell asleep.

After dinner, and the after dinner chores, if it wasn't too hot in the house, the adults would typically take seats in the living room around the mahogany Packard Bell console radio/record player. When they listened to a program they stared blankly at the console, like it was a TV, or a box actually containing the performers. If a commentator said something he disagreed with, Uncle Saint shouted his reply at the cloth covered speaker. Every member of the family had a special place, unlike at home, where the choicest seat went to the most fleet of foot. Uncle Saint sunk into his exclusive leather club chair with a woosh of air escaping vents in the massive cushion. He propped up his shoeless feet on its matching ottoman, feet fatigued from hours patrolling hard concrete cell block floors. He could reach the Packard Bell controls on one side, and his smoking stand on the other. There he sat, master of the household, enthroned, his cigarette smoke curling up through the shade of an onyx based floor lamp. There was never any question of who was in charge. "Uncle" Jack took his regular overstuffed chair deferentially placed out of range of the controls, near the bookcase and magazine stand. Aunt Marion sat on the couch, a coffee table separating her from the controls. Her hands were always busy knitting and sewing through conversation, music, and radio program. Visitors would sit on the couch, or on extra chairs drawn up to the inner circle. This was unquestionably an adult time. People and things were in their proper places. This microcosm of order and tranquility in a small house in San Rafael,

California, was repeated in millions of other American households, a ritual rebuke of the war and chaos that raged throughout the world.

Ironically, the first radio priority was war news and commentaries. Edward R. Murrow's static flavored reports from London were not missed. Two weeks before I arrived in San Rafael, on June 7, 1944, 175,000 Allied troops landed on Normandy beaches in the first D-Day wave. Twenty-four hours later 6,500 American soldiers were dead on the beach. By June 30, 1944 there were 413,000 American troops in Normandy pushing the German defenders back having already suffered 40,000 casualties. Uncle Saint kept maps of Europe and the Pacific handy to follow the progress of the Allies. Censorship kept the family from knowing exactly where relatives and friends were fighting. Occasionally I would stay up and listen to Jack Benny and Allen's Alley. Most of the humor was over my head, but the adults enjoyed it. Eventually, I had my own exclusive place, a smallish arm chair, at the fringe of the inner circle, near a separate mahogany cabinet where the collection of 78 rpm records was kept. To my delight, some of the album covers depicted sujaro cactus and cowboys. Being aware of my cowboy fantasies, Uncle Saint would occasionally play a Tex Ritter or Gene Autry record I brought to the top of the pile. My favorites were "Tumbling Tumbleweeds" and "Don't Fence Me In." To me these were authentic songs of the romantic West. Later I learned that "Tumbleweeds" was composed by an unemployed caddie from Bel Air Country Club during an LA wind storm that kept the golfers away. Likewise, "Don't Fence Me In" was written by that quintessential non-cowboy of Tin Pan Alley, Cole Porter.

A baby grand piano of undistinguished lineage sat forlornly in the darkest corner of the living room. It was draped with a mangy tapestry throw on which sat a small bronze reproduction of Auguste Rodin's "The Kiss". The sculpture was more important as mass than art. It kept the throw from sliding off. No one in the house played the piano. It was a relic inherited from Aunt Marion's family. She was forced to practice on this very piano as a child and hated making music ever since. She knew my mother wanted me to play the piano, and that mother herself was attempting to teach me. So Aunt Marion went about trying to find lessons for me so when mother got back I would have progressed. This was a very close call. Fortunately, no professional instruction was available in the neighborhood that summer since the local piano teacher joined the WACS (Women's Army Corps). I couldn't figure it; to teach the soldiers piano? I imagined waves of poorly played Steinways advancing on the Japanese lines. Hardened Imperial troops, on hearing Gershwin, panic and commit Hari Kari. It never happened. I told Aunt Marion about my fantasy. She explained the patriotic piano teacher went to war to find a patriotic husband with good post-war job prospects.

FRIENDSHIP AND FIREPOWER

Soon after I arrived in San Rafael a rhythm in lifestyle began. The family rose early and ate breakfast together in the big country kitchen, usually hot oatmeal mush with an apricot preserve topping. Uncle Saint and Aunt Marion rushed off to work after breakfast. This left "Uncle" Jack and me to leisurely attend to the "victory" garden, the apricot mess, and other chores. Aunt Marion left sandwiches in the refrigerator for our lunch. We all had dinner together exactly at 6:00 P.M. The best part of the day began after dinner.

Most weekday evenings after dinner 'Uncle" Jack and I would take a walk to the neighborhood park. The best time for a walk was in the cool of the evening. "Uncle" Jack wore his big Stetson and leather vest. Folks recognized him. People paid their respects when he passed. I was very proud to walk next to such an imposing figure. Buck, the old family dog, a medium sized shepherd of mixed pound pedigree, would join us. Most of the day he slept. Whenever the word "walk" was spoken in his earshot in the early evening he would get very excited. I came to realize that both "Uncle" Jack and Buck looked forward to the walks for similar reasons. As soon as we left the yard "Uncle" Jack would pull out a big after dinner cigar, sniff it from end to end, and light it succulating in a cloud of pungent smoke. In Buck's case he would sniff from street tree to street tree for his olfactory after dinner delights, usually leaving his sign for the pleasure of the next dog.

The park was just 4 blocks from the house. If I was lucky I would be the beneficiary of the right pocket of "Uncle" Jack's leather vest. He always wore a gold chain slung between his vest pockets. Attached on the left was his gold engraved Hamilton watch. Attached on the right was a big gold nugget, a souvenir from his cowboy days. He also kept his small change in the nugget pocket. It was uncanny. He always seemed to have a nickel available at the crucial time of the walk, when we passed the Good Humor Truck. The Good Humor man stationed himself in the shade of the mature elm trees park-side to serve his regular after-dinner customers. "Howdy Jack" said the Good Humor man enthusiastically, like greeting a well-liked old friend. "Uncle" Jack told me he knew the Good Humor man a long time ago when he was an inmate of Alcatraz. Maybe he was kidding. To play it safe I always was very respectful to the Good Humor man. These walks brought great joy to the three of us. "Uncle" Jack and Buck got the best smells of the day, I got a Popsicle, and we all enjoyed each other's company.

One Friday evening when we returned from our walk "Uncle" Jack asked me if I would like to help him clean his guns. Aunt Marion shouted to us as we left the living room for the kitchen; "be careful Jack"! Ever since I saw the guns I wanted to get my hands on them. I had never touched a real gun. Toy pistols seemed so phony after I saw the real thing in "Uncle" Jack's room. "Uncle" Jack ceremoniously removed the holstered guns from the rack and brought them into the kitchen for disassembly and cleaning on the kitchen table. He carefully checked to make sure they were not loaded. Taking one, he cocked the hammer a few times, spun the cylinder, then handed it to me butt first. It was a

Colt Peacemaker chambered for .45 long Colt. The unexpected heavy weight of the gun took me by surprise. My unsuccessful efforts to pull back the hammer were embarrassing for an aspiring gunfighter. My imagination raced on anyway. There I was, confronted by a marauding band of Indians out to kill the peaceful settlers. The only thing between the settlers and death was me with my trusty .45's. Naturally the kid won the day and peace returned to the range.

My fantasies were interrupted by "Uncle" Jack handing me an oily rag. He asked me to carefully wipe the blued metal until it shone brightly. As I polished I noticed two carved notches in the walnut grips. I asked the obvious question. Who were these notches for? Did Uncle Jack dispatch an outlaw or two? He thought for a while, probably assessing whether the truth would be too ordinary for an inquisitive kid. I had visions of a dusty street with "Uncle" Jack walking slowly toward a group of cold blooded killers out to rob the bank where all the townspeople had their life's savings. People cowered behind closed doors and occasionally peeped out a window to watch their defender, too afraid themselves to challenge the outlaws. Then the roar of gunfire broke the dusty silence of the street. Hot lead streaked toward flesh and bone. When the smoke cleared the tall cowboy stood there with his twin .45s still pointed toward where the bad guys had stood. They were all down. He returned the mighty weapons to their holsters and pulled his gold watch from the left pocket of his leather vest, the very same leather vest he wore now. Still before noon he thought, not a bad morning's work.

"Uncle" Jack brought me back to reality by saying it was my bedtime. At that moment I would have done anything for "Uncle" Jack, from standing by him in a shoot out to even going to bed. However, before heading out to my porch room I asked again for the story behind the notches hoping it would be as good as my imaginary gunfight. He promised to tell me the whole story before my stay was over.

The next afternoon, when the chores were done, "Uncle" Jack fetched a big pitcher of lemonade from the refrigerator that Aunt Marion made the night before. He placed it on the table in front of the glider with two ice-filled glasses. It was hot! After wiping the sweat from his brow and the inside brim of his Stetson with his ever ready handkerchief he poured both of us a frosty glass of lemonade. I reminded him of his promise of the night before. We sank into the glider clutching our drinks. He wore his Stetson and leather vest. No matter how hot it was he always wore his hat and vest! The glider creaked as we settled in. He began to speak — slowly, as if assaying words like they were gold nuggets, to be valued properly before dispensing. And the words were rich, igniting my imagination syllable by syllable.

INDIAN JOE AND THE LOST TREASURE

He said it was a hot day on the range, a lemonade day, like the past week in San Rafael had been. That afternoon the cowboys finished branding stray dogies near Ogallala, a cattle town with numerous saloons, rickety wooden buildings, cattle holding pens, and dusty streets. Ogallala's excuse for existing was the Oregon Trail. Settlers moving West needed to resupply here for the trip over the Rockies. The town got its second big boost when the Union Pacific Railroad established a rail head in 1880 to bring cattle to market in the East. "Uncle" Jack said he hired on with a local rancher who needed extra hands to ready his herd for market. The Double Bar Ranch spread out 20 miles north-west of town on the North Platte River. He said he gladly left the small second floor hotel room where he stayed between jobs. Tonight he would camp on the plain with twelve other cowboys. He always liked to be camped out in the summer when the stars in the sky were so clear that it seemed you could pick them off with your Winchester, one by one, constellation by constellation.

This night was the beginning of one of his great adventures in the Old West said "Uncle" Jack. It started out ordinary enough. The men prepared their bedrolls after caring for the horses. They always slept with their heads on their saddles and a coil of lariat around their bed rolls to keep the rattle snakes away during the night. Even in the summer the high plain nights could become quite cold. Many a cowboy woke in the morning with a rattler or two curled up with him trying to stay warm if he forgot the lariat trick. The lariats had horse hair that bristled. The snakes didn't like the feel of it on their bellies; it tickled. "Uncle" Jack said that because rattle snakes couldn't laugh, they were very careful not to cross the lariats.

The cook had prepared the chuck wagon the previous week with extra victuals because he knew the men would be working very hard. This night he cooked his special chili made with fresh steer meat from one of the lame steers that had to be put down that morning. He spent the day butchering beef, salting most of it and packing it in casks for future meals. He was hot, tired, and in a foul temper. An oozing bloody rag wrapped tightly around his left hand covered a nasty cut taken when his knife slipped on a bone.

The cowboys knew the cook to be as short tempered as a startled rattle snake. They also knew he was a very good cook, a talent rare in those parts. This offset his irascibility in the eyes of the cowboys. He also had a great respect for Indians, even taking a squaw for a wife at one time. He did not tolerate any unkind or bigoted comments about Indians. The trail boss said the cook was one of the few white men to ever see the Sioux do their ghost dance, a surreal ritual the Sioux believed would restore their traditional way of life by bringing the buffalo back to the plains.

Most of the cowboys knew that back in 1889 the cook was a scout for the Seventh Cavalry when they attacked Chief Big Foot's Sioux band at Wounded Knee. It was a massacre. He shielded a young hysterical squaw from the rampaging troopers. They lived together in town for a while, under the yoke of the slights of townspeople obsessed with hatred and the fear of Indians. Unfortunately, she was killed the next year in the cross fire of a bar room gunfight. That's when the cook left town for good to work the big herds. The men trusted his cooking and trail savvy. His knowledge of Indian ways came in handy when renegade Apaches were on the warpath. The men treated him with exaggerated respect and "kid gloves" so as not to set him off.

At sundown the dusty tired cowboys gathered around the fire to eat. They scooped up huge portions of chili from the boiling kettle. Everything went along fine until "Cookie", as the cowboys called him, offered the men a special treat. That morning the Train Master of a passing wagon train traded Cookie a keg of whiskey for a side of beef. Cookie brought out the keg. The cowboys filled their tin cups with the throat burning "redeye", attempting to quench their great thirst after the day's hot work. The fiery whiskey was consumed at an alarming rate. Soon the crowd became boisterous and then a little insane. A normally quiet half-breed named Charley called Cookie an insulting name, something to do with his dead Indian wife. Cookie went berserk! He grabbed the offender by the shirt and threw him into the fire. He crashed through the metal cooking frame knocking over the caldron of chili. The half-breed went for his gun, but not before Cookie drew his. Four point blank shots echoed in the canyon. The half-breed died before he hit the ground. The cook wreathed on the ground mortally wounded clutching a crimson hole in the belly of his dirty collarless shirt. Any wound to the gut was fatal, it just took time, very painful time. They bound up the cook's midsection with clean rags and a lariat. That night the cowboys kept watch over the dying cook in turns. At three in the morning it was "Uncle" Jack's turn to watch over the dying man.

He lay there on the sandy earth, his head propped on a saddle, softly groaning. He motioned to "Uncle" Jack to come closer. The cook could barley be heard. "Uncle" Jack put his ear up to the cooks mouth to hear the cooks last words. First he said he wanted to be buried out on the plain with his boots on. "Uncle" Jack agreed. Second, he wanted "Uncle" Jack to avenge the death of his old cowboy friend Tex who was killed by Indian Joe last year while searching for treasure. Before "Uncle" Jack could answer, the cook hesitatingly went on and said that there was a map showing the location of the lost treasure of the Apache in the chuck wagon. It was "Uncle" Jack's for killing Indian Joe. Without saying another word the cook choked up blood, convulsively heaved in a breath, exhaled gangrenous fumes, and lay still. He was dead.

"Uncle" Jack told me he was not a gunslinger and had not agreed to kill Indian Joe, but he did have an interest in the lost treasure. At first he thought the tales of treasure were just a way for cowboys to end a boring day of hard work with a little fun. But after hearing the treasure story around countless camp fires "Uncle" Jack's curiosity and imagination got the best of him. The cowboys had a tradition of telling "tall" tales. Could Cookie's death-story be true? The legend said the Apache originally acquired the treasure by massacring one of the regiments of Coronado in the Sierra Madre in Mexico. The Spanish regiment was sent to hide the plunder of the great Spanish conquistador rumored to be gold bars, silver ingots, and the gold vessels of Montezuma's Court. The Apache brought the treasure to the Southwest Territories and later to the high plains. The Apache had little use for treasure. They took it to deny others it's possession until they discovered the gold could be traded for horses and rifles. After only a few trades a smallpox epidemic hit the tribe. The medicine man said it was caused by the evil spirits in the white man's treasure. He said the treasure's bad medicine would prevent any rifles acquired from the treasure's gold from shooting straight. In addition to the white mans curse, the treasure was also a logistic burden, slowing down the rapid movement of the nomadic tribe. The Chief had only one choice. He ordered the treasure to be hidden forever.

To insure the total secrecy of the location of the treasure, the Chief entrusted the task of hiding it to his oldest son, Running Fox. The plan was to take two braves to the hiding place; hide the treasure, then Running Fox would kill the braves to keep the secret. Just before they left, Running Fox learned from his mother that his father, the Chief, intended to kill him on his return to assure absolute secrecy. Running Fox had no choice. He had to obey his father, but after hiding the treasure and killing the braves he ran away. Nothing more is known about Running Fox except that before he died he drew a map of the treasure's location. It was suspected that Cookie took the map off of a dead Indian at Wounded Knee. "Uncle" Jack knew that Cookie made several attempts to find the treasure. Each time he failed, almost losing his life on each attempt. The last try cost the life of his good friend, Tex.

"Uncle" Jack and the other cowboys dressed the cook in his best clothes and buried him on the plain with his boots on. As was the custom, the cowboys divided the worldly possessions of the cook among themselves. He had no known family or relatives. The cowboys all respected this tradition. They believed that the spirit of the dead cowboy would live on in the lives of their comrades as they used the dead cowboy's gear. Drawing by lot, "Uncle" Jack was third to select an item. The guns and saddle had been claimed. He always admired the cook's Bowie knife with the stag handle. He took the knife and told the cowboys about the cooks last words. No one wanted the map or anything to do with Indian Joe, a well-known renegade Apache killer.

The next week "Uncle" Jack on his horse Blacky left the Double Bar Ranch and his cowboy friends to search for the treasure. The night before he left, the cowboys cooked him a hearty farewell feast. With the crackling campfire lighting each of their leathery faces, each cowboy solemnly removed a .45 caliber cartridge from his gun belt and handed it gravely to "Uncle" Jack in the remote hope that theirs would inflict the fatal wound to Indian Joe. In this modest way the cowboys confirmed their solidarity and became a small part of avenging a cowboy's death.

It was now getting near supper time. Aunt Marion told us it was time to wash up. The story was over for the moment — to be continued the next day. "Uncle " Jack reached into his vest pocket and asked me to open my hand. He reverently placed a heavy .45 cartridge in my outstretched hand. It was tarnished, not shiny like those on his gun belt.

Yes, he said, it was one of the bullets given to him by one of the cowboys long ago.

After dinner we took our languid walk to the park —"Uncle " Jack puffed on his cigar, the smoke curling around him before vanishing into the warm evening air. He bought me an ice cream pie. We sat down on a park bench and enjoyed the tranquility of sunset while thousands of miles away, both to the East and West, family members waged war in Europe and in the Pacific. It could have been on that very evening that Uncle Jack Phelan, flying his P-51 Mustang, raked the hedgerows of Normandy with his six .50 caliber machine guns in support of the D Day landings. It could have been on that very evening that my future step-father was huddled behind a landing craft's steel ramp as it plowed to the beach on Tarawa with the first wave of Marines. In retrospect the sweetness of our oblivion was total! Buck, contentedly sprawled out under the park bench below us, matched our mood, but then he always lived for the moment. The next afternoon "Uncle" Jack continued the story.

The treasure map lead Uncle Jack Southwest. He rode down the backside of the Rockies passing through Fort Collins, Denver, Pueblo, and finally linking up with the Santa Fe Trail at Trinidad. It was late summer and just beginning to cool off a bit. He camped out as he traveled, preferring the range to primitive hotels and frontier city life. He also preferred the company of Blacky to the kinds of people he would likely encounter in the hotels and cafes he could afford.

He rode the Santa Fe Trail south to its terminus at Santa Fe, in the New Mexico Territory. Here he picked up the old Spanish Trail that headed northwest. He wanted to cross the continental divide before the first snow. This would be the only area where the high altitude might bring him foul weather. He crossed the divide at Jicarilla.

Near the top of the pass he met a grisly old gold prospector heading east for Santa Fe. The white haired, bushy bearded old man was leading a heavily loaded sad looking pack mule bristling picks and shovels. "Uncle" Jack asked the smiling toothless prospector to camp with him for the night. They were both glad to have company. This was Indian territory that the prospector knew well. "Uncle" Jack wanted to be on the alert to any news about hostile Indian activity. Traveling alone had its advantages in dangerous territory. He could move quickly and left little sign for trackers. The downside was not being able to keep watch at night.

They built a small camp fire in a depression so it would not be seen. The men shared "Uncle" Jack's last bottle of whiskey, most likely the only bottle of whiskey within hundreds of miles. They both took many long pulls on the amber liquid turning the trail dust in their mouths to mud, then to a polluted river of sediment that washed down their parched throats. The old prospector finished the last drop with a mighty satisfying deep swig. So refreshed, the prospector became talkative, overcoming his usual caution on the trail. They both knew that only the cautious survived where they were. He proudly showed "Uncle" Jack a big gold nugget he found near Durango. He admitted that beyond the nugget, after 6 months of prospecting he only had a few ounces of panned gold dust and a sore back for all his work and risk. The prospector told about a renegade Apache band lead by Indian Joe. He was the son of the great Nez Perce Chief Joseph who lead the last free roaming band of the Nez Perce Nation. In 1877, after being harassed by the 7th Cavalry and beset by famine and disease, Chief Joseph spoke the famous line: "My heart is sick and sad….I will fight no more forever". He and all the Nez Perce Nation were forcefully placed on reservations in Oklahoma, with the exception of the Chief's son by his Apache wife. Indian Joe (as he was called by the white man) escaped. He recruited a band of Apache warriors and continued to fight, mostly preying on hapless settlers and wagon trains. The place called Four Corners, where four states now meet, Utah, Colorado, New Mexico, and Arizona was where Indian Joe resourcefully evaded military expeditions sent out to capture or kill him. The prospector said this place was very dangerous and that he would never go there. This place had thousands of hiding places in blind canyons and rocky labyrinths said the prospector. Unfortunately, this is where "Uncle" Jack's map was taking him.

In the morning "Uncle" Jack wished the prospector good fortune as they each headed in opposite directions, the prospector to the east, "Uncle" Jack to the west. The first landmark on the map to the west was the "Rock With Wings." The Navajos named the rock for a legend that the rock took off, soaring onto the heavens saving the trapped Navajos on top from their enemies below. Now this place is known as Ship Rock. The formation protrudes from the high plain and appeared to be a ship in an ocean to the early settlers heading for California. After a long days ride "Uncle" Jack camped at the base of Ship Rock. He was bone tired, having ridden over 30 miles. As he skirted the dry Mancos River he saw many Indian pony tracks. He was wary and didn't want to stop. He once saw smoke in the distance, possibly an Indian sign. These of course could be peaceful Indians or Indian Joe's dreaded band.

Late that night he was awakened by a strange bird call that he recognized as an Indian signal. There were several more bird calls from different directions. Blacky, pawed the ground showing he was getting nervous. Silently "Uncle" Jack rearranged his bedroll to make it appear that he was still asleep. He then slipped on his boots, strapped on his guns and grabbed his Winchester. He concealed himself under an overhanging rock nearby. In the distance a coyote howled. "Uncle" Jack said he never felt more alone.

That was all for this evening. "Uncle" Jack liked to keep me in suspense . This is how it went, chapter by chapter, day by day, week by week. The only real break that Uncle Jack had was his regular visit to the local saloon. Every Saturday the old cowboy would spend 4 hours by himself at the saloon quenching his thirst. I was never allowed to see what actually went on in "that place" as my Aunt Marion called it. I did know that it was very special.

In preparation "Uncle" Jack would take a leisurely morning bath. Then he shaved. Usually he left the bathroom door open so the steam from his earlier bath would not obscure his image in the big mirror over the sink. The stropping of the straight razor echoed down the hall, alerting me to the ritual about to begin. There were three leather strops hanging from the bathroom wall. He always knew exactly which ones to use. With a special brush he lathered up his face and neck until all that could be seen were two sparkling blue eyes and a craggy nose. I watched as he skillfully maneuvered the shiny steel straight razor through the white foam covering his craggy face. He gripped his nose with his left hand to turn his head to the right angle. Miraculously the engraved steel blade took the whiskers and not the face! After the whiskers were cleanly shaved off he slapped his face with a pungent lotion from a fancy corked bottle. Sometimes he would dab a little lotion on my outstretched hand. I would gingerly rub it onto my disgustingly smooth cheek. I craved for whiskers and a straight razor. After shaving he put on a starched white shirt with a detachable collar so stiff that I couldn't see how he turned his head without being cut by it. He wore a dangling black string tie, a dark brown western cut suit with leather accents, and polished cowboy boots. Topped off by his big Stetson he made a very fine sight!

He didn't drive so my Uncle Saint or Aunt Marion would punctually take him to "that place" in the tenderloin part of town every Saturday. I often went along for the ride in the big Hudson, but I was never allowed to get out of the car. I yearned to see what went on inside that mysterious place with the studded leather door and dark windows. They never let me go on the trip to fetch Uncle Jack. He would not join us for dinner on Saturdays. Sometimes Uncle Saint helped him to bed. While the Barkers were not teetotalers, they took their godparenting as seriously as "Uncle" Jack took his libatious outing. It was morally incorrect for children to observe the consumption and effects of alcohol. The way I figured it, because of "Uncle " Jack's great age, wisdom, and heroism on the range he was allowed this mysterious worldly gratification by God.

The story continued.

They attacked! Three Apache arrows pierced the bedroll as Indians approached from three sides with war hoops. Blacky was going crazy. "Uncle" Jack leveled his .45's on the three warriors from under the ledge as they cautiously approached what they thought was the dead body of a cowboy. The .45's roared. Two Indians died instantly as the 275 grain slugs cut through flesh and bone. The third Indian lay on the ground with a gaping wound in his leg, tomahawk still in his hand. "Uncle" Jack knew that had he not heard the bird signals his scalp would have been hanging from this Indians belt having been roughly removed by this mean looking tomahawk. Fearing other Indians "Uncle" Jack remained silent and in place. The wounded Indian struggled.

A sinister silence crept back over the camp. The bird call was heard again, only this time it seemed farther away — then the sound of horses galloping in the distance. The Indians had left their comrade to die rather than risk trying to save him. "Uncle" Jack thought back to a time when other cowboys got him out of a jam; they would never let one of their own die at the hands of a foe, particularly an Indian brave.

"Uncle" Jack carefully circled the camp, from rock to rock to make sure the other Indians had left. He then approached the camp and disarmed the wounded warrior who had crawled 100 feet into the rocks. He was easily found by the trail of blood. The warrior gave up his weapons after a persuasive blow to the head from the butt of "Uncle" Jack's Winchester. He bound the Indian's wound while he was still unconscious.

At daylight "Uncle" Jack buried the dead and released the wounded warrior to fare as best he could. He gave the Indian matches so he could light a signal fire. The other warriors took all of the ponies figuring the cowboy would kill the remaining wounded brave. From this experience "Uncle" Jack knew that he was in very dangerous territory. He would have to be very careful to cover his trail and plan his camps defensively. His next landmark was Black Mesa where the treasure search would begin.

The story had to be continued because Uncle Saint and I were invited to go boating on San Francisco Bay by Everett. Everett was a prison guard at San Quentin and the Captain of "SEA SHARK". I was very eager for adventure on the water. The name "SEA SHARK" conjured up visions of tall ships like the one in the old oil painting over the fire place in the living room—a fiery Maxwell Parrish sky back lighted the "CUTTY SARK" slicing through steep , white-capped waves at full speed . Aunt Marion packed us a lunch and we were off. The boat was tied up to a rickety drift-wood dock in a tidal slough just off Highway 1 to San Francisco. The slough doesn't exist now. The whole area was filed in the 50's and developed as a shopping center. The first sight of the "SEA SHARK" was a disappointing shock. The "SEA SHARK" turned out to be a shabby, home built 20 foot plywood cabin cruiser. Its source of power, like much of its equipment came from wrecked cars. The floorboards in the cabin were floating. When I unsuspectingly stepped onto them they sank, filling my shoes with a mixture of salt water and oil. While my Uncle and I pumped and bailed the Captain removed a greasy tarp that covered an exposed car engine and coaxed it to life by poring gas down the carburetor throat. I was instructed to stay clear of the engine since parts of it were very hot and the whirling pulleys and belts might easily take off a finger or hand. I found a safe corner and grabbed hold. Captain Everett in his wool watch cap and navy surplus pea coat looked very salty. He skillfully steered the "SEA SHARK" out of the slough, increasing my confidence , that just maybe, power boating might be as much fun as sailing in a clipper ship. He looked impressive man-handling the old car steering wheel attached to clothesline pulleys that controlled the rudder. When we got to the bay he added more power by forcing a small wedge of wood farther into the carburetor linkage on top of the engine.

The Bay was rough that day. The wind tore the whitecaps off the tops of the famous San Francisco Bay chop. Icy spray came over the bow . The plywood hull oil-canned into each trough. In the smaller waves the

Captain expertly ducked the flying water. Then we hit the big mid-bay waves. We all got soaked. I went into the cabin, but had to come back on deck because I was thrown about like a bouncing basketball. When the bow dropped off a big wave there was zero or reverse gravity. I hit my head several time on the overhead. The little craft plowed on. Uncle Saint suggested that we head for Mare Island where there was shelter from the wind and some interesting old wrecks to explore. We headed for an anchorage behind a big mud flat that had many hulks on it. Captain Everett let go the anchor, a rusty exhaust manifold from a Chevy pickup. Remarkably it held! We were about 150 feet from the shore. The low tide exposed the massive rusting iron cylinders of a Fairbanks diesel between the plankless ribs of an old lumber coaster. A short distance away, the "walking beam" of a derelict ferry poked the sky. Looking up I saw the bridge door of a listing freighter swinging in the wind revealing glimpses of peeling paint and signal tubes. The rough boat ride was quickly forgotten by the prospect of exploring the intriguing wrecks.

Uncle Saint asked if I could swim. I said no. He said he would teach me. I didn't realize that Uncle Saint was of the school that believed all animals and humans swam instinctively. We put on our swimming suits. When I came out of the cabin Uncle Saint effortlessly picked me up and tossed me into the cold, murky water. I distinctly remember that frozen moment in time when I was still in the air hoping his theory was correct. I quickly proved his theory incorrect. I thrashed the water in terror. He jumped into the 5 foot deep water and carried me to shore. The wrecks were interesting enough, but I was worried about the return trip to the boat. The great Olympic Club swimmer carried me on his back. It was like riding on a whale. Uncle Saint seemed disappointed by the failure of his favorite nephew to confirm his theory of swimming instruction. He prudently put a mildewed orange life jacket on me for the return trip.

We had lunch on the bobbing boat, and what a great lunch it was! Aunt Marion packed jumbo Spam sandwiches, pickles, potato salad, cookies, and soft drinks. We all ate heartily. The men drank beer. The Captain teased my Uncle about my swimming ability and the instruction method. On the way back to the slough it was still very rough, although we were now going with the waves. Uncle Saint sent me below so I wouldn't fall onto the engine . It didn't take me long to become seasick, throwing-up on the Captain's sleeping bag. When he saw what had happened, he glared at me in disgust. This partially offset the obvious pleasure Captain Everett took in watching my swimming lesson. All-in-all my first boating experience was enough to eliminate any interest in boating, swimming, and ship wrecks. The allure of the dry Old West was assured, at least for that summer.

The next day after lunch "Uncle" Jack continued the story. He sat in his oak rocking chair. I sat on the Apache rug,

His keen black eyes surveyed Marsh Pass from the rim of Black Mesa. He was on the lookout for patrols from the 7th Cavalry. He knew they would come through the pass soon after they found out that his braves killed an old prospector and the settler family he was visiting at Jemez Springs, near Santa Fe. His ten braves returned with the scalps of two blond children, two brown haired adults and a woolly white trophy from an old prospector. More importantly they brought back three repeating rifles, ammunition, and dried food. These supplies would help sustain his band for another month.

Indian Joe was puzzled by the story of a wounded brave who turned up several days after the raiding party returned. He said a tall well armed cowboy let him go after the raiding party killed his sleeping partner. He was surprised that he wasn't killed by the cowboy. Indian Joe wondered what the cowboys were doing in his territory. He wasn't pleased that two of his braves were lost in the attack on the cowboys. He thought back to the previous year when he killed one cowboy and chased off another. They seemed to be looking for something, but they were not prospectors. They were looking for something else, perhaps the rumored treasure of the Apache. He was unaware of the possible connection his father might have had with the treasure map. He was sure he would not let anyone scout his territory lest his security be compromised. This was the last free place for Indians in the Southwest, at least for his band of 23 outlaw braves. As the white man continued to settle in the region his space was shrinking. The homesteaders were easy prey, but being forced to kill the white man to survive increased the pressure on the cavalry to attack him. For six years he managed to evade the Cavalry. He knew when they came, where they were, and either hid from them or ambushed them on his terms inflicting many casualties. A single skilled stalker was a more serious threat because he would be harder to track.

Sooner or later, there had to be a showdown between the relentless cowboy and the ruthless renegade, or I didn't know my "Uncle" Jack.

Chore time! The weeds in the victory garden beckoned. The story would continue . The next afternoon I was back on the Apache rug for the next installment.

"Uncle" Jack traveled at night now, relying on his compass and the stars for navigation. He slept by day wherever he could find cover and shade. It was dry barren country, good for rattle snakes, coyotes, and spiny cactus. The treasure map lead to a large box canyon that ran east/west on the rim of Black Mesa. The sandy floor of the canyon was strewn with large boulders. Uncle Jack proceeded cautiously, doubling back from time to time to see if he was being followed. This was Indian country! An ambush could be expected if a clear trail was left. He set up his own ambushes on his own trail several times without any takers, save for a curious coyote that sniffed its way into his gun sights. He had the sinking feeling of being trapped. He knew quite well that there was no way for him to escape the canyon if discovered.

When he approached the end of the canyon he studied the map and terrain. The map showed an "x" on the rim of the mesa on the south side and a "x" on the wall of the canyon opposite. "Uncle" Jack carefully scaled the south mesa. When he reached the mesa rim he found no landmarks that would be probable treasure locations. The ground was solid rock. Huge boulders were scattered at random. That is when he came to the idea that the treasure may not be on this side of the canyon, but rather on the opposite side. But why the two "X" marks?

After a long search he found a faint horizontal scratch on a boulder. This was the first sign of possible human presence in the canyon. More searching revealed another boulder close by with a horizontal scratch. He lined them up like a rifle sight. In one direction they pointed to the sky. In the opposite direction they pointed to a spot on the opposite side of the canyon, about half way up where the other "X" was marked on the map. He sighted in on a small rock strewn shelf completely hidden from the canyon floor below. He thought this would be an excellent hiding place—very hard to get to and invisible from any normal vantage point. He was confused though because the box canyon wall was pure rock, making it impossible to dig a repository for treasure. The next morning after a sleepless night he scaled the north side of the canyon where the primitive rock sights pointed.

The climb was difficult! It was 10:00 am before he reached the shelf. He searched the whole shelf carefully, even crawling under the small patches of manzanita brush for signs of human activity. Nothing. He was becoming discouraged. He took a swig from his canteen and ate a piece of jerky. He began to study the pattern of boulders on the ground out of boredom. The rocks always laid on their largest surface. He noticed one that seemed to defy this rule. It was tipped up against the canyon wall and was almost invisible due to overgrowth. He took his shovel and excavated around the rock until he could move it. To his amazement he discovered a small natural tunnel behind the rock. This might be it he thought, as treasure fever gripped him!

He squeezed his tall frame into the hole. It was dark! He felt his way along. The tunnel turned right and opened up into a larger chamber about 60 feet long where he could stand. It appeared to be a natural formation. The floor was sandy. Since the cave turned there was no light from the entrance to illuminate the larger chamber. He lit a candle. The cave had smooth dry walls. There were no signs of human presence in the cave, even the sandy floor was smoothed by decades of tiny mouse feet. He reminded himself that the rock was positioned in front of the opening concealing it as only a human would. He started to dig in the sandy cave floor. After an hour of hard labor his shovel hit a fragmented wood plank. This was a sure sign that humans had been in this place. In a semi-frenzy he dug until the whole floor of the cave was explored to the sandstone bed rock. It was now late afternoon; he slumped against the cave wall exhausted. Still no treasure.

There I was left hanging again. It was time for dinner and the treasure was within "Uncle " Jack's grasp, if there was one. "Uncle " Jack said that he would continue the story the next day after the apricot picking was done.

Indian Joe and his band had been tracking the lone cowboy for three days. It had been difficult to track the elusive intruder. The Indians could not catch up because "Uncle" Jack hid his tracks, retraced his tracks, and set up false ambushes to slow any would be followers. Finally, on the fourth day the Indians found Blacky hidden in mesquite brush at the foot of the box canyon. There would be no escape now for the cowboy without his horse. A fight was sure to ensue.

The band spread out to look for signs showing where the cowboy went. After several hours they found the ledge and the entrance to the cave. Indian Joe told his braves he wanted the pleasure of dealing with the cowboy himself. He also thought that if this was a treasure hunt, he wanted all the treasure for himself. The band obediently returned to the canyon floor to wait by the horses. Indian Joe drew his pistol. He turned the cylinder slowly, checking to make sure the gun was fully loaded. An instinctive fear of the evil spirits that all Apache know live in the underworld gnawed at him. He took a final look out over the canyon as the sun slipped behind the rocky rim. Like a cat stalking prey, he bellied to the ground and cautiously pulled his powerful body through the opening.

"Uncle" Jack was sitting quietly so he was able to immediately hear the Indian as he entered the cave. He knew he was trapped. He extinguished the candle and stealthily moved to the very end of the chamber. Now it was pitch dark leaving only smell, sound, and touch. The two men could hear each other breathing. "Uncle" Jack was relieved to hear only one Indian in the cave with him. Indian Joe smelled the candle smoke. Uncle Jack smelled Indian Joe. They were not able to locate each other by sound because of the echo from the concave ceiling. Uncle Jack eased his .45's out of the holsters and pointed them in the direction of the entrance. Indian Joe had his pistol at the ready listening for any sign of the cowboy. Both men realized that the flash from either of their guns would give away their positions and unless the first shot was fatal the second shot would be from the enemy with deadly effect. They both unsheathed their knives. "Uncle" Jack silently slipped out Cookie's Bowie knife thinking that he would not be here in this mortal danger, and he would not have to use this very knife if that senseless fight back at the ranch had never happened. There was no escape now. Indian Joe and "Uncle" Jack knew this would be a bloody hand-to-hand fight to the death. A slight advantage was with 'Uncle' Jack because he knew the size and shape of the chamber.

"Uncle" Jack tried an old Indian trick. He tossed his shovel toward the Indian hoping to draw his fire or hear some motion. The shovel landed with a deafening crash against the far wall of the cave. The Indian didn't move. With a .45 in his left hand and his Bowie knife in his right "Uncle" Jack moved toward the silent crouching Indian. The Indian slashed out first cutting him on the arm. "Uncle" Jack responded with a plunge and miss as both men rolled away from each other on the sandy floor. There was only one chance for the cowboy. He fired all six rounds as blood gushed from his limp right arm. The flashes briefly illuminated the cave. The combatants lost contact and all went silent.

The breathing of two men could still be heard. One was wheezing and began to cough, then stopped breathing. "Uncle" Jack remained silent for several minutes until no sound was heard. This could be a trick he thought. He smelled human blood, probably his own, he thought. He knew he had to attend to his wound soon. Blood was soaking his shirt flowing like an artery had been severed. He cross drew his other gun with his good left hand, cocked it, and leveled it at the last place he saw the Indian. Painfully he lit a match with his bloody right hand. There was Indian Joe leaning up against the opposite chamber wall. He was dead with 3 hunks of deformed lead in his chest; perhaps the underworld spirits were on "Uncle" Jack's side after all.

"Uncle" Jack needed a thong for a tourniquet to stop his bleeding arm. He crawled over to Indian Joe and cut a leather thong from India Joe's neck with his Bowie knife. The thong had a gold nugget suspended from it. "Uncle" Jack recognized the nugget as the one the old prospector showed him two weeks earlier. Might make a nice watch fob someday, he thought. He tied the thong tightly around his arm. The bleeding stopped, but he was not yet out of danger. The rest of the band was probably waiting outside the cave.

In the end it was Indian Joe's greediness and the evil spirits of the underworld that saved "Uncle" Jack. All of the rest of the band obediently remained at the foot of the canyon wall. In addition to their leader's orders, none of them wanted anything to do with the evil spirits of the underworld. Of the many faults that Indian Joe had, the lack of courage was not one of them. "Uncle" Jack dragged Indian Joe's bleeding body out of the cave by a limp muscular arm, an arm that had to its credit countless scalps. He rolled it to the edge of the precipice and pushed it over. In a bounce, skid, and a roll it came to rest fifty feet the from the waiting braves. Seeing that their leader was slain the braves lost the will to continue the fight. They dejectedly departed with the remains of Indian Joe draped over his pony. All the spirit had gone out of them. They seemed a forlorn bunch as "Uncle Jack" watched them

silently disappear down the soft canyon floor into the growing dark-
ness. "Uncle" Jack felt sad, not only because there was no treasure, but
more profoundly because he killed the last real leader of free Indian
warriors on the plains. He had killed part of the "wild" west and part of
himself. Melancholy was not part of his nature, but he realized he accelerated the passing of an era, and that his cowboy world, and the open
range was itself passing into history.

"Uncle" Jack retrieved Blacky and rode for Santa Fe. He thought as he
rode of a story he heard one night in a Durango saloon—many of
"Uncle" Jacks best stories came from the denizens of saloons. His
Saturday excursions to the saloon in San Rafael were merely research.
The story told of a wealthy Apache living in luxury in the West Indies
off a stash of gold. "Could this have been Running Fox?" he asked
rhetorically as he lifted his creaking body out of his rocking chair. There
were many mysteries in the Old West that never would be solved, and I
could see that "Uncle Jack' was not about to attempt any further specu-
lations at dinner time. As for "Uncle" Jack, he told me he was never
tempted again to seek hidden treasure as we both headed for the
kitchen table.

FAREWELL TO THE SUMMER OF '44

My army surplus duffel was packed for the return home. It was late
Saturday morning. "Uncle" Jack had bathed, shaved, and dressed for his
trip to "that place". Uncle Saint would drop the old cowboy off at the
saloon on our way to San Francisco. No need for a separate trip on
rationed gas. I felt sad to be leaving and also eager to get home.

Uncle Saint rolled out the big blue Hudson. The "super six" on rich
idle, spit out noxious liquids from the chrome tail pipe. Aunt Marion
saw us off. She gave me a cardboard box full of apricot preserves in
Mason jars for mother. Looking at all those jars reminded me of how

sick I was of picking apricots, cleaning up apricots, and eating apricots. It appeared that I would not be spared gastronomic patriotism for the next several weeks.

As we headed for the tenderloin the sweet smell of shaving lotion wafted through the car. "Uncle" Jack looked and smelled his best! We pulled up in front of the saloon. "Uncle" Jack and I both got out since I wanted to ride in the front seat the rest of the trip. He bent down and hugged me. His steel blue eyes looked into mine. I almost cried, but remembered that there were two notches. I solemnly asked "Uncle" Jack about the second notch. He drew himself up to his full height and said "that was another story". He tipped his Stetson and went through the studded leather door. That was the last time I saw "Uncle" Jack. He died in his sleep the next winter in the bed with the cowhide bedspread under the gaze of the cowboys still holding off the Indians.

The Hudson purred passed the slough were the " Sea Shark " was tied up, then across the Golden Gate Bridge. The fog was thick to the west out toward the "Onion Patch". On the bay side the sky was clear. White caps sparkled against the gray hulls of anchored war ships off Treasure Island. It was an ending and a new beginning.

My Aunt Marion died unexpectedly in 1951 of a virulent form of cancer. Uncle Saint died in 1960 of a heart attack. When Uncle Saint died I was an Architecture student at The University of California at Berkeley. The family asked me to be a pall bearer. The ornate metal coffin with big Uncle Saint in it was extremely heavy. The other pall bearers were all burly prison guards from San Quentin. When one of them stumbled we almost dropped the casket going down the stairs of the church. I imagined Uncle Saint getting a good laugh out of our toil. My mind flashed back to the summer of 1944 when Uncle Saint took me to the prison for a haircut. On the way he said that the trustees who worked in the prison barber shop were usually careful when they used the straight razor in the final shaving of the neck. But, sometimes they slipped, he said, particularly if they didn't like you, and they didn't like anybody who moved when they were cutting their hair. In explaining how sharp the razors were, Uncle Saint said one poor fidgety man didn't know his throat was cut until he tried to turn his head. That image was enough for me to sit as still as I could during my haircut. It was a win/win situation. I got a good haircut and Uncle Saint got a good laugh. Even though I was the brunt of many of Uncle Saint's jokes, I already knew I would sorely miss my Godfather.

After burying Uncle Saint in the family plot next to Aunt Marion the immediate family returned to the house. I hadn't been back for many years. The apricot orchards were all gone. New subdivisions surrounded and pressed in on the bungalow. Was it my imagination or was the house, like the apricot trees shrinking away? My room still looked the same, but smaller. I searched for the glider. Rusted metal framing and springs behind the garage seemed to be the only remains.

As the relatives dealt with the business of dying in the living room I continued to explore. I entered the basement. My head almost hit the floor joists overhead. The stoves were still there, rusty and obviously not used in years. No preserves were in sight, just empty dusty Mason jars on filthy shelves. There were stacks of boxes full of junk scattered about. My Aunt Amanda, who seemed to be in charge, had been sorting real junk from stuff that Good Will might pick up. In a corner where she had yet to sort was a small wooden box with papers and a cigar box jammed in one side. I pulled out the cigar box, opened it, and found five tarnished .45 pistol cartridges and a photo of "Uncle" Jack taken with my mother in 1937. In the photo they were sitting on a big log. Uncle Jack had on his leather vest. He held his big Stetson on his lap. Mother wore a print dress. I dug deeper. There under old magazines and books lay the stag handled Bowie knife that belonged to "Uncle" Jack, the knife he acquired from Cookie all those years ago. It was still in its tooled scabbard. I rushed back to the living room and asked Aunt Amanda if I could take these as a remembrance of "Uncle" Jack. She said that all that old stuff was going to the dump anyway, so why not?

In the process of settling the estate, Uncle Saint's house in San Rafael was sold to a developer. It was torn down a year later and the property re subdivided. Five new houses were built. Like the passing of a ship over an ocean, who's wake inexorably disappears leaving no physical trace, the lives of the Barker's and "Uncle" Jack passed through San Rafael, leaving no physical trace, only these memories recorded here.

CHAPTER III

UNCLE ED

VICTORY AT SEA

Humid salt-air blasted down the SARATOGA'S 800 foot flight deck. The venerable 36,000 ton carrier, her keel laid by workers of the New York Ship Building Company in Camden New Jersey in 1923, shuddered as she drove into the oncoming South Pacific seas at thirty knots. Originally intended to be a heavy cruiser, but converted to a carrier in 1927, the SARATOGA was the first "fast" carrier in the US Navy. Now, 21 years after her construction, she had just played a major role in defeating the Japanese Imperial Forces at their main supply base in the Pacific. Only one of her aircraft was still airborne.

War weary sailors stood at their battle stations in gray life jackets and steel helmets, they steadied themselves as the SARATOGA pitched and rolled. On the bridge Rear Admiral and Captain, Frank Fletcher alternately paced and squinted through his binoculars. His Squadron Leader was still out there. On deck, the Landing Signal Officer's orange jumpsuit audibly snapped in the wind. Like the conductor of a apocalyptic orchestra, he stood vivid against the sky, flags ready for action. The missing Squadron Leader's "ground crew" huddled like cowed dogs under the edge of an anti-aircraft gun-turret; four men ready to rearm and repair Eddie's F6F Hellcat, that is if he could put it on the pitching deck. Could he cheat death again, they wondered. Fire suppression teams and "Airedales" were ordered on deck.

It was late Sunday afternoon, February 18, 1944, one more vicious, but decisive, day of warfare between the combined Imperial Japanese forces and the US 3rd Fleet. The target had been Truk Island, the Japanese Gibraltar of the Pacific. In the past 24 hours the SARATOGA lost 12 of its best pilots. The ship itself took two hits from Kamikaze Zeros. The superstructure was damaged, but the critical teak planked flight deck and the old hull survived unscathed. Now, only one plane remained out there, shot-up and running out of fuel.

The SARATOGA plunged on into the rising white-capped seas, an ominous squall line bearing down. It was almost sunset. There would be only one chance at recovery for the Squadron Leader, assuming the maimed airplane held together long enough to reach the carrier. The Admiral nervously turned to his Exec and said, " If anyone can land a lame Hellcat in a nasty squall it would be Eddie ."

At first only a speck appeared on the horizon slightly behind one of the picket destroyers cruising two miles astern. The speck grew in size. It was leaving a faint trail of smoke. The destroyer identified it as crippled Hellcat 476. The Executive Officer announced the good news through a bull horn so the gun crews would know the craft was not hostile. With a sense of relief the Kamikaze-nervous gun crews clicked on their safeties. Emergency landing procedures were ordered. It was clear that the pilot was having control problems and engine trouble. The tail and rudder were shot-up. The starboard stabilizer was shattered, a section dragging by control cable. Smoke streamed from the starboard cowling. The engine coughed, surged, and sputtered.

On board Hellcat 476 the pilot dropped the landing gear, pulled his goggles over his steel blue eyes and slid open the canopy. Immediately oily smoke blowing back from the engine swirled into the cockpit coating him with a film of burned oil, but more ominously partially coating his goggles obscuring his vision. He quickly wiped a hand over the lenses when he dared to remove one from the bucking "stick". The fighter was becoming harder to fly by the moment. The fuel gauges showed empty. In his bones he could feel the fourteen red hot aluminum pistons screeching oil-less against scorched steel cylinders. If he overshot the carrier's 800 foot deck in two heart-beats he would be in the Pacific Ocean upside-down. The ship would plow over him, shredding man and machine in its four giant bronze screws. If he undershot and crashed in the churning wake, he would have at best, a slight chance to get out of the overturned plane before it sank. If hungry sharks didn't get him a destroyer might pick him up if he was very lucky. He said a quick prayer and focused all his skills on slamming down on the pitching deck.

The flag man waved furiously, indicating wing up, wing down, too high, too low. His gyrations were in vain. All the pilot could do was to stay airborne, going in the general direction of the ship. Bright orange flames intermittently scorched the starboard side of the aptly named Hellcat. From a perch high on the superstructure war weary squadron pilots watched the day's final dance with death....there, but for the grace of God…. silent prayers were said. The Catholic Chaplain, overcome by the moment, shouted prayers, as if God could hear them better over the rush of wind and roar of engine. The words were torn from his mouth by 40 knots of wind and sent on their way over the vast Pacific Ocean. That very morning Eddie served as the alter boy at the mass before the launch and made his confession; as usual, he was well be prepared for any eventuality!

The huge cylinder fins of the Double Wasp radial 2,200 hp. engine could now be seen under the cowling behind the spinning prop. The engine snarled like a caged tiger in defiance, its lifeblood oil supply shot away. The plane pitched, rolled, struggled level. It was over the deck! The plane crashed onto the deck doing 140 knots, snagged the arresting hook, and barreled ahead into the wire safety netting. For a moment the craft stood on its nose, prop bent back, helpless, like a giant deadly bird caught in a net. The tail fell to the deck with a crunch. Instantly the crew chief was on the wing pulling the pilot out of the smoking cockpit. The fire suppression crew, looking like asbestos zombies, sprayed carbon dioxide under the engine cowling. On the deck under his own power the pilot pulled off his goggles and flight cap revealing his short wavy blond hair. Joyous pilots rushed onto the deck to greet their leader patting him on the back, sharing their mutual ecstasy of survival. The Captain, still on the bridge, bellowed out on the bull horn, "Well done Eddie!" The approaching squall line hit the Saratoga square on the nose! Blinding rain lashed the men as they ran to get below.

After all missions the flyers assembled in the ready room for debriefing. Squadron Leader Eddie Hobrecht started with a prayer for all those who didn't make it. Several of the Saratoga's pilots were seen bailing out, but this was little consolation. Ever since Doolittle's raid on Tokyo, captured pilots were treated especially cruelly by the Japanese. Only 5% of those captured alive survived the officially sanctioned torture and starvation in the Japanese prisoner of war camps. His trusted friend, skiing buddy, and wing man was blown out of the sky by a 4" anti aircraft shell from a Japanese destroyer in Truk Lagoon; bits of the shrapnel hit his own Hellcat. At least he went quickly thought Eddie, trying to make sense out of the senseless.

In the swirling air battle Eddie engaged two Mitsubishi Zeros downing one and damaging the other before a third jumped him, peppering his tail almost causing him to bail out! Two nearby Hellcats came to his aid. Using the famous Thach weave maneuver they blasted the attacker out of the sky with lethal bursts from their six .50 caliber machine guns. His rescuers stayed with him on the way back to the SARATOGA until their fuel ran dangerously low. The last 75 miles he was on his own. Now merely minutes after his crash landing, in the calm of the ready room, he had his first opportunity to thank the pilots who came to his aid for their bravery and loyalty. It was deadly business as usual. His case was just one of many. Heavy air action was routine in the Pacific theater as the Japanese desperately fought to stall an inevitable defeat. Each pilot in turn reported their experiences and coolly gave their assessment of the damage inflicted upon the enemy. Truk Lagoon became the watery grave for 12 SARATOGA Hellcats and over 60 Japanese ships that day. Not one of the 12 SARATOGA pilots shot down on February 18, 1944 survived the war. The destruction of Truk from the air marked the end of the Japanese ascendancy in the Pacific.

The weary pilots retired. This was the end of their day, but the beginning of the day for the mechanics and "ground" crews that rushed to repair and rearm the planes for the next launch. The Captain wanted to put 36 Hellcats up at dawn. The SARATOGA'S experienced pilots were to fly air cover for the fleet to defend against more expected suicidal dive-bomber attacks. On average one out of four Kamikazes got through the air cover. After that the anti-aircraft guns took over. The pilots stoically accepted the mission, dreading the possibility of loosing their ship. At dawn Squadron Leader Hobrecht catapulted into the rising sun to begin another deadly workday.

Squadron Leader Edward M. Hobrecht of San Francisco, was my favorite uncle; to me just plain old Uncle Ed.

CHRISTMAS 1944

Christmas 1944 was as gala a family holiday gathering as could be produced in the aura of the sickening tragedy of global war. On the "Western Front" there were 4 million soldiers facing each other. Most were Christians; Protestants or Catholics. In trenches, in the coldest winter in Europe in 40 years, praying to the same God, they fought and suffered. The American troops lacked winter uniforms. General Bradley and the other American Generals, deceived by early successes after D-Day, decided that the war in Europe would be over before Christmas 1944. They employed scarce transport to the front for equipment, ammunition, and fuel to sustain the drive into Germany, not winter clothing for the troops. But that was before the Battle of the Bulge, the last great German offensive of the European war that ground to a halt at its maximum extension just before Christmas 1944. In the fox holes and bunkers on both sides Christmas trees were set up by homesick soldiers, mostly young men in their late teens and early 20's. On Christmas Eve "Silent Night, Holy Night" was sung in the trenches echoing out over no mans land to the German emplacements. The young German troops sang "Stille Nacht, Heilige Nacht" back, as the corpses of fallen comrades of both sides froze and were slowly covered by snow. Because Germans were the largest immigrant nationality in America one-third of the American troops facing the Wehrmacht were of German ancestry. This irony was not lost on the Hobrecht family who themselves immigrated to America from Berlin in 1880, just 64 years earlier. To the Hobrechts, Christmas in the romantic, un-American German tradition, was the only way they knew how to celebrate the religious and family holiday.

The Hobrecht family, headed by my stern grandfather and energetic grandmother, was hosting the most grand family Christmas celebration of the war at their home near Golden Gate Park in San Francisco. A flag draped patriotic poster was prominently displayed in one of the bay windows overlooking the street. It showed that the family in this house had two sons serving in the military. Every third house on the block boasted a similar poster. The spacious four level house was built in 1924 to plans and specifications prepared by my grandparents. By that time my grandfather's medical career was as successful as his marriage was productive. They had two sons and four daughters. With ample funds and a need for more space they built their dream house on a hill two blocks from Golden Gate Park, quite near The University of San Francisco campus. The stucco sheathed house was framed with redwood timbers for fire retardation and resistance to rot. Exotic wood wainscoting, leaded glass doors and windows, and fine oriental carpets all bespoke of a prosperous professional's residence, one superbly fitted for family gatherings.

For months grandmother saw to it that food ration cards were pooled among family members to acquire the necessary groceries. The presentation and consumption of copious amounts of heavy food was basic to a German style Christmas. All members of the family were expected to attend and eat their share. In addition to the religious meaning, Christmas was a ritualistic feeding of family by the family matriarch, presided over by the patriarch. The presiding role was traditional and not to be taken too seriously. My grandfather was well aware that in matters of the home, grandmother was in charge.

Both of my uncles, my mother's brothers, were home on furlough, alive and well. Uncle Ed was exposed to the most danger, flying off a carrier in battle after battle. Uncle Cyril was a Doctor and seemed to be relatively safe working a Honolulu army hospital. In my young imagination I could see Uncle Ed diving his Hellcat out of the clouds, machine guns cutting a swath through a Japanese bomber formation, like the war posters at the post office; while I imagined Uncle Cyril dancing with my future Aunt Marty at the Royal Hawaiian to Harry Owen's big band like the scene on the album cover of Harry Owen's latest recording. My mother and her sisters, with the exception of Aunt Loraine, would all attend. Aunt Loraine lived in Miami, Florida, where her husband learned to pilot a P-51 Mustang, courtesy of the US Air

Force. This Christmas he was in Europe escorting B-17 formations over Germany, and Aunt Loraine was too pregnant to make the long journey home. Aunt Marion, a defense plant worker, and Uncle Jim, a drafted Technical Sergeant could attend since they lived in San Francisco. Uncle Jim served most of his army tour at the San Francisco Presidio making sure the large base had water. In the 30's he was a construction worker on the Hetch Hetchy project, that to this day, still provides the water for the San Francisco Bay Area, all by gravity from the High Sierra. Aunt Clare, the youngest of my mother's sisters was not yet married and lived at home. In sum, five of the six Hobrecht children and their immediate families would be present for the gala of '44.

Those that did not live close by stayed over. The big house was quite full. Even Father Augustine Hobrecht, my great uncle and Prefect of the Franciscan Order in the Western Hemisphere, honored us with his presence. He came all the way from Santa Barbara Mission, his headquarters. He slept in the sun room at the back of the house. This special room captured sun, whenever there was any, from large windows on its three sides. Normally this was my grandfather's study. My mother, sister, and yours truly (see photo #7) slept in the penthouse. My mother shared the penthouse with her sisters growing-up. The bedroom had access to a roof deck with a great view of the city. My sister and I shared one of the two enormous feather beds, mother and Aunt Clare slept in the other. The sense of being totally enveloped by soft feathers was a new and memorable experience. Behind one door was a sink, kind of a mini bathroom without the necessities. Behind another door were the necessities, a toilet and tub/shower. Mother spoke of the keen competition for these facilities when she and her two sisters were dating. For me it was like observing the great pyramids of Giza, a kid archeologist finding traces of earlier civilization. This was the first time I realized that in the dim past mother was a girl at home growing-up in this very place!

Photo 7—Author, mother, and sister Helen—backyard of Hobrecht grandparents house—San Francisco (1943)

Uncle Ed and Uncle Cyril stayed in a large bedroom on the main level; the one they shared growing-up. The room-size walk-in closet was crammed with Uncle Ed's sports equipment. Three laminated wood tennis rackets in hardwood presses hung from the back wall. The main tennis courts of Golden Gate Park were 5 blocks from the house. Before he went to war, Uncle Ed could hold a court for a full Sunday morning by taking on all challengers, winning set after set. Now the equivalent of a missed overhead could mean sudden death in air combat. The "civvies" clothes and idle tennis rackets were a striking reminder of life as it was before war changed everything.

Uncle Ed's journey from war in the Pacific to 1941 Grove Street in San Francisco took just 48 hours of plane hopping travel. On the leg between Hawaii and Seattle he flew in the bomb bay of a B-29 with a bunch of deadheading bomber pilots who were returning to Seattle to pick up a new batch of B-29s they would fly back to the Pacific front. He asked for and received permission from the captain to take the controls. I heard him tell granddaddy that it was like flying a boxcar, and no fun at all. From a daily routine of war where chance of survival, mission to mission, was about 70% to his own secure bed at home, civilian clothes, and family must have been a shock. If he felt a time warp in the transition from total immersion in warfare to domestic life he didn't show it. At least I couldn't detect it. In 5 weeks he would return to battle, in a war that had reached its maximum intensity. There was already speculation on the date for the invasion of the Japanese mainland. General Douglas MacArthur, whose estimates of projected casualties, had been remarkably accurate in the past, projected the US invasion force would suffer a minimum of 400,000 casualties.

The house was sumptuously decorated. The illuminated star on top of the Christmas tree touched the ceiling. Lights and tinsel festooned the traditional blue spruce, cut in the foothills of the Sierra Nevada. At the base of the tree, on one side, a miniature Bavarian village was constructed, complete with a lake made from a mirror that reflected toy ice skaters. On the other side a crèche with antique German figures nestled into the snowy white landscape of sheets. The manger was made from real little logs. My Uncle Jim, a railroad buff, set up an HO scale model train to connect the crèche with the Bavarian Village. Under his careful surveillance I was allowed to operate the train. I would place baby Jesus and a wise man or two on a flat car and give them a scenic ride past gaily wrapped presents to the Bavarian village. In the spirit of the holiday the incongruity escaped me.

The piano was garlanded so heavily it partially obscured the top of the Christmas music propped above the keyboard. By the heft of the sheet music even a kid could tell that a lot of singing was expected. Dozens of candles sprouted from evergreen boughs on the Chippendale fireplace mantel. It was definitely a fire hazard. To top the living room off Grandmother removed the see-through plastic covers on her embroidered, light blue Louis XIV furniture. This was not done unless something very big was happening. The dining room table was fully extended to seat 16. The best crystal, silver, and china sparkled at the place settings. A centerpiece of ribbons, bangles, and ornaments held front stage on the German lace table cloth. Large sterling silver candelabra anchored each end.

Presents were opened early Christmas morning. My sister and I were very excited about receiving presents. The adults were outwardly less so, not wanting to acknowledge a materialistic distraction during a religious holiday. The gifts were quickly opened revealing what shaking and squeezing had not revealed the night before. Granddaddy played Santa, passing the gifts around so everybody had something to open together. When the last box of candy and pair of socks was unwrapped Grandmother took over. My sister and I found out that the real task Christmas morning was not enjoying presents, but rather getting ready for church.

With the efficiency of a drill sergeant, grandmother mustered the household through bathing and dressing. Doctor, priest, daughter, son, son-in-law, what-have-you, it didn't matter, she directed, cajoled, and badgered until everyone was ready. The bathrooms became production lines. The Hobrecht men, starting with my grandfather, were always late, seeming to enjoy the prodding to get them moving. Good humor prevailed. Christmas would not be spoiled by any ill temper this morning. As the deadline neared the men appeared one at a time in the entrance hall in dark suits, stiff white shirts, and spit-shined black shoes. Spit was also used by the women on my head several times in vain attempts to paste down my unruly hair. Family saliva could not do the job of my normal Brilliantine hair paste which was left at home in the rush to leave for San Francisco. When the whole troop was assembled the symbolic conclusion of the dressing ritual was performed by grandmother. She officiously wrapped her Kolinsky sable stole around her shoulders, clipping the mouth of the last beady eyed sable to the tail of the hindmost. Wearing animal skins with heads and tails harkened back to when families came out of caves to hunt, fight, and socialize I thought. The animal skins on the Hobrecht matriarch signified her status in the tribe and that the tribe was ready for action. No food or drink could be taken prior to receiving communion. So it was a hungry well dressed crowd that piled into four cars and headed downtown.

I rode with my grandfather in the front seat of his doctorly gray four door 1940 Oldsmobile. We went to Saint Boniface Church, a baroque mishmash built after the great earthquake and fire of 1906. Saint Boniface was the spiritual focus for the German Catholic community in San Francisco. Father Augustine was the guest celebrant. My mother and her sisters and brothers went to the grammar school attached to the church. Everyone knew each other. It was a place where German could be spoken without having one's patriotism challenged. It was my lot to be admired by friends and acquaintances. The unrelenting burden of being the first born of the next generation was, as always at these events, excruciatingly trying. I pushed my little sister forward to fend off the worst attacks. My cheeks were bright red from admiring tweaking. The old German nuns pinched the hardest. Having arrived at church only five minutes before the 12:15 mass the gauntlet was passed quickly as grandmother hustled us to the family pew, so marked for family donations during construction.

Attending Christmas high mass in Latin is a test of religious fervor even in normal circumstances. With the celebrant being my great-uncle-celebrity-priest the ecclesiastical test would be supreme. The choir, having prepared for weeks for the Christmas celebration, couldn't resist showing off. For his part, Father Augustine liked nothing better than a captive audience to display his off-key booming bass voice. He would sing a few lines in Latin that would be answered by the choir. There were even a few singing lines for the faithful, presumably to make sure that the congregation was still awake. Every few minutes one of the assisting priests with the help of an alter boy would present an elaborately decorated incense burner in front of Father Augustine. With gold and silver embroidered vestments accentuating his theatrical motions my great uncle reverently poured spoons full of incense powder onto the glowing coals. The billowing smoke enveloped him and the alter. He swung the clanging contraption before the alter producing graceful contrails of holy smells. Fat cherubs grinned grotesquely through the rising cloud as they peered over the encrusted baldachino. Behind the alter extravagant murals depicted swirling scenes of damnation and salvation. Remarkably, at first the fancy vestments, incense, sparkling candles and pageantry against the baroque decor kept my attention. However, soon even the religious excess could not prevent my mind from wandering to more sublime subjects, like the toys that were left un-played-with under the tree and my growling stomach. I became restless. The mass dragged on. I thought forward to the dreaded obligatory after mass socializing in the church hall—another gauntlet for me and my sister, but at least there would be donuts.

Luckily, I was sitting next to Uncle Ed who came to church in his own car directly from an early morning test run on Skyline Drive. I could see he felt the same. After signaling granddaddy of our intent, we high-tailed it down a side aisle as Father Augustine was putting the finishing touch on the final blessing. We ran out of the church to the church hall where Uncle Ed grabbed up half a dozen donuts while the church ladies behind the serving tables looked on disapprovingly; jogged to Uncle Ed's cobalt blue 1936 Chrysler four door convertible and sped away top down, cold and sporty. The day after he arrived home he took the car off blocks. Somehow he was able to get aviation fuel for the straight eight from the Navel Air Base on Alameda Island. No questions asked. On the way home we took a detour out to Ocean Beach through Golden

Gate Park. It was cold, windy, and foggy. I shivered as I slouched down in the leather bucket seat munching on a jelly donut. Riding in the sleek open car seemed like heaven compared to the oppressive socializing at the church. I felt sorry for my sister, but not too sorry.

We stopped at the GJOA, the first ship to make the Northwest Passage. The decrepit 47 ton ex herring boat squatted on a concrete cradle in the park facing Ocean Beach. It looked like it could have come right through the surf, across Ocean Drive, and into the depression where it rested and rotted. We parked next to the hulk. Mountainous Pacific swells could be heard crashing on the beach 200 yards off after 5,000 miles of fetch. Exploration and adventure by sea interested Uncle Ed. His enthusiasm for geography was infectious, and he knew it. He explained that Roald Amundsen departed Norway in 1903 on this very boat to find the North West passage. He said Amundsen left secretly to escape creditors. It took three years to complete the historic voyage that ended in San Francisco Bay, not on this beach where the boat was later trucked, thereby disabusing me of any thought that it plowed across the beach. Amundsen survived the perilous Northwest Passage and man's first journey to the South Pole as a young man only to die in mid-life flying his plane near Spitzbergen in a futile attempt to rescue the crew of a downed Italian dirigible. Adventure always meant risk said Uncle Ed. He whispered to me that one could never know when your number was up, then winked, a fleeting thought of air war no doubt crossing his mind.

Years later I remembered his wink, and began to understand what he said. He was telling me that he was quite aware that he might not survive the war, but worrying about it was not going to ruin his Christmas! Twenty years later, when I had my own family, Uncle Ed provided for our continuing education in geography with his annual Christmas present—a family subscription to "National Geographic". In 1978 GJOA was shipped back to Norway where it began. Uncle Ed sent me a photograph he took of GJOA hanging from a sling as it was unceremoniously loaded on a container ship. He liked ships and docks and never forgot that he infected me with this same interest that chilly Christmas day of 1944.

Back at the house the women were busy in the kitchen. The men relaxed, talking sports and politics. Uncle Cyril began to interview the guests on his new wire recorder. Helen and I sang "Silent Night". Listening to tapes of these old wire recordings transcribed by my half-brother Hilary 50 years later, one cannot help but be impressed by two things; how terrible we sounded and how circumspect the interviewees were about war related topics. The national paranoia about espionage created an atmosphere of self censorship when discussion turned to the whereabouts of fighting family members. The whole family knew Uncle Cyril had orders to ship out the following week but in response to several questions he declined to say where he was going or what his assignments would be. The old recordings show that on politics the family was divided. President Franklin Delano Roosevelt was reelected to an unprecedented fourth term on November 7, 1944. Granddaddy voted for his opponent, New York Governor Thomas E. Dewey, and proudly so stated for the record. In the previous election in 1940 he voted for Wendell L. Willkie. Roosevelt, he explained, was too liberal and too generous with the public's treasury. In the Hobrecht house there was never a shortage of contrary opinion, no matter how banal the subject. Sensing the coming of a good debate Granddaddy served cocktails; Manhattans and martinis to "sharpen" appetites, he said. After all the candy I thought mine needed a little sharpening. Granddaddy instructed me in a tone reserved for impudent children that children's appetites were quite keen enough without sharpening. In our family hard liquor was for adult ceremonial consumption, whereas wine was food. Later my grandfather would pour me my first and second glass of wine during dinner, Christian Brothers Chardonnay sent by family friend and cellar master Brother Timothy from Napa Valley.

One present I received was a model kit of a jeep. The opened box revealed several scrappy pieces of flat wood, some wheels, and an instruction sheet showing the steps to attain the realistic finished product as photographed in color on the box. I felt shortchanged! While the present was better than socks, there was no way I could turn this stuff into the finished product on the box. I beseeched Uncle Ed to help. He took me down to the basement workshop, an extra large appetite sharpener in hand. I liked the workshop. Coffee cans of nuts, bolts, screws, clamps, and nails stood in rows on shelves. A faint smell of paint and lacquer thinner teased the nose recalling projects past. I could also smell the gin in Uncle Ed's big martini. Tools hung ready on the paneled wall. Precisely driven nails conformed to the shape of each tool, evidence of my grandfathers sense of order. We began to work on the model. In truth Uncle Ed worked; I perched on a stool and watched.

We were called for dinner several times. Assembling a few critical parts delayed us. My grandmother came down. She chewed Uncle Ed out for always being late, delaying the most important dinner of the year and the war. Mother told me later that as a kid, Uncle Ed would be in constant trouble for being late for dinner. He tended to get so involved with the project he was working on that he would forget time and the necessity of eating. A more sophisticated observer would have seen a mother enjoying a scolding, unintentionally revealing her happiness that her son was safely home to scold. As we washed up in the sink in the corner I thought she would get after me, but Uncle Ed absorbed all the tongue lashing. He appeased my grandmother by saying I didn't know any better. He took full responsibility. My uncle's reputation for bravery under fire in the war was academic to me until I saw with my own eyes his cool manly response to my intimidating grandmother. I knew the Japanese could never win!

The dinner was grand! Turkey, ham, mashed potatoes, gravy, three kinds of vegetables, Waldorf salad, white and red wine, aspics of various kinds, freshly baked rolls and scads of trimmings. The candles gave a church-like glow to the whole scene. The food waited under the watchful eyes of my grandmother while Father Augustine in his Franciscan robes said grace. He seemed to play "chicken" with the assembled faithful, stopping the blessing just short of a hunger rebellion. My sister and I, Great Depression born, were the only kids. The inevitable boom in Hobrecht babies was on hold until the war was over. The dinner conversation focused on the impact of the war on various members of the family. In the heat of an argument on the proper strategy to finish off Germany my grandfather mistakenly poured me more wine as he refilled glasses around his end of the table. The whole family seemed to be immersed in the war, either fighting, or at home working in the defense industry. I must admit my childish needs for non-war related fun at Christmas, and my very limited view of the world, enticed me to take a few pokes at my sister under the table just for amusement. She kicked me in the shins, then snuggled up to a surprised and appreciative granddaddy. She understood power! The grand finale was apple pie a' la mode, as much as one could eat.

After dinner my grandfather offered the men Cuban cigars and cognac. My sister and I had cigar rings for our fingers. The women cleared the table and began to clean up. This was the first reunion of the Melody Sisters trio as they called themselves in show business before the war. Aunt Clare, the youngest stood in for Aunt Loraine. They began to sing as they worked. The voices blended perfectly as only sisters can. The three part harmony reverberated in the tiled kitchen. Most of the songs were of the time, about separation from lovers due to the war—" I'll Be With You In Apple Blossom Time", "I'm In the Mood For Love", "I'll Be Home For Christmas". I enjoyed being in the kitchen. There was a lot of action and nice singing, but nothing for me to do. My sister was given a dish towel to play-dry with the big girls. I was just underfoot. I checked out the living room.

The men had gravitated to the living room in a cloud of cigar smoke and hearty well fed laughter. The prospect of fitting into the men's group was dismal. They were talking way over my head, literally and figuratively. The top of my head came to belt level on Uncle Cyril, the shortest of the lot. Then I reminded Uncle Ed about the jeep. We went back down to the basement. Uncle Ed puffed on a big stogie and sipped cognac as he worked. Two hours later I had a beautifully lacquered model of a 1943 Jeep, complete with authentic military decals. We went back upstairs to an unoccupied corner of the living room, found an empty overstuffed chair, and fell asleep, thereby ending a memorable Christmas celebration. (see photo #8)

Photo 8—Uncle Ed and author after Christmas dinner—Hobrecht house (1944)

THE DOWNHILL SKIER

Four men stiffly climbed out of the 1934 Ford and peered over Donner Summit at the sparkling waters of Donner Lake some three miles distant and 2,500 feet below. It was an early mid-winter morning. The year was 1935. The crisp mountain air further rewarded them with a spectacular view of Lake Tahoe 15 miles further to the East. Sucking on the pitifully thin 7,000 foot air, the flathead V-8 barley pulled them up the last grade. When the thump and clank of tire chains and the wheezing engine ceased, it left them standing there in a high altitude cold vacuous silence. They stared in awe from their perch on the top of the world, or at least as close to the top of the world as a fully loaded Ford could get in a 1935 California winter. They saw what they were looking for; a 2,500 foot vertical drop to the valley below over fresh powder snow 10 feet deep. They shoveled a space for the car off the narrow road. Being sea level creatures they winded quickly with the sudden exertion of pushing back the snow bank that loomed over the car.

They unloaded their gear breathing deeply and coughing, like old men whose lungs had been clogged by excessive tobacco smoke. They were not old (in their twenties), and didn't smoke. Excitement and fear, two close friends on this mountain, bound the men together as they struggled with their own demons and equipment. Seven foot long hickory skies and bamboo poles were removed from their lashings on the top of the car. Square toe, ankle high leather boots in wooden presses were pulled out of the crammed trunk. The equipment came from Austria where the sport of downhill skiing was more advanced than anywhere else. One of the men was an Austrian Jew. His family fled the Nazis, but still had enough contacts back in Austria to obtain the latest ski equipment. Downhill skiing was in its infancy in the US.

Each man would carry a back pack that contained food, water, and spare clothes. They wore World War I Army surplus aviation jump suits with fur collars. If all went well they might get in two runs on this beautiful day. The second car, a 1932 Chevy, was parked at the edge of Donner Lake some three miles away. The plan was to ski to the second car that was dropped off earlier. The four would drive back up the pass. One unlucky skier who drew the short straw would take the car back down and three skiers would have a second run.

Skiing in those days was not for the faint of heart. The mountain was unforgiving with the constant threat of avalanche and bad weather. In this remote location there would be no help if one of them was injured or lost. The equipment was equally unforgiving. "Bear trap" bindings fixed the skis to the men's boots without any safety release mechanism. Steel cables jammed the boot's square toe into the metal "trap". They would be using the Telemark turn, a technique developed by the Norwegian Army. This required the skier to be able to lift the rear of his boot off the ski.

Tramping out to the cornice was difficult in the waste deep drifted powder. Their adrenaline was pumping in anticipation of the high speed run ahead. They all shook hands and wished each other good luck, like men might do before battle. They all were experienced skiers and knew the thrills and risks before and below them. Finally, they lined up four abreast on the cornice with ski tips pointed out over the sheer drop. Then they were off!

Each of them wanted to make new tracks in the light virgin powder. They snaked down the mountain doing large radius turns at very high speed only occasionally crossing each other's tracks. Their ski tips surfaced on the traverses cutting a line in the snow ahead in the fluffy powder. The big bowl was well above tree line. A mile into the run they stopped at a cornice to catch their breath and to plan the next part of the run. Here the light surface snow on top of a heavy layer of older more dense snow created an obvious avalanche danger. The Austrian joked that he didn't want to be in a reenactment of Hannibal's crossing of the Alps in the Second Punic War in 218 B.C. when Hannibal lost 18,000 of his 90,000 men to avalanche. One of the others noted that in addition to the men, 2,000 horses and dozens of elephants also tumbled down the Alps in avalanches never to be seen again. The thought while sobering, prompted little more than unconvincing laughter.

Not intimidated, one man kicked turned his skis over the precipice and dropped over the cornice. The others traversed to a bowl on the left. The plummet off the head wall immediately started a small avalanche that followed the speeding skier as the others looked on in horror. The skier's track took him into a small valley with a rock escarpment on each side before the bowl opened up again. The cascading snow mass grew as it tumbled. The skier looked over his shoulder and saw the danger. He realized that only by schussing did he have any chance of staying ahead of the roaring mass. Near the foot of the valley he was overtaken by the onrushing snow. He doubled over holding his knees to his chest with his arms. He chaotically tumbled keeping his skies as close together as possible.

The avalanche stopped shortly after it buried the skier on the flatter slope. The mountain grew peculiarly silent and peaceful having expended its enormous pent up energy. The other skiers gingerly approached the last place they saw their comrade. Under the snow the buried skier struggled. He strained to compact the snow around him so he could get right side up. He felt his legs and arms for fractures—all seemed OK! It was slightly light. A good sign that he was not too deep. But he could barley move. He was out of breath, the snow pressed on his chest. After several minutes of intense effort he managed to make some space around himself by banging back the snow that seemed like concrete. Only a minute ago it was dry fluffy powder. He moved to a more upright position and began to maneuver to reach his ski bindings. He knew that there would be no escape attached to his skis. Ten minutes later he was successful. With the skis released he managed to work his way upward, poking ahead with his pole.

On the surface his friends searched frantically. They were relieved to see a ski pole poking skyward 200 feet from the toe of the avalanche.

They quickly dug out the trapped skier who was fortunately buried in the lighter upper layers of snow. Then they dug down and retrieved his skis and backpack that had the days supply of wine. Still, two miles of skiing remained to get back to the car. They decided to rest and have lunch before taking on the lower mountain. The Austrian joked that the only reason they worked so hard to dig out the buried skier was to retrieve the wine skin he carried in his backpack. They ate lunch as the last rays of the sun disappeared behind Donner Summit. Somehow the mountain seemed a lot more ominous in the shade. Many spills and thrills later they arrived safely back at the car to late for a second run.

It was Uncle Ed who was caught by the avalanche. It was Uncle Ed who told me this story. His friends good-naturedly teased him about spoiling their opportunity for a second run observing that the vote was very close between searching or skiing. Later the Austrian would go to Navy Flight School with Uncle Ed and become his wing man in the Pacific. He was killed in action over Truk Lagoon. Another, Ken Staley, would join the Marines, land on Iwo Jima, and in 1945 go to art school in LA with Uncle Ed on the GI. Bill. The fourth man, Jack Douglas, was killed in action on D-Day. Of the four men on the slope that day in 1935, only Uncle Ed and Ken Staley (the artist) would survive the war.

In 1986 I was sailing my sloop from the Chesapeake Bay to Lake Champlain in Vermont. The ocean part of the voyage went smoothly. Our landfall after leaving cape May, New Jersey, was Ambrose Light off New York harbor. Our route required sailing past New York City up the Hudson River and through the Champlain Canal. Uncle Ed was visiting my new Vermont home from San Francisco. He borrowed my car to visit his old skiing and art school friend Ken Staley in Schenectady, New York. Ken finished art school and eventually became the chief illustrator for the General Electric Company, performing award winning scientific illustration. Staley had recently retired with many accolades.

When we arrived at Troy lock on the Hudson River, the first of 16 locks we would have to lock-through, the boat's engine stalled just as I reversed to stop. The butt-end of the mast that was lashed to the deck rammed the newly painted steel lock door with a resounding crash. Paint chips flew! As we neared the top of the 20 foot lift we peered over the slimy lock wall and saw a uniformed man sternly approaching us. We thought we would be reprimanded for hitting the lock door. Instead, the Lock Master told us that Uncle Ed had stopped by several hours earlier and asked him to tell us he and Staley would take the crew out to dinner in Mechanicsville that evening. The City of Mechanicsville was at the next lock. We arrived in a thunder storm. Sure enough the two old buddies, Uncle Ed and Ken Staley were huddled on the dock fending off the rain with a huge golf umbrella. They came aboard. The crew including my youngest son, an architect friend, a sailor writer friend, and myself crowded around the big table in the saloon with Uncle Ed and Ken Staley. Under the warm glow of the oil lamp we took cocktails to sharpen appetites and adjust attitudes. We then all walked in the rain to a highly recommended Italian restaurant in Mechanicsville.

Staley and Uncle Ed reminisced about their adventures skiing in the Sierra Nevada Mountains almost before the sport had been introduced in the US. They were both greatly amused by the new popularity of the Telemark technique, a technique they gladly abandoned when they learned the Arlberg Technique imported from the Austrian Alps in the late-thirties. They told many humorous stories of their experiences in art school in Los Angeles in the late 40's. They were too poor to afford professional models so they asked their skeptical girlfriends to pose for the required nude sketching. Staley eventually married his model. They also recalled the war and its impact on their lives. All of us could sense that Staley was pleased to be with his old, still feisty, friend. At the time Uncle Ed was fighting with the Federal Aviation Administration (FAA) over retaining his pilot's license. He was 74. Uncle Ed said he told the FAA inspectors that he was flying before any of them were born, and was shooting down Japanese fighters before the inspectors could walk, let alone fly. He said they had the nerve to tell him that was the point. We sympathized over double cognacs. It was truly a grand evening for us and the old skiing buddies.

Uncle Ed skied actively well into his 70's. In the late 1960's, when I lived on the West Coast near San Francisco, he joined my young family on day trips to Squaw Valley. My two rambunctious sons were just as impressed with their great uncle's skiing technique and his unforgettable stories of adventure in the High Sierra as I was 20 years earlier.

THE ARTIST

He was mistaken for a circus performer as he cleared customs and immigration at Rome, Italy. The occupation line on his US passport simply read, "artist". His athletic build lead the impertinent officials to incorrectly conclude that he was with the recently arrived troop of trapeze artists from Barnum and Baileys that had top billing at the Great International Circus visiting Rome. He was treated with exaggerated respect and quickly cleared through when the officials found out he spoke Americanized Italian with a Hollywood B-movie Sicilian accent.

This artist had more than swinging high in the big top on his mind. He was a "fine" artist—a painter and sculptor. It was 1951. The artist, Uncle Ed, had several commissions for religious sculptures, including several pieces for the 21 Spanish California Missions that were being restored. The works were already executed in clay back in his San Francisco studio. Now he would seek Italian carvers to duplicate the clay models in marble. He favored the famous white Tuscan marble quarried in Alpi Apuane near Carrara, the center of the Italian marble industry in north central Italy near the Ligurian Sea. He visited the quarry and personally select the stone for each piece. If Michelangelo could take a flawed blank of Carrara stone and carve David, then surely his work could be carved in perfect blanks.

He spent many months in Italy and in other parts of Europe in the 50's. He became a "fine artist" rather late in life. To catch-up he took every opportunity to study the great works of the masters, even as he pursued his own work. He received his formal serious training in the "fine Arts" at a time in life where one can really appreciate the struggle for creativity. His youthful adventures at sea and his World War II flirtations with death brought a sobering maturity. He realized his time was limited and valuable. Like a religious zealot, he was consumed and obsessed with the discovery of art. It was as if he suddenly knew what his life's work would be, truly a metamorphose.

As a young boy he had a natural talent for drawing that was unfortunately unmatched by the patience necessary for formal education. When he was 14 he had a regular cartoon strip in the weekly *San Francisco Shopping News.* He was paid $3 for each four window strip; big money for a kid in those days. Grandfather, who was a believer in education, was disappointed that Eddie would not go onto university like his brother and sisters. At 17, after graduating from technical high-school, he went to sea to find adventure and himself. With the Great Depression at its deepest, shipping out was an affordable way to find adventure and see the world. He started as an Engine Wiper and worked his way up to Third Engineer on the tramp steamer, STAR OF CHINA. He sketched and water-colored his way through the ports of the world. After 3 years of globe trotting he began to realize that he wanted to develop his artistic talent, and perhaps even earn a living at it.

In the Spring of 1933 the STAR OF CHINA docked at the Port of Long Beach, California. Uncle Ed called an old girl friend who was living in LA at the time. She told him that William Randolph Hearst was looking for artists. He caught the next train for San Francisco. His portfolio contained engineering drawings done at technical high school and the sketches and watercolors he did at sea. Hearst's Art Director particularly liked the sketches done in the Mediterranean and South Pacific.

The Art Director hired him on the spot. The next day he was working for the *San Francisco Examiner* doing ad design and page layout.

His natural talent was sufficient to gain him recognition in the advertising field. For the next 7 years he worked for the Hearst System, moving up to fashion artist. This was the longest and last time he ever worked for someone else. Then Pearl Harbor! His passion to fly lead to his enlistment in the Navy Air program. He was already a recreational pilot. At 29 years old he was one of the oldest students in the Navy Flight School. He decided that if he survived the war he would go to art school and move from commercial art to the "fine arts". The G.I. Bill did the trick! Uncle Ed again became one of the older students.

On July 25, 1946, his beloved ship the SARATOGA was sunk by an atomic bomb at Bikini Atoll in Operation Crossroads accomplishing what three Japanese torpedoes and six kamikaze hits could not do. Many years later he told me the ignoble end of the SARATOGA helped him close the chapter of his life on the war. He seldom spoke of the war. He did not cling to the past or his past heroics and accomplishments. He preferred living life for the future. In 1948, at age 36, he graduated a "fine Artist" from the Los Angeles School of Art. I wonder how he stayed awake in art history lectures after the exciting life of a fighter pilot in war.

Growing up I had two special opportunities to see Uncle Ed making art in the field. In 1952, when I was 14, after I graduated from Mount Carmel Elementary School in Redwood City, I visited Uncle Ed at work in Malibu. The other opportunity, four years later in 1956, after I graduated from Serra High School in San Mateo, I visited Uncle Ed at work in the Napa Valley.

The location is a 1928 Hollywood style mansion on the hills just above Malibu Beach. The year 1952. The 40 room mansion is being converted from a ostentatiously extravagant home for a movie mogul to a religious retreat house for the Franciscans. The mansion is in the Spanish Colonial style. Stucco walls, heavy red tile roofs, and rustic timber framing give the three story building a solid and peculiarly theatrical look. There is a 60 foot tower with a lookout. The view is spectacular—to the West, the Pacific Ocean and the Channel Islands; to the North, South and East, the rolling California foothills. The three upper tower rooms, about 20x20 feet, served as Uncle Ed's studio and quarters. This is where I stayed when I visited Uncle Ed.

His assignment was to make this symbol of material excess into a religious retreat by remodeling and redecorating with appropriate inspirational art. A large crucifix was affixed to the rustic timber entrance structure, with a sign carved in redwood that said, "Franciscan Retreat House". Religious statuary he had carved in Italy was placed along the winding, eucalyptus shaded driveway leading to the forecourt. A parking area was graded using the old tennis courts as a base. Impulsive Uncle Ed became so frustrated with the grading contractor that he jumped on the bulldozer and did the finish grading himself. The huge vaulted living room was converted into a chapel. The dining room that overlooked the ocean became a lecture hall. He painted murals, created sculptural pieces, hired and supervised a staff of carpenters, produced architectural and interior design drawings for contractors, and designed the landscape plan for the 15 acre property.

I stayed with Uncle Ed for two weeks. My job, artist's assistant. I hauled material, cleaned brushes, prepared surfaces for paint, and stayed underfoot. On a typical morning, after the mandatory 6:00 am mass in the chapel, we took breakfast with the prefect and a score of Franciscan brothers, all attired in their church going brown habits. Speaking was not allowed! Scriptures were solemnly read aloud by different brothers each day; their mellow voices echoing in the vaulted ceiling. The food was super! Bacon, sausage, eggs, muffins, several juices, and steaming hot coffee. The work day started at 7:30 am. Well fed and spiritually nourished, the brothers went out to the fields after changing into work clothes. Most of the food was grown by the brothers. Several acres were dedicated to row crops and a few more to a modest orchard. There was a barn to store the mechanical farming implements and house a few dairy cows, several sheep, an old goat, and a coop of chickens out back. In essence, the brothers did all the manual labor to keep the facility in operation, from farming to housekeeping to grounds maintenance. I don't recall seeing a female the whole 2 weeks I was there. In the afternoons the brothers attended classes, meditated, and assisted with retreats.

In the morning, Uncle Ed met with contractors first, pointing out details on his drawings and reviewing the progress of the work. Then he drew, painted or did sculpture for the rest of the day. The weather was hot an dry, typical of the semi-arid Southern California coast. Our reward came at end of the exhausting workday when we jogged down a winding path to Malibu beach for a plunge in the Pacific Ocean to cool off. I tried to learn body surfing from Uncle Ed who seemed to have a knack for it. One night when the surf was really up, a 10 foot roller caught me driving me to the rocky bottom. I surfaced gasping for air almost not noticing my bloody nose and abrasions. Back on the beach I quickly learned how painful salt water was on open wounds. A fresh water shower and hearty dinner fixed me up. The next afternoon we went back to a beach south of the rocky beach to continue our afternoon plunges. Uncle Ed was not one to mollycoddle himself or his nephew.

The most important work for Uncle Ed were the tympanum murals over the bedroom doorways. There were 20 in all, each of a different Saint in a scene recollecting the Saint's life. Writings on the particular Saint were provided in the room to stimulate meditation. The luminous fresco painting was done on freshly prepared plaster with water soluble pigments. Uncle Ed felt oil paint, while easier to use, lacked the brightness needed in the rather dimly lit hall. I remember several: St. Paul rejecting material wealth, St. Francis of Assisi ministering to the animals, St. Paul of Cilicia being cured of his physical and spiritual blindness in Damascus, St. Clare of Assisi forsaking worldliness, and St. Ignatius of Loyola writing his *Spiritual Exercises.* While each fresco was done in one session on the plaster, each required a detailed miniature, painted earlier as a guide to the final work. The tympanum frescos were completed over 18 months. I watched Uncle Ed rework two miniatures during my stay. The retreat house was open while the last of the murals were completed. The Franciscans were proud of the murals using a photograph of tympanums above the room entrances in several post-cards. For over 25 years the Franciscan Retreat House served Catholic laymen in need of spiritual nourishment.

In 1977 the Franciscan Retreat House burned in a huge conflagration that destroyed virtually all the structures in the Malibu Hills, but not before providing inspiration and peace to thousands of souls. The art and the building were totally lost. Only sketches and photographs remain of Uncle Ed's work, but times have changed. Religious life and religious retreats are fading in our secular, sexually neutral, materialistic society. A retreat house for men only, and operated by men only, would be an anachronism today; maybe even against the law! Given the character of the old mansion, it would most likely be prohibitively expensive to convert it today to a handicapped accessible structure. But more fundamentally, where would the motivated young men be found to become brothers? Where would a population of men be found that regularly seek spiritual renewal? The ground that in the fifties and sixties supported a seemingly permanent contemplative religious structure is now covered with luxury homes for the very materialistically endowed. The statues of Saints that provided visual interest among the eucalyptus trees on the entrance drive (now a municipal street), have been replaced by three car garage doors, high concrete walls, and security signs warning that intruders will be promptly arrested and prosecuted.

Scene two: The Christian Brothers Vineyards and Winery in Napa Valley. To be invited to the vineyards as an artist's assistant and hunter was a great honor for me. It was 1956. I finished my senior year at Serra High School, an all male Catholic school on the San Francisco Peninsula. The artist's assistant part was due to Uncle Ed. He was redesigning the tasting room, the Brothers' cemetery, and general landscaping for the Christian Brothers Winery. At the same time he was commissioned by the Order to paint a monumental mural covering an entire wall in the chapel. The hunting part was shooting the deer that squeezed through the "deer proof" fencing protecting the grapes. Uncle Ed knew my step-father taught me to shoot and hunt, and in spite of many hunting trips, I had taken no serious game.

The Christian Brothers were among the first Napa Valley vintners, making wine originally for sacramental purposes. The product was so good that after several vintages they began commercial production on a modest scale. The profits from the sale of wine supported the Brothers novitiate school at the winery. As the reputation of Napa Valley wine grew so to did the Brothers' operation. More acreage was planted in varietals. The quality and quantity of wine increased. The school expanded to 125 students on the profits. Tourists then began to arrive in Napa Valley in great numbers. This required the wineries to provide tasting rooms, parking, and escorted tours. Uncle Ed was the main design consultant for the Brothers. He worked under corpulent Brother Timothy, the Provincial Head and cellar master. He was provided with a small house on the winery grounds and access to affable Brother Timothy's private wine cellar.

I stayed at the guest house where visiting faculty would be accommodated. It was an old tree shaded bungalow, one of the original farm buildings on the site. We took our meals in the nearby faculty dining room that was attached to the recently constructed and incongruous International Style dormitory. Somehow the design of this building was slipped by Uncle Ed who let Brother Timothy know that the Brothers growing purse greatly exceeded their growth in design sense. The food was very good, most of it grown by the students, who needed to develop sustenance skills for their future assignments in the teaching missionary Order. Venison appeared frequently on the menu.

Uncle Ed was about half way to completing the chapel mural. The chapel was in the style of Simplified Spanish Colonial. The mural rose above the altar to the ceiling, some 40 feet above. It ran the full width of the chapel, 30 feet. Steel scaffolding had been erected so that Uncle Ed could work on any section of the mural at will. It was like a giant jungle-gym. He would swing from one section to another, and clamor up and down like an acrobat. A movable curtain concealed the work and scaffold. The altar had been moved forward so the chapel could function during the painting. The mural depicted the teaching missionary orders of the Catholic Church. Members of each of the orders were shown in their correct working habit and working environment. Getting the dress right required a considerable amount of research. The winery attracted a great many visitors, among them clergy interested in both spiritual and corporal matters. Consequently, many clergy of differing Catholic orders visited the chapel. A slip-up in dress detail would be most embarrassing. The work was meant to show the aspiring Christian Brothers that they had dedicated company throughout the world.

This was a mammoth work. Uncle Ed painted miniaturized versions of the mural and its sections in his San Franciscan studio. These were organized by a grid system at reduced scale. The grid was established on the chapel wall with strings in both the horizontal and vertical directions. The technical problems of maintaining a consistent pallet over the huge expanse, and of crafting a consistent sense of perspective and scale so that the whole appeared to be painted at the same time was horrendous. He faced the same problem that Michelangelo faced in the Sistine Chapel, except he could work upright and his boss was only the provincial head of a relatively small religious order, not the Pope. His studies of the techniques of the masters of murals in Europe, including Michelangelo's, paid off for this commission. I mixed paint, sharpened pencils, carried material up and down the scaffold, and cleaned up the artist's mess.

On my second evening after dinner, Brother John, the vineyard manager, and Uncle Ed said it was time to go hunting. There had been reports of severe night-time deer damage to grapes and vines in the Cabernet Sauvignon vineyard. We climbed into the Dodge Power Wagon, a 4-wheel drive open truck, used for vineyard maintenance and hunting. The truck had a roll bar over the driver's seat. Two operable spotlights were mounted on the roll bar. I loaded my 30-30 Winchester model 94 and off we went. Fences 12 feet high all around the grapes failed to keep the ravenous deer at bay. Each day the fencing would be inspected and repaired, but still the deer got through. Using spotlights at night to hunt deer is very illegal except in enclosed vineyards as a last resort to protect priceless vines.

We cruised the rows of vines shining the spots down each row. I stood above and behind the driver, with delusions of being the great white hunter! Soon we saw two big bucks gorging luxuriously on Cabernet Sauvignon. They were downed with two shots. We took 6 deer that evening in the space of 1 hour, but this was only the beginning of the process. When we got back to the barn I learned from Brother John that there would be no rest until the deer were skinned, butchered, and wrapped for freezing. What God provided and fattened with Cabernet Sauvignon would not be wasted! The deer were hung in a row from a beam erected for the purpose. Brother John, Uncle Ed, and I began. It was 10:00 pm. By 2:00 am we were still at it when Brother Tim showed up with some of his private cellar sweet wines. We sampled Muscatel, Port, Sherry, and several brandies. The work and we were finished at 3:00 am.

We "hunted" one more time during my visit. That time we bagged only two deer. Instead of 5 hours of butchering we did the job in two hours with the same level of refreshment; a definite improvement! The venison was one of the main sources of meat for the school. The cook excelled in venison dishes such as sausage laced ground venison hamburger, venison stew in wine sauce, and venison and sausage meat loaf. These dishes did-n't require "aged" meat. It was good eating!

Uncle Ed was fun to be with. I was sorry to leave, but my summer job would not wait. Being with him I always learned something about art, sports and the outdoors, all of which he relished and shared. Brother Timothy, Brother John, and the novitiate school have all past into his-tory. New wine makers and new tourists have taken over Napa Valley, bringing an intensity of activity that has totally changed the relaxed rural character of the Napa Valley we knew in the 50's. Traces of Uncle Ed's architecture, landscaping, and art remain as a reminder that he passed that way.

REFLECTIONS ON A LIFE

On January 24, 1997, Uncle Ed died at home. He was 84. He just got too old to be Uncle Ed. There was nothing pathologically wrong with him. When he turned eighty-two his physical strength diminished, his eyesight failed, and by then all of his old friends had gone, except Staley. He told me it was now time for him to move on. He felt God had over-looked calling him. This world held little attraction for him because his deterioration prevented him from engaging life the way he wanted to live it. And perhaps more importantly, the world had changed too much for him. President Clinton's escapades in the White House he saw reported on TV only added to his feeling that what he fought for and believed in was passing, if not being mocked by a self-indulgent society obsessed with sex and materialism. He saw his specialty in art, new and recon-structed religious works in the tradition of the masters, had few patrons in the dot com world, although I did send him good books on classical art whenever I found them to inform him that all was not lost. Finally, on a Friday afternoon in his 84th year he took his final breath in the bed-room he slept in as a young boy. What Japan's best pilots couldn't accomplish, time eventually did. The same day 1,000 other American WW II veterans died. Each year about 360,000 American WW II veterans die as their cohort moves up the narrowing population pyramid, eventually to the pointed top where it ends. Tom Brokaw has called them *The Greatest Generation,* in his book of that title. These men and women who survived the end of the Great Depression, defeated Japan and Germany, and lent a big hand to those defeated through the Marshall Plan and other forms of foreign aid is relentlessly becoming history. In 10 years they will almost all be gone. Uncle Ed passed in good company.

In his last years he was attended by two pretty Irish nurses. These two wonderful women, Margaret and Cecilia, grew to love Uncle Ed. His increasing frailty was matched by a growing crustiness. But they could see underneath through to the real Uncle Ed, to the spirit of the man once so full of life, the Uncle Ed I knew. God bless them!

This has not been the complete story. Left out were my many other adventures with Uncle Ed, like driving up the Alcan Highway to Alaska in an old Willys Jeep, skiing in the Sierra dumbfounding the Ski Patrol with Telemark turns before they were rediscovered, and moving furniture in an old truck at 3:00 am being apprehended by the cops as possible burglars. We have also enjoyed many hours playing the banjo together. He played the plectrum style on his 1929 Ludwig in the manner of Eddie Peabody. One balmy evening on my boat in Saint Michael's Harbor off the Chesapeake Bay we sipped Grand Marnier he made from brandy and orange peels. When it came to providing the right refreshment for an occasion he was the most resourceful person I have ever known. I pulled out my 1895, 5 string Washburn banjo. He started playing tunes of the 20's and 30's. Soon many dinghies came alongside to hear the sweet music.

Uncle Ed never married. He was too busy. His art and other interests took him all over the world. It wasn't his nature to stay in one place and raise a traditional family. He had the large families of his brother and sisters to enjoy family life when he wanted. When the time came, he unselfishly returned to the family home on Grove Street to care for my grandmother and grandfather in their last years. Back in the old family house he presided over his art collection, gave to charities, and personally maintained my long deceased grandfather's 1946 Fleetwood Cadillac. After grandfather and grandmother died (4-26-66 and 7-31-68) he traveled quite a bit, visiting far off relatives, fishing in Mexico, and occasionally driving his 450 cubic inch Olds muscle-car to LA to see a lady friend of many years. When I asked him why he needed such a big powerful car, he said "to get over the Grapevine at 85 miles per hour and to keep those pesky little Japanese cars at bay." He drove like he flew a Hellcat. Horse power meant a lot!

Uncle Ed's funeral was a memorable family gathering, the kind Uncle Ed might be tempted to come back for. The crowded funeral mass was held in St. Ignatius church, just 3 blocks from the family house. For over 20 years Uncle Ed served as an usher. He was well know by the Jesuit clergy and many parish members. After the mass I saw a jaunty man in his late 70's I didn't recognize, dash out the side door. I asked who he was. One of my cousins who was sitting next to him said he flew with Uncle Ed off the SARATOGA during the war. The man said he saw Uncle Ed's obituary in the *Chronicle* and wanted to pay his last respects to a real hero who risked his life to save his some 50 years earlier. He said he had not seen Uncle Ed for 40 years. Racing out to catch him and invite him to the reception back at the family house, I only saw him disappear around a corner. I couldn't pursue him since I was a pall bearer, and the Funeral Director was impatient to get out to Holy Cross Cemetery for the grave side rituals. We probably will never know who this man was, and what he and Uncle Ed experienced together in war all those years ago. Fortunately, several old vets did come to the reception, and many others sent E-mails to be read at the service. We heard many stories, some extremely funny, some very sad. We heard things about Uncle Ed that were surprising and not already part of family lore. It is a shame to have to wait until after a man is dead to learn things about him that would have enriched our living appreciation of him.

Back at the house, as I surveyed the crowd of friends and relatives, I thought how Uncle Ed touched each of their lives. My two sons came up from LA. At 30 and 32, they had the opportunity to know their Great Uncle in his elder years; a man who knew unequivocally what he liked and disliked, a man who wasn't reluctant to share his views, nor inclined to hold his punches to curry favor. He called their high volume rock music "screaming babies". They learned not to ask him about Communism, civil aviation, and Japanese cars unless they were prepared to spend whatever time it would take to be properly educated on the subject. My sons learned to appreciate the opinion of someone they knew loved them, even if they absolutely disagreed with that opinion—a great lesson for life. In his will he left me his collection of his own artwork. He was aware of, and partially responsible for, my interest in art. The hundreds of watercolors chronicle a life of adventure; from exotic ports of call of a tramp steamer in the 30's, to the battered flight deck of the SARATOGA at war, and finally to 1970's fishing trips to Baja. It's all there through his eyes! I am framing one of his watercolors for each member of the family.

The family house was sold. I call it "the family house" because it was the anchor for the Hobrecht side of the family for 72 years. It was the nerve center. All during those 72 years any member of the family could call or visit for the latest family news. After grandmother and granddaddy died, Uncle Ed took over the house and family switchboard. It was a commodious, hospitable place where any family member or friend could reliably find a room and a good meal. We all attended frequent family events there, from baptisms to funerals. Whenever I stayed at 1941 Grove Street I was reassured that the family had a solid home base. I'll miss the familiarity of the Louis XIV living room, the cozy kitchen with the big Regulator on the wall, the sun room overlooking Twin Peaks, the '46 Fleetwood and the Olds 98 parked in the dim light of the cavernous garage, Uncle Ed's studio, darkroom and the work-shop. I'll miss most of all the funky 1924 vintage telephone nook off the central hall, with its padded bench, writing desk, gooseneck lamp, and bulletin board, where so much family business transpired in war and peace. Courtships, marriages, births, funerals, socials, business deals, travels, and much other family communication was conducted by a family member planted firmly on that cushy upholstered bench.

The revolution in communications, smaller houses, and job mobility have largely undermined the need for a solid physical central family place. The kind of imagined and real family connective tissue lost when 1941 Grove Street was sold has not, and will not, be regained. Nostalgic and sentimental, maybe; but not enough to inspire me or any other family members to move back to San Francisco to carry on the family tradition as successor to Uncle Ed. No, the house, like Uncle Ed is of a bygone time. It is far too large to make any sense for me or any of the cousins. I hope that another family may take the grand old place over and make it the center for a new extended family for the 21st century, as it was for ours in the 20th. Uncle Ed would have wanted it that way.

CHAPTER IV

THE MELODY SISTERS

OPENING NIGHT AT BARKER FRIVOLITIES

Spotlights stabbed the foggy San Francisco sky in front of the Rococo facade of the Marconi Radio Hall. White hot shafts of illuminated water droplets disappeared into infinity, if not infinity, surely as far as Oakland across the Bay. Three special arc floodlights played on the facade of the hall setting the building apart from all the other ornate buildings on Van Ness Street. Under the marquis, the drone of generator engines feeding high voltage to the powerful arc lamps blended with the hyped voices of the gathering crowd. The scene was alive with excitement and anticipation. Tonight was the gala opening of the third season of Cecil B. Barker's popular variety show; "Barker Frivolities". Over 15,000 fan letters were received the previous season! The audience was coming by trolley, cable car, automobile, and on foot. Those that arrived early could see the stars gracefully alight from sleek Packard limousines. Cheers went up as stars and celebrities passed the straining line of nattily uniformed ushers that looked like officers from an extravagant production of "The Student Prince". Occasionally a star would stop to shake a hand or two and sign a quick autograph. Live radio was at its peak in 1935 and so was Cecil B. Barker, my father.

Three short years earlier he was broke and newly back in his home town with only a dream to enter show business. The Great Depression may have beggared him, but it did not kill his boundless optimism and good eye for an opportunity to make some money. Show business, particularly radio and motion pictures, boomed as a demoralized country sought escape from the harsh realities of depression living. With the help of his old show business friends in Hollywood he became the creator, promoter, and MC of a new radio show loosely based on Major Bowes' Amateur Hour. These same singers and actors would appear regularly on the show guaranteeing its success. They also had a great deal of faith in Cecil B. Barker who developed some of the choicest real estate in the Los Angeles area until the Great Depression wiped him and his kind out. (see photo #9)

One-half hour before show time the last of the poshly padded 1,200 seats were filled. No latecomers were allowed in the auditorium as preparations for on-the-air radio became serious. The "no-smoking" sign flashed. Uniformed ushers patrolled the isles. Any violators would be escorted out of the theater. Coughing in the audience was not tolerated on live radio. My father came ebulliently on stage without introduction, to slight applause, the kind of recognition a professor might receive in anticipation of a brilliant lecture. Indeed, Cecil Barker would profess, he came out to instruct the live radio audience on their expected behavior during the show. With humor and showmanship he coached and warmed-up the audience. If they liked him, they would like the show. He tested them on their response to lighted cues that appeared over the stage. The Stage Manager triggered the signs that blinked "applause", "laugh", or "silence". The audience was taught to break into hysterical laughter and enthusiastic applause at the right moments, even in response to the not-so-good warm-up artists my father would introduce. At show time, the theater doors were closed and guarded by officious ushers. No one would be allowed to enter or leave when the "On the Air" sign flashed. The audience would not only enjoy a superb show, they would also be part of it.

Photo 9— Cecil B. Barker, author's father at age 27—Los Angeles (1927)

The show was heard live at 8:00 pm by over a quarter of a million listeners on station KYA, San Francisco's major station, an affiliate of the National Broadcasting Company (NBC). The 50,000 watts of transmitting power from the antenna on top of Radio Hall reached an invisible arc of over 35 miles. From Santa Rosa to the north, San Jose to the south, and Oakland and Alameda to the east, people gathered faithfully around their radios to hear the stars and enjoy the search for new talent. Being scheduled immediately after NBC's most popular weekly shows like "Amos 'n' Andy", "Allen's Alley", and "The Shadow", guaranteed a large audience. Advertisers vied for the best 30 second slots coming twice every 15 minutes in the one-hour program. Advertising fees and the ample box office made the show profitable. Each season over 50,000 people purchased tickets to see the show live at the Marconi.

The show's production schedule was brutal. It aired 5 days a week. A season was 180 unique shows. The audience loved the variety. The "Frivolities" was never boring. It couldn't afford to be. The need to find new talent, sign up proven talent, and write scripts required a full time staff of 12 people. The advertising sales staff of 5 brought the total staff up to 17, excluding my father, on-air talent, theater staff, and security. The office and audition studios were located at 222 Kearny Street, a few blocks from the theater. The staff worked 7 days a week, 10 hours a day, and were all very happy to have steady work when the national unemployment rate hovered around 40%.

Up until that time, theater productions, and vaudeville shows were repeated for changing audiences. Bad shows could be improved or canceled. The new radio technology changed all that by requiring new shows each night for a hopefully growing repeat audience. Each individual show could only be rehearsed once—the afternoon of the performance. If a show ran too long during rehearsal, it was not uncommon to eliminate acts, cut musical numbers, or restructure a skit. Tuning up a difficult show might continue up until the final minutes before "air time". The rehearsal of a show that "clicked" would wrap up by 4:00 pm giving the performers and support staff a rest before going on air live. The whole operation demanded discipline, working under pressure, flexibility (for example, when an act didn't show up), very long hours, and a sense of style, all of which Cecil Barker accomplished with alacrity.

My father was keenly aware that a good chunk of the profits needed to be invested in proven talent. Talent meant a large audience; audience meant advertisers; and advertising meant more profits. For the opening of a new season, the advertisers and the audience knew that the show would be star studded. It had to be. A weak show to start the season could sap the sales efforts and undermine the advertising rates. Advertisers closely followed rating polls of listeners in the highly competitive radio market. One good sign of the prospects for a successful season was advance sales of theater seats. "Barker Frivolities" sold out the first three weeks of performances at the Marconi a full two months before opening night in 1935.

The Melody Sisters, a local San Francisco vocal group, lead by my mother Helen Hobrecht warmed up in a cramped dressing room. They were clearly excited and nervous. Unlike the big stars they would make no arrival at the curb. Just as well, my mother thought. The time before the show tended to concentrate the attention of her sisters who were still hesitant performers at the tender ages of 17 and 19. The "Sisters" wore matching satin, peach-colored floor length gowns. They made the gowns themselves using a design mother improvised from a Ginger Rogers costume in the movie "Flying Down To Rio".

It was at the end of the last season that they were invited to stay on with the show and be "regulars". This was a great honor and opportunity. To my mother's chagrin, Aunt Marion and Aunt Loraine under appreciated this big break. They placed show business well below their desire to complete their educations and find suitable husbands. Living at home under the strong influence of their father, Doctor Charles Hobrecht, my grandfather, they were dutifully following the prescribed path established by tradition. They had not had the mind-expanding opportunity of living away from home, like mother, who was living at Berkeley. Grandfather attributed my mother's interest in show business to the corrupting communist influence he believed virulent on the Berkeley campus.

Nevertheless, grandfather was proud of the talent of his daughters and reluctantly let mother form them into a performing trio.

Being a "regular" meant good pay and the prospect to advance a show business career. My mother was always an organizer. The lot of a first born daughter she claimed. She persuaded her sisters to join her in performing in amateur shows when she decided that a trio of sisters was her best chance of breaking into big time show business. Audiences liked the close harmony of pretty sisters with good voices. The mid-thirties saw the rise to stardom of the Andrew Sisters, the Boswell Sisters and The King Sisters. The "Melody Sisters" were on the same track, and within grasp of success. This opening night could be the "big break"!

Like the trios that attained fame and fortune, the Melody Sisters also came from a musical family. Singing in the home was a family tradition. All the Hobrecht sisters were born with a good ear and nice voices. They were also pretty. My mother was a 5'-5" blond with a slim big-busted figure. Her sisters were equally shapely brunettes. But it was my mother that had the show business bug and the drive to organize. It was her drive that finally landed the Melody Sisters on my father's show in 1934. They were contestants in the talent search. If the audience liked your performance, you were invited back. The applause meter was the harsh judge. Like Major Bowes, my father would strike a large gong to send off acts that failed, to the great amusement of the audience. Being only a gong away from failure, did not intimidate my optimistic and confident mother.

Now the "Sisters" were "regulars". The meter was kind to them the last three shows of '34 -'35 season. Tonight they would sing two popular songs, "Chapel in the Moonlight" and "Pennies from Heaven". My mother would also play a part in a western skit with Jack Kirkwood and W. C. Fields.

The house lights dimmed. The "on-the-air" sign blinked on. The audience became silent as the "silence" cue flashed. The Stage Manager paced stage front holding his fore-finger to his lips. The mellow voiced announcer, Harry Vonzell, introduced my father. The "applause " cue flashed. The Stage Manager waved his arms like a conductor for maximum volume. The audience responded with thunderous applause. After a modest thank- you, my father reviewed the evening's line-up of stars and other talent. The Melody Sisters were part of the "other talent". Again the "applause" cue roused the audience to a crescendo of enthusiasm. As the applause faded a prerecorded commercial came on. It was a jingle for SUDS washing powder followed by a commercial skit on clean teeth by Colgate.

The show headlined Mr. W.C. Fields and Edgar Bergen. They did a skit that ended with rambunctious Charlie McCarthy being attacked by woodpeckers. After the skit the Melody Sisters performed to the accompaniment of Guy Lombardo's big band that happened to be doing a two week gig at the Fairmont. Later in the show an old Vaudeville friend of Fields, Jack Kirkwood, led the cast in a western skit satirizing Tom Mix, the popular cowboy film star. The talent show featured a comedian from San Jose who was gonged to oblivion. My father was quite taken by the performance of the Melody Sisters, and especially their leader.

After the show my father invited my mother to join a special dinner for the headliners at the fashionable Cliff House. That evening the Cliff House, like the city, was shrouded in fog. The landmark Seal Rocks were totally obscured by dense, wet fog. The fog horns bellowed as W.C. Fields and my mother rode out to the ocean front restaurant with my dad in his Franklin touring car. Jack Kirkwood and his wife rode out separately in a cab with Edgar Bergen and his wife. Guy Lombardo wasn't able to attend the dinner. He dashed off to the Fairmont Hotel for his show. Years later mother told me how shocked she was by the heavy drinking, crude off-color jokes, and foul language. She said even the women joined in. My father must have seen mother's bewilderment with the crude behavior and with unusual self control, restrained his own natural tendencies to be in the thick of it. After dinner they went dancing at the Fairmont; guests of Guy Lombardo himself. They danced until 2:00 am. The next day she was back at Berkeley, tired, hung over, and facing a history exam.

A BERKELEY EDUCATION

Times were tough! Nevertheless, my strict grandfather thought his children should be well educated, and he was willing to stretch the modest family budget as necessary to achieve this end. This meant private schools run by religious teaching orders of the Catholic Church for all 6 of his children. The nuns of Saint Boniface elementary school took off the early rough edges. This school was downtown attached to the German parish that served the city's German population. The children rode the street car to school, about 2 miles. The next step for the daughters was Presentation Academy High School. This was an exacting all female school taught by the Sisters of the Presentation. The school sat on the top of a hill in a magnificent Beaux Arts building one mile from the family house on Grove Street. The daughters walked. The two brothers, Cyril and Edward, went to Saint Ignatius High School. The campus of the University of San Francisco was just three blocks from the house. Saint Ignatius High School was attached to the Jesuit University as a feeder facility. After one year Edward left Saint Ignatius for San Francisco Technical High that better suited his lack of enthusiasm for academics. This greatly disappointed my grandparents. For the Hobrecht family, religion and education were inseparable.

The almost cloistered existence of my mother during her early education didn't prepare her for the openness, experimentation, and liberalism of the Berkeley campus of the University of California. She went there because my grandfather couldn't afford a proper private religious school for her. If scarce money was to be spent on advanced education then it was better spent on my mother's older brother, Cyril, who was becoming a doctor in the footsteps of his father. My mother's younger brother, Edward, was more interested in adventure than education at the time. When he turned 17 he went to sea on a tramp steamer.

My grandfather allowed that Berkeley had some good professors in the sciences. At the same time he was very suspicious of the liberal arts crowd. He thought that many of the Professors embraced the idealism of the Soviet revolution without looking very closely at communism in practice. The same might have been said about democracy at the time. The biggest underlying problem grandfather had with the Communists was the Marxists total rejection of religion, and especially Catholicism. He could not imagine himself a successful father if even one of his children lacked German Catholic values. Liberal politics and sex was an explosive mix for him. Without Catholic religious values to control behavior, natural urges, like sex, might lead to unconfessed debauchery and lives of sin. He seemed to believe that only conservative Catholics should be entitled to sex, and then only under the sanction of sacramental marriage. I was never sure how he singled out the communists as exclusive promoters of sexual promiscuity, but he seemed to. He dreaded the prospect of "free love" on the Berkeley campus. In his mind he saw bemused liberal faculty looking on with valueless good humor as fornication took place right before their noses. However, the cost of going to Berkeley was affordable. There was no tuition, cheap housing was available, and transportation home was a walk and a short ferry ride from the Berkeley Mole; and this was the Depression.

He reluctantly allowed mother to enroll as a History major with a German minor, maintaining the unrealistic hope that a secular education would not totally eliminate any possibility of a religious vocation for her, for which there was strong family precedent. His younger brother became a Franciscan priest, the famous Father Augustine Hobrecht, Prefect of the Order in the Western Hemisphere. Three of his four sisters joined missionary orders leading adventurous lives bringing The Faith, sanitation, and guilt to countless Indians, Africans, and Filipinos. I heard Uncle Ed grumble one time that grandfather, the first born of his generation, was considered something of a black sheep in his family for only becoming a doctor and getting married. Grandfather damned the Great Depression that kept him from putting his first daughter, a potential nun according to family tradition, in a proper religious college. Without the Great Depression, mother would not have had a Berkeley education. Without the Depression, the "Melody Sisters" would have never been. Without the Great Depression, my mother and father would have never met. Without the Great Depression, I would have never been born. On the last point, clearly, the effects of the Depression on our family were not all bad.

In absolute contrast to grandfather, mother relished the opportunity to go to Berkeley! The great University of California at Berkeley was a hotbed of new ideas and coeducation. She looked forward to new experiences, new friends, and making decisions on her own. She was excited about living away from home, out of the demanding and increasingly stifling atmosphere of the family. Ominously, grandfather made it clear that his daughter was to do well or be brought back home. Mother was not one to muff an opportunity for freedom. In her first year she made the deans list—straight A's. She was invited to join Phi Beta Kappa and never looked back. Her scholarship was her ticket to freedom. Grandfather thought she was quenching a thirst for knowledge cultivated by the nuns and her good family upbringing. Closer to the truth, the nuns provided an intellectual bank account that mother cashed in at Berkeley.

She studied world history and languages. She already spoke German fluently when she started Berkeley. She added Italian and Spanish to her language skills. She also continued her musical studies. The romantic languages and their cultures were very attractive to her. Later she would write love songs in Spanish and Italian. Her German studies maintained her credibility with grandfather who would engage her in discussions of German history when she visited home. His examinations were tougher than those in her course work. He grudgingly acknowledged she must be getting something constructive out of the liberals and communists, but he also saw her potential religious vocation, if there ever was one, vanish.

Mother shared a two bedroom apartment with three other coeds. The building still exists. It's a stucco bay-windowed 4 story walk-up on Euclid Street two blocks north of the rambling eucalyptus and redwood shaded campus. In the morning she would be awakened to the tolling of the Campanile, just as I would be some 30 years later. They lived very modestly, cooking simple meals on very limited budgets. All during her college years she worked when she could. She clerked and occasionally modeled clothes for a department store. When she could, she also found work as a waitress. As her singing skills grew she began performing at weddings and clubs. She discovered that her singing talent could earn more money in a shorter time than all her other jobs put together. This is when she got the idea for a sisters trio.

The Depression had a deep impact upon the University. The faculty seemed to be as threadbare as its students. She told me about a time when all the Phi Beta Kappa history students were invited to the home of the Dean of Studies for an honors seminar. There were about 20 students there. At the end of the seminar the professor's wife served each student a glass of wine. Then she embarrassingly passed a small plate around so that each student could kick in 5 or 10 cents if they had it.

She graduated in 1935 with honors. She would never be the same. By this time she was performing as a solo, and with her sisters. She had many boyfriends, but was far from ready to get tied down, particularly in a strict family situation that was the expected option for a woman of her age and background. Find a good Catholic boy. Get married. Have children. This was not for her. She liked the freedom and excitement of show business and performing. But now she would have to move back home until her career would make her independent. Enter Cecil B. Barker.

COURTSHIP ON THE AIR

1936 was a banner year for the Melody Sisters, particularly my mother. The trio had steady work on KYA. Mother's talent for arranging and acting was being put to use on the program with greater frequency. She was making records for Columbia as a pick-up singer, mostly with country and western groups. She recorded singles with members of the Sons of the Pioneers, a new group headed by Sylvester Sly, who later wisely changed his name to Roy Rogers. This was the best, and sadly also the last year of the sweet singing Melody Sisters.

My father's romantic interest in my mother continued to develop. My Uncle Ed told me that Cecil B. Barker would come calling at the house on Grove Street in his Franklin. He would run up the stairs taking them two at a time, a huge fistful of flowers in one hand and a big smile on his face. For grandmother there was always a small gift, perhaps flowers or tickets to his show. He shamelessly cultivated the family power structure where he sensed the most receptivity. Uncle Ed said my father's boundless optimism and good humor lit up the old house with his presence. He made it a point to greet all sisters and brothers enthusiastically, dishing out personal compliments easily in a family where grandfather thought a compliment was the absence of criticism for a very short period of time. Grandfather and grandmother would let the couple visit in the front parlor. The pecan wood French doors with pebbled glass would be closed behind them. Nevertheless the courting couple could still be seen out of focus in dimly pixilated light if an indiscrete family member wanted to spy. Cecil Barker's dashing style added to mother's feeling of oppression in the family.

Grandfather was uncertain about my father's commitment to Catholicism. The Barkers were Catholic all right, but leaned toward their liberal Irish roots. They belonged to the Star of the Sea parish in the Richmond District. Their liberal Irish pastor was in constant conflict with the Bishop. This could spell trouble if these two ever married.

He was also worried about my father's age and experience. He was 14 years older than my mother and worldly. Further, Grandfather was haunted by the potential affects the Berkeley communist influence might have had on mother in this situation. He was glad she was at living home under his strict moral guidance.

In absolute contrast mother delighted in my father's worldliness, his sense of humor, his polished outgoing manner, and his spirit of freedom. She detested moral guidance, after all she did have a college education, had lived away from home, and was no longer the innocent child her father imagined her to be. She committed the absolute act of rebellion! They eloped.

The Hobrecht family was shaken to its orthodox roots. Grandfather waged a battle of containment. If this could happen to his eldest daughter, what might happen to his yet unspoiled daughters? He put great pressure on Aunt Marion and Aunt Loraine to leave show business, put their lives in order and to search for proper husbands or religious vocations. Predictably the Melody Sisters vanished into the dustbin of memories of just another singing group that could-have-been. The good news is that ultimately the sisters did find proper husbands and raised big happy families.

Mother and father took an apartment in the Bohemian community on Telegraph Hill. The show went on without the Sisters. Mother stayed on as a regular. Then in early 1937 tragedy struck. My father had a severe bout with pneumonia that led to a mild heart attack. He was just 37. His doctor ordered him to leave San Francisco if he valued his health. San Francisco's damp-cold climate encouraged more pneumonia attacks. The pressure of producing the radio show and performing live on stage prevented any sort of normal healthy life style. Too much pressure, too much booze, too little sleep, and too much cold-damp weather forced the decision to leave radio. They moved to Bakersfield, California, and opened a restaurant. I was born in fogless Bakersfield a year later.

CECIL B. BARKER'S PAST

The restaurant was built with family housing, guest facilities, and a studio on the second floor. The whole building was air conditioned, an innovation at the time, but a practical necessity in hot Bakersfield. The menu featured steaks and chops. The decoration was all show business. The place was called "Mr. & Mrs. of Radio Fame". (see photo #2) From the very beginning family life was stressful. Cecil B. Barker had show business in his blood, more specifically the lifestyle of show people. This contrasted greatly with mother's idea of proper family life. My father continued his show business lifestyle. Hollywood cronies visited. They drank too much; stayed up all night, and enjoyed off-color humor—none of these fit into mother's idea of family values, values considerably less stringent than her parents, but nevertheless violated by life at "Mr. & Mrs. of Radio Fame". In May of 1937, mother became pregnant. While she was pregnant she prepared for the new arrival. Baby clothes and equipment were purchased. A special room was furnished for baby Barker. Just a few feet away in the studio the parties rolled on. The restaurant was successful on the first floor. The mix up of functions on the second floor with children coming along proved unhappy. Regardless, I was born on January 26, 1938, and 18 months later, my sister Helen was born on August 11, 1939.

On their second wedding anniversary my father gave my mother a Baldwin studio piano. (see photo #10) The smiles in the photo disguise the tumultuous marriage just under the surface. There were good times and bad times, a roller coaster mother later told me she was committed to for life. After all she was Catholic, and married—period! Living in Bakersfield, away from family, reduced the support and commiseration mother might have received from her sisters. On the other hand, her disapproving parents were not there to add to her burdens. Her aspirations to sing professionally seemed to fade with each pregnancy, although some faint hope for a break lingered. She married into the excitement of show business, a business of illusions and delusions. Life without an applause meter in Bakersfield was not only dull, but carried with it, through my father, the hard living down side.

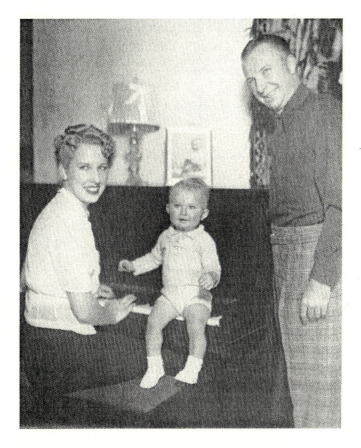

Photo 10—Author's mother and father, author sitting on piano—Bakersfield, California (1939)

My mother and father were separated in 1941 after mother was shocked to learn my father had been married before. My grandfather, quite by accident, discovered that my father had been married prior to coming north in 1932. He stumbled upon medical records that indicated that Cecil B. Barker was a married man in 1930! It turned out to be a spur of the moment quickie marriage in Reno, Nevada. Neither the Barkers or the Hobrechts knew anything about it! It was such a bad idea that my father and his bride divorced immediately in 1930. There were no children. Divorce of any kind was not possible according to the strict precepts of the Catholic church. When confronted by the news my father admitted the truth. I believe that my father truly thought that his past was just that; that his embarrassing secret would never be discovered, and that this short mistake marriage was inconsequential. Mother was precipitated into action! She accepted that in the eyes of the church (and her father) she was not married. Grandfather and Uncle Cyril hurried to Bakersfield to take my unmarried mother back home to San Francisco. Mother packed and left Bakersfield forever. The church annulled the marriage. That is how my sister and I became illegitimate in the eyes of the church. The civil authorities were less harsh.

Mother, my sister, and I moved into a second floor apartment in San Francisco's Richmond District. We lived there one year until our new house was completed in San Carlos, on the San Francisco peninsula. My father hired a well known San Francisco residential architect, Richard Baker, AIA, to design the house. The design called for a modern two story, elevated bedroom house, resembling a San Francisco terrace house designed to be abutted on each side by other houses. Curiously, our new house was sited on a spacious single family corner lot without abutting houses. In fact our house was the only house for many blocks. When the war started the subdivision was essentially complete, roads, sewers, sidewalks, and all utilities were in place. Missing were the houses. The war stopped most building. Our house was the last built until after the war. It was completed in 1942. The house was so prominent in the flat empty subdivision that Uncle Ed said he used it for a target on practice strafing runs. I think he was joking, but I distinctly remember mother calling me outside one time to see Uncle Ed do aerobatics, then drop down, canopy open, upside down, to wave at us. Father deeded the new house to mother. In the end I think both mother and father understood that they had unchangeable conflicting natures, natures they would not change for each other. Grandfather's prediction, that getting mixed up with the liberal Irish Catholics from Star of the Sea Parish could come to no good, proved correct in the end, although he proudly loved and accepted my sister and me, the first of his 26 grandchildren. The separation and civil divorce was amicable. Father always generously supported us financially.

Cecil B. Barker did not remarry. He lived in Bakersfield until he died in 1948, at the age of 48, of a pneumonia induced heart attack. He operated the restaurant, Mr. & Mrs. of Radio Fame until his death. My sister and I visited him in Bakersfield for a few weeks each year. We also saw him in San Francisco when he visited the Barkers. A hard drinking romantic to the core, he delighted in writing flowery poetry on how much he loved my sister and I until his untimely death. He could love, but not reform.

AND THE MELODIES LINGER ON

The use of talent is joyous. To not use talent is sad. The "Sister's" false start in show business did nothing to dampen their pleasure in using their talent. Whenever my mother and her sisters were together they sang for the pure joy of it. They seemed to transform themselves once again into the Melody Sisters. With a little imagination one could see them on stage in long dresses gathered around a huge studio floor microphone. It became a family tradition for the sisters to sing after a family get-together as they did the kitchen chores, and later around the piano for the appreciative men. Their songs were mostly of the late thirties and early 40's. Sometimes they would belt-out war-time love songs with a special poignancy, having lived it. They never lost the instinctive talent to blend their voices into perfect harmony. The sounds, sentiments, and syncopation's of the music of the late 30's and WW II are indelibly etched in my brain. Friends my age remark on my ability to croak the lyrics and melodies of the generation that suffered the Depression and won WW II. This undeserved ability was the result of being surrounded by the music growing up, not personal effort.

The children of the Melody sisters, who were born after the war, did not establish a connection to the music of the Sisters. Rock and Roll came along, drowning out all that came before. In the post war baby boom years the country wanted to get on with the future, forget the Depression and war, and move to a different beat. All of my 16 cousins are of the post war culture. They have little attachment to the music of the Melody Sisters. Uncle Cyril, a recording buff, made many wire and tape recordings of the Melody Sisters at family occasions. These are now on modern tape cassettes, thanks to my half-brother, Hilary, who is an electrical engineer and aficionado of recording history. Perhaps someday the cousins might take an interest in their parent's generation and its music. Most of it is there for them when they do.

During the war mother entertained at USO (United Service Organizations) functions for the troops. Off came her defense plant coveralls (she worked for IMAC, an electronics military contractor in San Carlos), and on went one of her old show biz gowns. She'd primp up her page-boy, and drive to the "City" to sing solo for the "boys". After the war she never sang in public again. For her, any prospect of a show business career for herself or the Melody Sisters was finished. She moved onto a new husband, 4 more children, and a rural suburban life style. She continued to write and sing songs for her own pleasure, and to amuse family and friends at social occasions. Some yellowed sheet music and scratchy recordings are all that remain.

END OF PART I

PART II—GROWTH

CHAPTER V

HAMPTON GLEN

A NEW BEGINNING

The Second World War ended with Japan's unconditional surrender to General MacArthur on September 2, 1945 on the deck of the battle ship Missouri anchored in Tokyo Bay. The Germans surrendered unconditionally earlier on May 7, 1945. The war was over! Truman was president. The great US baby boom was about to begin on a wave of unprecedented American prosperity and a remarkable pent-up demand for making children. My mother remarried. The family moved into new digs auspiciously named Hampton Glen, on the San Francisco peninsula. The Glen and mother had a new name. Both took the name of my step-father, E. David Hampton. The "E" stood for Elmer. He didn't like to use Elmer, his real first name. It seemed too rural. It was a name made sport of in Disney cartoons as backward. The animated Mr. Elmer Fudd was a stupid, ignorant, gun totting farmer that always got outsmarted by a rabbit, Bugs Bunny. My step-father was called "Dave". (see photo #11)

For a house-warming present Uncle Ed made a sign to hang in the entry gable declaring that this place will hence forth be called Hampton Glen. The wooden sign had Gothic calligraphy on a blue-green background. The sign was not as presumptuous as it might at first seem. Most of the houses in our new neighborhood had names. "Summer In",

"Shangri-La", and "The Doll House" are a few that come to mind. The proliferation of house signs could be traced back to the 1920's when this "remote" area on the San Francisco peninsula was a desirable resort for "City" people. City folks wanted their summer houses, however modest, to be special, so they named them. After the war, when housing was scarce, the summer houses were rapidly converted to full time housing. Times changed, but the house sign tradition didn't.

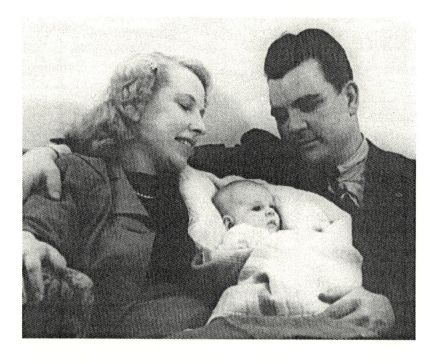

Photo 11—Author's mother and step father holding Loraine, their first child—Palo Alto, California (1946)

In the late 40's the San Francisco Peninsula boomed with new construction. Development began to fill in the flatlands on the San Francisco bay shore and bump into the foothills. Merchant builders were mass-constructing "homes for heroes" with generous financing by the federal government. At the southern end of the peninsula, some 40 miles away, San Jose still slumbered in agricultural bliss. In between, about 20 miles from "The City", is Redwood City, so named for the cities' port that shipped the last of the locally harvested redwoods in the 1920's. "Climate Best By Government Test" boasted the sign placed at the city limits by the Chamber of Commerce. The tests were never challenged. Everyone knew that the climate was mild, usually sunny, and never foggy. Before the war, for many well-to-do San Franciscans, this was the place to get away from the famous San Francisco summer fogs that reliably rolled in through the Golden Gate, shrouding the "City" in a depressing dismal dampness.

It wasn't corporate Redwood City itself that "City" sun seekers sought, but rather, the unincorporated foot hills above and to the west of the old port town on the bay, and more specifically the area around Emerald Lake. Here was the oasis they sought, The Emerald Lake Country Club. For my mother and step father the area offered a semi country atmosphere, cheap housing, a good place for kids, and an easier commute to the Palo Alto VA Hospital, where Dave worked. In 1948, shortly after my father died, the house my father built for us in San Carlos was sold for $19,000. Dave Hampton was probably glad to be out of a house haunted by the ghost of my father. Hampton Glen was purchased for $12,500, resulting in a nest egg that supplemented my step father's annual salary of $2,900. The extra funds went mainly to cover the medical costs of mother's four additional pregnancies over the next 8 years.

When we arrived, the Emerald Lake neighborhood was a mixture of seasonal summer houses, year-round conversions, and new houses built on the recently subdivided Emerald Lake Country Club golf course. Years of slow decline during the economic depression of the 1930's followed by wartime stagnation, forced the Emerald Lake Country Club's Board of Directors to sell off club property bit by bit until only the lake itself remained the property of the Emerald Lake Country Club. But what a lake! Emerald Lake was formed in 1923 by an earthen dam impounding 10 acres of green murky water, about 60 feet at its deepest point. The lake provided swimming, boating, picnicking, a social center, and modicum of flood control for the flatlands of Redwood City below. Outside of the dam and beach areas the lake was edged with a thick growth of tulles and over hanging willow trees. At the upper end of the lake, a luxurious tulle swamp of several acres, fed by polluted runoff and effluent from failed or non-existent septic systems provided a mini overgrown nature preserve. Birds, blue-gills, bass, perch, green turtles, and dragon flies abounded. The lake seemed immense and a bit mysterious to me.

Summer houses and summer people were on the decline, occupying about a third or less of the houses. Those summer people that remained seemed to be bound by tradition and old friendships. Second generation wives and children settled into flimsy thin-walled cottages around the lake each summer. Husbands commuted from San Francisco to the lake on weekends on the Southern Pacific Railroad that ran up the bay side of the peninsula. It took the old steam driven trains an hour to cover the 20 miles between the Redwood City station and San Francisco, including 6 stops at commuter stations along the way.

The annual across-the-lake swim race was the ultimate athletic challenge. A big silver perpetual trophy, as imposing as the America's cup "mug", memorialized the names of the great swimmers of Emerald Lake going back to 1925. There was a race winner every year, including the war years. All of us aspiring freestyle swimmers longed to be named on the venerable trophy. It was hard to imagine that one particular flabby old man who came to the beach in dress shoes, dark socks, and a baggy swimsuit, actually competed and won the race in 1932. His name was Bob Walsh. No matter what he became in later life he could always find some appreciative old weekend "lakers" that remembered him as the champion he was. The lake had history. It had tradition. It had an aroma of past glory and decaying tulles.

We moved into a 1927 vintage wood framed summer house, 306 Park Road, about a quarter mile from the lake. Park Road curved around our bowl shaped yard as it followed the contours of the end of the valley that was damned to make the lake. The narrow roads and heavy tree canopy gave the impression of a Hansel & Gretel forest that sprouted quaint cottages at random. Our dark brown ship-lap sided house was located on one side of the one-third acre lot. On the opposite side was the garage with a shop tucked under, taking advantage of the slope. A six foot high boxwood hedge screened the road frontages except in front of the house and the ramp to the elevated garage. Gangly cantilevered limbs of mature white and red oaks spread over house and yard, filtering out most direct sunlight. The previous owner might have been a retired Italian stone mason by the look of the meticulously crafted contour hugging stone terraces stepping down from the hedged road frontages to the large half-oval concrete patio. The view uphill from the patio was softened by English ivy clinging to the stone walls of the terraces. Like an afterthought of a landscape architect with too much stone, a section of the underground storm water pipe was exposed next to the house in a stone lined artificial creek that cascaded white water when it rained heavily. One wet spring I had the idea of blocking the outflow pipe to make a small swimming pool. It was excessively successful flooding our yard and our neighbor's. At night the yard was illuminated with exposed colored light bulbs strung tree-to-tree along the terraces and patio. Many of the other yards in the neighborhood were similarly illuminated creating a festive ambiance, reminiscent of the popular Russian River resort, Rio Nido.

When our house was constructed in the 20's it had only one level. In the 30's two bedrooms were built underneath the main floor. The two floors did not have an internal connection. This impracticality for a full time residence was corrected by my step-father by an ingenious stair he built that ran from the lower hall to a closet in the living room. Later when my sister Helen was dating, she would miraculously appear in the living room out of a closet to the astonishment of her date. Much to my step father's credit, he made many improvements to the house, but none as ingenious as the hidden stair. On the lower level he also designed and personally constructed a bathroom, a laundry, and hall. This required excavating the hillside under the house by hand, mixing, hauling and pouring concrete retaining walls, constructing bearing walls, framing and finishing the new rooms and wiring and plumbing the lot. On the main floor he converted a sleeping porch off the master bedroom to a much needed nursery. With these improvements 306 Park Road was no longer a summer place. It was a year round residence fit for the growing Hampton family.

MOTHER AND STEP FATHER

If grandfather Hobrecht was shocked by mother running off with a liberal Catholic from Star of the Sea parish in 1936, he must have been apoplectic when she married an avowed atheist from Kentucky in 1946! Would there be no end to the communist mischief imposed on his family? Fortunately, grandmother tempered the tempest. The senior Hobrechts resignedly accepted Dave Hampton as an opportunity to do penance on this earth for real and imagined transgressions through penitential suffering. By focusing on his good points family unity, while strained, was not lost because of the Hobrechts. The Barker side ignored the whole affair, doing what they could to keep Cecil's children (Helen and me) in the Barker sphere.

For five years mother was a single mom, from 1941 to 1946. She was in her late 20's and attractive. She carried on an active social life. Dave Hampton was not her only suitor. There were two proposals of marriage in those years, one from an Army officer who was a banker before the war; and one from an old college boyfriend who was a Navy doctor. She was crushed when the ex banker tragically succumbed to a fatal illness acquired from tainted military vaccine injections. I don't recall exactly what happened to the doctor, but it had something to do with his desire to postpone marriage until after the war. He could have been of faint heart. The war seemed to mess everything up. On the other hand were it not for the war mother would have never met Dave Hampton, from Lexington, Kentucky. Their lives simply would have never intersected. I am still amazed how these two people, so unlike, determined that they had needs the other could fulfill. It must have been love!

Dave Hampton, the eldest of five children, grew up on a tobacco farm outside Lexington, Kentucky — his parents were poor rural sharecroppers. He was a bright kid, but his family background and economic circumstances precluded higher education. He certainly was not dumb! His IQ exam on entry into the military showed him to have an IQ of 136. In Lexington at that time, graduating from high school itself was considered quite an academic achievement, attained by less than a quarter of young people his age. The Great Depression was at its depth in 1932, affecting Kentucky's' rural areas particularly hard. Dave Hampton dropped out of high school in his sophomore year to help support the family. After several years of farming he started to look for non-farm work at age 18. The unemployment rate stood at over 30%. He sought work with the federal government. A Government job was secure and paid very well in comparison to private sector jobs. He took the federal civil service examination with 350 other hopeful job seekers in the Lexington Armory in an attempt to land one of 17 government jobs available in the Lexington area. He was very proud to have finished 10th highest!

He became an orderly at the local Veteran's Administration Hospital. Working for the government meant security and good money. Any regular paycheck in those days was good money. He married in 1935 and expected to move up to a middle class family life in Lexington. Mary was her name. She died unexpectedly of uterine cancer in 1940. They had no children. His family life shattered, with war looming in the Pacific and Europe, he decided to enlist in the Navy. He told me the alternative would have been to wait, be drafted, and have no choice of service. The Navy offered him training as a medical corpsman which he gladly accepted; an assignment similar to his VA job. He wanted to stay in the medical field, and if war came he said he certainly didn't want to be a foot soldier.

He joined the Navy in the Summer of 1941, six months before Pearl Harbor. Contrary to his wishes, when war came he was assigned to the Marines as a medical foot soldier. He landed on Tarawa in the Gilberts November 23, 1943 with the Marine invasion force of 5,000 men; 2,700 would be killed. So much for picking a service to stay out of harm's way! In that battle Dave Hampton became one of the millions of unsung combat heroes of WW II that our generation and succeeding generations too often fail to properly honor. Near the end of the war he sailed into San Francisco Bay on a troop carrier for R&R (Rest and Recuperation). The fickle hand of fate now steps in! The next day he met mother at the USO in San Francisco, where she was singing in the USO variety show. Dave Hampton was ruggedly handsome, standing just under 6 feet. His jet black hair combed straight back accentuated his dark brown, almost black eyes. He was strong and muscular. He took a liking to my sister and me. We also liked him. My mother and Dave Hampton began a courtship that led to their marriage in 1946.

They shared physical attractiveness, an interest in family life, earlier tragic marriages, an interest in "country" living, and a desire to start a new life after the war. What they didn't share was 1) religion—mother was Roman Catholic, he was an atheist; 2) education—mother was college educated, he was not; 3) geographic perspective—mother was from the West, he was from the South; and 4) family background—mother was from an urban professional family, he was from a rural farm background.

Eventually the strength of the shared interests could not overcome the areas of differences. They still managed to have four children in the 15 years they were married. A fifth child died at birth. (see photo #12)

Photo 12—Mother and her children—left to right: Hilary, Michael (author), David (on floor), Philip (on mother's lap), mother, Loraine (on floor), and Helen. (1953)

My step father was very fatherly to me. When mother became Mrs. Helen Hampton, my sister and I were too young to rebel against a new father figure, as often happens in remarriage situations. The fact that our father died shortly after mother remarried further reduced the potential 2 father problem. Nevertheless, we were still Barkers in a growing sea of Baby Boom Hamptons. Helen and I remained close to the Barker relatives.

Dave and I had a good relationship, except when some of the parental issues got in the way. For example, mother made sure all her children were brought up Catholic. Dave had little tolerance for religion and the religious. He felt that priests, even my much revered great uncle, Father Augustine Hobrecht, were only witch doctors exploiting human weakness. Surprisingly, when Father Augustin visited he and Dave got along very well. Dave told me that the only religious he respected were the witch doctors he met in the Pacific Islands during the war who had not yet been corrupted by the hypocrisy of Christianity or other organized religions. Most of the time he held his tongue, and I mine. However, inevitable conflict arose. This lead to heated arguments, never physical violence. If that happened I might not be writing this. He was powerfully built and knew how to handle himself in hand-to-hand conflict; they called him at the hospital whenever a deranged knife wielding marine or other miscreant had to be disarmed and subdued. He never used his immense physical power to punish or abuse in the family. In fact, after mother read Dr. Spock, even she did not use corporal punishment—unfortunately too late for my sister and I.

He worked night shifts to earn the extra pay that night work offered. He built a bedroom next to the workshop under the garage where he could sleep during the day away from the main house that was full of his young boisterous children. On several occasions I thoughtlessly decided to work on my car in the garage over his head when he was trying to sleep. The reason I say "several", is that I remember only the occasions when he got up, came up into the garage in his plaid flannel bathrobe and asked me somewhat plaintively, to please be more quiet. If it were me trying to sleep, I am sure I would have been far less temperate in my demands for silence. My step-father was at base a gentle, insecure man struggling with step children and a strong wife. He taught me chess. We had many marathon matches. He taught me to fish, to shoot, and to hunt. He exposed me to a unique view of the human condition that I could not embrace. Without reading the books he recommended, or arguing with him about current events, I would have missed understanding a point of view that I would not have been able to hear anywhere else. An atheist, a cynic, an underachiever, a man who relished the exposure of corruption in high places, particularly the Catholic Church, he unflaggingly did the best he could for his stepchildren, particularly in the first 10 years. Although he was never a father to me. I already had one. He was however, a true step-father.

HOME LIFE

Mother thrived in our semi- rural life style at Hampton Glen. While she was raised in the City, she loved the country life. One of the common interests mother and my stepfather shared was a joy in the land. Gardening bound them together with the same force religion split them apart. We had chickens, rabbits, dogs, cats and even some ducks at one time. The excitement of show business and city life was behind her. In this new life she was creative and highly productive. She filled the house with children, music and good cheer.

She was pregnant and taking care of babies much of the time. The thought of materialism never entered her mind as she practiced what she and the Catholic church preached — that the biggest gift of all was life, particularly children. She never complained about some material deprivation due to so many mouths to feed, or the pure work and struggle of it all. Maternal love in the deepest spiritual sense was her nature. Today, many would say that a big family is too expensive, demanding, compromising and stifling. Not her! She made an art of loving and caring for six children. How she treated all of us as though we were the most important persons in the world is a mystery to me, but she did!

Family and friends marveled at how she had time to instill self confidence in each of us. Part of her talent was to spend time on things that were important, letting lesser matters slide. Important things included stroking and caring, homework, church, athletics, music, and character building. Character building included discipline. Until she read Dr. Spock, she was not reluctant to use corporal punishment to make a point in an extreme case. When she did, she would not do so in anger. The coat hanger would be applied to the backside with an explanation that it was her responsibility to free us from the misconception that it was sufficient that all transgressions would ultimately be punished by God at the last judgment. I found out her time frame was shorter than God's. Less important things included housework, cooking, ironing, shopping, and boring people. As kids we were non-ironed, shabbily dressed, sometimes dirty, self-confident and happy lower middle class; too full of ourselves to realize how bad we looked. The only reasonable explanation for each of us turning out to be successful adults was her love; and not because we were lovable. It was that she loved without condition, took the time to love, and loved lavishly.

It's in the walls, in there like the ancient spruce wood of a Stradivarius violin. All the past sounds are locked in the wood. All future sounds are sweeter for the earlier resonance. Violins could be made out of the wood in the living room walls at Hampton Glen. She played, she sang, she composed and she instructed in this modest space. It could well have been Carnegie Hall, but for her choice to answer her maternal instincts. The Baldwin Monarch piano that she received as a second wedding anniversary present from my father brought joy every day. This was a talented woman. She could play in any key, transpose and create. Music was integral with family life, and all of us are richer for it. When family and friends visited music was usually part of the fun. How I longed to play myself when I saw what great joy there was in it. She tried to teach me to play. In frustration she said I was like my father, who loved music, but had little talent for making it. I now have the Baldwin. I play out of sheer stubbornness and love for it. The walls in my house will never aspire to a higher calling than to be recycled as kindling wood.

Every house has an attitude, a spirit. An architect uses wood, stone, glass and other materials to create spirit and feeling simply by the arrangement of elements. The first century Roman engineer, Vitruvius, who set the standard by which all architecture is measured until this very day, said that good architecture should have three elements: "...firmness, commodity, and delight"; meaning structural strength, a functional plan, and aesthetic appeal. By these standards, Hampton Glen had no architecture at all. Hampton Glen was so architecturally deficient that it provided only a void for mother to fill with her presence, her cheer and optimism. Her aura created exquisite space that projected out into the void even when she was not physically present. Consider the living room. There was always something happening. Whether it be family, relatives, or guests, the place bustled. It was never a showplace—far from it. It was seldom clean and neat. Good living seemed to get things out of order. The eclectic furnishings ranged in style from Regency to nouveau Naugahyde, (reflecting mother's practical side). The piano, the Packard Bell recorder (mother made records), and the books were of high quality, but the rest was Salvation Army and Good Will retreads. Mother would have thought that all the effort to produce a room worthy of *ARCHITECTURAL DIGEST* a pure waste of time, when there were so many more important things to be done. But then, these magazine rooms are designed by experts for people whose presence alone cannot make any space glorious as she did.

In 1952 mother purchased our first TV set, an Admiral 13 inch black and white, a good set for the time. A 20 foot mast was erected on our roof supported by two levels of guy wires. A rotating antenna on top of the mast brought in two and sometimes three stations. Our antenna proudly joined the other sprouting rooftop neighborhood status symbols. The motor mounted immediately below the festoon of aluminum antenna tubes added mass to the maze, thereby accentuating our symbol of arrival in the modern world of TV. Because we lived in a valley the weak signal we received bounced off land forms before being ingested by our set. The Admiral could not filter out the ghost images produced by these slightly off cycle signals. The greatest stars, no matter how fleet of foot, could not shake their lighter other selves appearing slightly offset and behind them. Neighborhood traffic, we never particularly noticed before, became a problem. When a car approached its electrical interference caused the picture to roll up, slowly at first, then flipping up faster and faster as the car closed in. The process reversed as the car past on. Folks who used to warm up their car in front of the houses before driving off soon learned that this practice was unacceptable TV reception sabotage.

Our first TV was not the first in our neighborhood by any means. The first TV in our neighborhood was owned by the parents of my friend, David Dent. He lived a hundred yards up the hill in direct line with the Channel 5 transmitter. His father, Gorden, had a passion for the latest gadgets, and there were many available after the war. The thousands of small start-up companies that produced war material looked for new ideas and markets. One company that made portable generators for the Army, tried its small gas engine on a scooter. They called it the Doodlebug, the 100 mile per gallon motor scooter. Mr. Dent bought one of the diminutive spring-less 50 pound machines for his commute to the train station. He drove it in his business suit till winter on 3 gallons of gas. The scooter was so small that Mr. Dent looked like he was magically gliding along the road sitting on nothing. When winter set in he moved up to a Crosley miniature car. The tiny Crosley in the neighborhood solidified Mr. Dent's reputation as being on the cutting edge of consumer innovation, an image he cultivated in his public relations firm. It was not unexpected then that the Dents acquired the first TV in Emerald Lake. Their first set was a 10 inch 1949 Munson Deluxe. David's father wasn't content with plain black and white. He installed a blue, green, and brown tinted plastic film over the screen to colorize western movies. It was pretty effective for outdoor shots. The sky was blue; the valley was green; and the ground was brown. Unfortunately, the film stuck to the tube so tenaciously it was seldom removed. Consequently, Howdy Doody had blue hair, a green face, and a brown neck.

In the early 50's there was not much on TV that could compete with the live action around our house. As TV programming improved we watched The Hit Parade, Roy Rogers, Dragnet, Milton Berl, The Cisco Kid, and most especially Faith of Our Fathers. My Uncle Frank's brother, Dan, a Catholic Priest, produced and directed a live, early Sunday morning religious TV program on Channel 5 in San Francisco. My sister Helen and I appeared on the show as attentive audience for the bible lessons from time to time. It was fun because we stayed over Saturday night at Uncle Frank's and Aunt Clare's house in San Francisco. They had no children. It was an opportunity to be spoiled a little. Once we acted in a biblical Christmas skit. Helen was the Virgin Mary. She wore a pillow under her bed sheet gown to effect pregnancy. I played Saint Joseph, unconvincingly. When told that there was no room at the inn, my literal Saint Joseph thought it was amazingly funny. The mock-up inn was a flimsy piece of painted cardboard supported in back by sticks that even a two dimensional Saint Joseph would never be able to enter let alone a pregnant virgin. Laughing at the wrong time, a handicap that has plagued me most of my life, guaranteed that Saint Joseph would be my last acting appearance on the show.

Frequently the show headlined a remarkable and very popular preacher, Bishop Fulton John Sheen, the national director of the Society for the Propagation of the Faith. "Life Is Worth Living", his widely read 5 volumes on life as a Christian occupied a conspicuous place on our living room bookshelf. He was the Catholic's answer to Reverend Billy Graham. His sermons attacking Communism, birth control, and Freudians left listeners either limp with overpowering argument if they were non believers, or intellectually reinforced if they were Catholics. Father Dan traveled in pretty fancy company in the TV business, a bit too fancy. He eventually needed clerical re-treading and a lower octane life style. He spent his later years as the Pastor of a very nice parish in South San Francisco. Around our house however, he was always remembered as our family's TV celebrity, a reputation only very slightly tarnished by the fading family memory of my rendition of Saint Joseph.

TV was limited at Hampton Glen. Mother felt it distracted from homework. She wouldn't allow any Barker or Hampton to idly watch the tube when any one of us had remaining schoolwork to do. All would be denied as an incentive for the quick to help the slow. On Sunday night, at 8:00 PM we saw the USA in Diana's Chevrolet, not a bad variety show for kids. Unfortunately at other times, mother had a knack for finding programming that featured her favorite tenor, Mario Lanza. There could have been no more powerful incentive for me to do homework or build model airplanes. The denizens of Hampton Glen missed a great deal of the cultural revolution sociologists attribute to malevolent influence of TV in the 1950s. It just went by us. We read while others watched. The *Redwood City Tribune* and the *San Francisco Chronicle*, delivered daily, provided the news of the outside world and entertained. All of us found something to look at in the daily papers, from cartoons to editorials.

Once a year mother made a concession to good housekeeping just prior to the annual visit from grandmother and other relatives. Each year we hosted a family reunion on the patio at Hampton Glen. As many as 45 relatives descended upon us in the "country" to enjoy a swim in Emerald Lake and a sumptuous barbecue featuring Dave's renowned stone pit. She vacuumed, dusted, removed piles of old newspapers, temporarily banished animals, and arranged the furniture. We were ordered to suspend living until grandmother inspected. This domestic constraint had a domino effect on the neighborhood. Our kid friends always gathered at our house, usually with their pets, because their mothers had nice living rooms. Mother was popular with neighbors, so she herself suffered from the non-living mandate till grandmother came. Even with all this effort grandmother could always find fault. Her own living room in the house in San Francisco was not for living. It was filled with fine furniture, art and accessories. Only on special occasions did the covers come off the furniture. She did not understand the concept of living in a living room. Grandmother was a great housekeeper and was surely disappointed in not passing this trait onto her eldest daughter. Mother, the dog, the cat, us kids, and the neighbors were glad to have the living room back after grandmother and the relatives left.

The yearly gathering of the relatives from San Francisco on our patio was graciously hosted by mother and my stepfather. In a big family, hosting a reunion for that many had to be a labor of love. The aunts and uncles and their children came to swim in Emerald Lake and eat barbecued chicken and hamburger provided by the Hamptons. Quite often mother killed some of her old laying hens before the feast. They were a bit stringy and tough but very flavorful compared to the tasteless chicken now available. Mother always made her famous garlic bread, half-loaves of broiled sour dough bread soaked with butter and garlic, browned to perfection. The rest was pot luck. The aunts and uncles brought many varieties of drinks—for the kids, Coke and Ginger Ale. A treat! Mother would never undermine our diet with chemically treated carbonated sugar water as she called it. The adults drank nutritious premixed Manhattans and Martinis, the maraschino cherries and cocktail olives supplying the vitamin rich vegetable component. None became inebriated, although some left as late as 11:00 PM, well after mother turned off the colored patio lights. The die-hards hung out in the kitchen drinking mugs of strong coffee before heading back to "The City".

My sister and I were quite tanned by mid summer and took great delight in teasing our young cousins about their whiteness. We didn't publicly notice anything about the adults out of outward respect masking inward ridicule. Their sagging white flesh rippled as they tender-footed into the water where buoyancy floated odd bits of non-descript white skin above the surface. Every year they suffered sun burn, almost as if their red skin, and later the skin peel, proved that they had done the country. All-in-all these were grand parties I enjoyed very much. It gave me a chance to show-off my swimming skill, socialize with my aunts and uncles with mutual affection, and lord it over my young "baby boomer" cousins.

Living space was at a premium at Hampton Glen. At first I slept in the boys bunk house, actually one of the two bedrooms under the main floor of the house. Helen and half-sister Loraine slept in a big double bed in the other. Our circumstances reminds me of the line Floyd Hyde, the former Fresno Mayor used in describing his low-income upbring-ing. He said "I never slept alone until I was married". The boys room had six bunks built by my stepfather out of military surplus parts. It was cramped. As each new half-brother arrived it became more crowded. Also the age difference made it difficult for me. All three were more than 11 years younger than me. The room also served as the guest accommodation for males. On several occasions uncles and family friends stayed over. They seldom availed themselves of our hospitality for long, although one of Dave's cousins, Everet, from Kentucky stayed several months due to a divorce. He rode a big Harley motorcycle all the way out from Kentucky. He rode it all the way back after a temporary job he had as a gas station mechanic in Redwood City went sour. Everet, though basically broke, was generous enough to give my friends in the neighborhood rides on the Harley while he was with us. My increase in status was well worth a little overcrowding.

One day I returned from school to find all the model airplanes I had built smashed on the floor. After completing each model I suspended it on fishing line from tacks in the ceiling. There were dozens frozen in banked dives toward the linoleum floor. My younger half-brother, David, wanted to show the models to his friends close-up. He sensibly used a broom to get them down since I put them as high as possible to keep them safe. There was little left but broken balsa and torn paper. This precipitated my move to a shed then occupied by my mother's loom. In all her spare time she wove. My step-father built an eight by twelve shed attached to the garage structure to house the big loom. With a little carpentry it became my private apartment. This apartment also provided needed study space and privacy. The model bashing was a blessing in disguise. From 14 on I had my own separate quarters and more importantly a private entrance. While primitive, the un-insulated shed granted me a freedom of movement and privacy unattainable by my contemporaries in more regular middle class digs. In the California winter a small 1,400 watt electric heater was just enough to kept the chill out. The socket, plug, and, cord became untouchably hot and added a little extra warmth. For bathroom needs I simply took care of those necessities in the main house. When it rained I was separated from the big collective rain drops coming off the overhanging trees by only by a thin layer of tar paper and a half inch of tongue and grove. Sleep came to the lullaby of splattering water. A very under appreciated aspect of living in an old summer house is flexibility. Hampton Glen was added to, modified, and upgraded to fit the needs of our changing family, much to the credit of Dave Hampton and his carpentry skill.

CHAPTER VI

THE NEIGHBORHOOD

THE PEOPLE

Diverse is the best adjective to describe the people in our hilly neighborhood. The human diversity reflected the great range of housing choices. There was something for everyone. There were wealthy and poor, educated and uneducated, old and young, married and singles, and the unconventional. Our immediate neighbors illustrate the point.

The Heflins—Doc, Beatrice and their son Bill, lived next door in a post-war house, built in 1946. Doc's real name was William. He earned the sobriquet in the army where he was a medical corpsman. He didn't see the bloody action my step-father saw in the Pacific. His military service was state-side, mostly in training camps giving injections to soldiers. The war seemed to define him in name only. Before the war he was a bank teller at the main office of Wells Fargo Bank in San Francisco. Nevertheless, everybody called him "Doc", Beatrice included. They purchased the vacant lot next to ours with war-time savings, and had a local contractor build a house from their sketches. The two story conventional wood frame building was readily identifiable missing the tell tale oddities of the converted summer houses that surrounded it. The Heflin's property abutted our property, down valley. They also had frontages on the two roads.

After the war Doc went back to Wells Fargo Bank in San Francisco as a junior officer. Every work-day morning at 7:30 AM, he left the house in a pin-striped bankers' type suit. He drove a 1936 Pontiac coupe (station car) the three miles to the Southern Pacific station in Redwood City for the 20 mile rail commute to the "City". In my first two years of high school, I rode with Doc to the station, where I caught the train to San Mateo and Serra High. The dirt parking lot at the train station was a showcase of reverse status jalopies, including a fair number of Model A Fords. A typical "station car" was old, rusty, dented and only locally reliable. Doc's Pontiac was almost paintless. Its universal joints were shot resulting in a whine that could be heard before the car was seen on Park Road. To start the car Doc pumped the gas pedal 10 or 15 times, then pushed the starter saying "come on baby you can do it". It worked.

Doc was friendly to the Hampton Glen kids in a condescending, establishment sort of way. His esteem for my step-father increased immeasurably one night when my step-father administed life saving first aid when Doc had a hemorrhaging ulcer. The ambulance came to take Doc to the hospital for emergency surgery. With half his stomach removed Doc quit drinking and chain-smoking. When I was a teenager Doc helped me acquire a car from the repo department of the bank. It was a 1952 De Soto Deluxe slightly marred by bullet holes in the trunk from a police chase. The trunk held a special bonus, loot from a burglary overlooked by the police. More about that later. Beatrice was a quiet lady who taught piano, the old fashioned way, by book and metronome. She drove the family '51 Packard like the great boat that it was, slow and steady. She never accelerated before a hill, relying instead on the big V-8 to maintain a constant 20 mph speed. If mother, a fast driver always in a hurry, found herself behind Beatrice on the way to our hilly neighborhood where passing was impossible, she lost her grip. Mother exhibited a lack of verbal self control she expected in all around her, but surprisingly could not suppress in herself in moments like this. Their son Bill, an only child about 10 years older than me, helped me fix my bike several times. I really didn't see him around very much. He was very studious. He earned a Ph.D. in electrical engineering from Stanford. Later he started a company in Silicone Valley and became wealthy. The Heflins, were proud that the famous screen actor, Van Heflin, was a cousin of Doc's. They were a solid Republican, Episcopal, middle-class, establishment family.

The Pasteurs—The Pasteurs on the other hand were blue collar working class fallen away Catholics. Harry, Muriel and daughters Judy, Darlene, and Michelle rented a rustic summer cottage across the street and up the hill from our house. Harry greased cars at Towne Motors, a Ford dealership in Redwood City. I learned a lot from Harry. In his youth he rode the rails, played semi-pro baseball and worked as a stunt man in Hollywood. He wanted sons, but fathered three daughters. I was the closest son substitute. He taught me baseball and fist fighting. He sported a dramatic scar that ran from eye to chin on the left side of his chiseled face. He showed me how to defend myself from a knife attack like the one that marked him in a fight in a rail car. The man was full of energy. The whole neighborhood would turn out for his bit-part performances with the local little theater group. His wife, Muriel, was a saucy waitress in a tavern on El Camino Real. Mother did not like the way she dressed, showing the things that attract men too obviously, things she had in abundance. It apparently paid off in tips. Of the daughters, Judy, my age and their eldest, was my on and off girl friend. She grew up fast passing me by on my slow journey.

The "Boys"—"The Boys" lived across the road at the end of our property. A huge climax bay tree obscured their tastefully remodeled summer house. My mother called John and Bob "The Boys", much to their amusement. John was a muscular balding warehouseman, about 35, Bob a thin television salesman, about 40. John and Bob were the first out-of-the-closet homosexuals I knew. They shared mother's enjoyment of opera. When mother acquired a new Mario Lanza record she would invite them over to listen appreciatively in front of the big speakers of the

Packard Bell. My mother liked them and they liked her. Race, color, creed, class, or sexual orientation made no difference with my mother. My step-father, extremely bigoted in religious matters, was generous and accepting of all other human conditions and frailties. At our annual neighborhood holiday cocktail party everyone came, and under my mother's influence, buried their prejudices at the door. John and Bob had several Pug dogs that were so inbred that they could barley breathe through their flattened snouts. When John and Bob traveled, I looked after the dogs and their garden.

The Crockers—The Crockers (alias) were well-to-do summer people from San Francisco. Mr. Crocker held an important political position in the "City" government. Since the 20's the family spent summers at Emerald Lake. In the 50's they just spent weekends. Their house perched across the road from our garage, high on the hill. A full width porch spanned the second level. It was from here that the Crocker boys would shoot their BB guns at passing cars, pedestrians and cats and dogs under the bleary eyes of their parents. The afternoons usually found the senior Crockers intoxicated. Fortunately, most of the shots were deflected by our big hedge and trees. The Crocker boys would also take delight in yelling profanities and racial and religious insults at passers-by. The most impressive thing about them was their unqualified dislike for Jews, homosexuals, blacks, Mexicans, animals (they killed several of our chickens), country kids and normal people. My sister and I had to ask mother what many of the swear words and racial epithets meant. They called me a spic mother fucker, which could have been a compliment as far as I knew. Mother explained it was unkind and showed their ignorance. Our vocabularies in this specialized disgusting form of communication gained whenever the Crockers were around. Their ambitious younger sister now serves in the US Congress. We were all glad when they went back to the "City". Later the house was rented year round to a couple of motorcycle riding lesbians, one of whom had a beautiful daughter. All the neighbors agreed that this was a great improvement to the neighborhood.

Mr. Price — He was an elderly eccentric writer of books never published and greeting card poems. We saw him when he trotted down to the ganged mail boxes to pick up his rejection notices—barefoot in his loin cloth, winter and summer. He lived alone, next to the Pasteurs in a rough hewn timber cottage that was totally obscured by trees and overgrown brush. He seemed to relish obscurity, even hiding his face behind a bushy white beard. He bought the place in the 30's to find solitude; found it, and never left. One Christmas he came to our cocktail party beardless in a going-to-see-a-publisher type business suit. No one recognized him. His masquerade must have failed because his beard and loin cloth soon reappeared. On another Christmas he brought me a present, a Howard Pease book, "The Black Tanker". I eventually read all 12 of Pease's adventurous sea stories. These books reinforced Uncle Ed's tails of his travels on tramp steamers in the 1930's. To make some "pin" money at Christmas time my sister Helen and I sold greeting cards door-to-door. Mr. Price always bought at least one box, although he didn't believe in Christmas and never sent any cards. Once he found two cards in a box that had poems he had written. My sister and I were impressed that someone so famous, modest, and generous lived among us.

The Bartletts — Mr. Bartlett was the head librarian of the famed San Francisco Library. He and his Aleut wife moved into an old summer house just above us on a very steep road in 1946. Mr. Bartlett commuted to the "City". In his official capacity he received complimentary tickets to "openings" at the San Francisco opera. He didn't like opera. Mother and Mrs. Bartlett would pile into our family car, Mrs. Bartlett was a notoriously bad driver, and head up Bayshore Highway. The openings of the San Francisco opera became a ritualistic ladies night out. The Bartletts had two sons, one a goof off three years my junior, and one, Peter, my age who was to become a grand master chess champion. To my mortification Peter beat me in the across the lake swim race of 1953. Adding insult to injury, he didn't practice! Unfortunately, Peter was murdered in Alaska by one of Mrs. Bartlett's lovers some years later.

Their house was about half way up the steepest hill around, 200 feet from our hedge. It was at the exact location were bicycle brakes would burn out on the unsuspecting flatland kids. There were many spectacular crashes. Bikers would hit our thick hedge at warp speed of 30 miles per hour. Lucky for them, the dense foliage cushioned their impact. The most serious bike crash I can remember resulted in a bloody nose and broken arm. One night a car blasted through our hedge, down two terraces, and into our chicken coop where 16 hens peacefully roosted. The drunk, and fortunately unhurt, driver fled the scene. With their roost upset and an alternative shelter at hand a dozen chickens re roosted in the wrecked car. When the repo men came to fetch the car three days later the chickens seemed genuinely sad to see their white-walled coop dragged away. I saw the men flip a coin to see which of them would sit in the wreck as it was towed.

Jesus Garcia — Jesus and his wife Maria lived about a mile from us. Mr. Garcia worked for the utility district. He fixed leaky water pipes. The iron pipe system installed in the 1920's in Emerald Lake was well passed its useful life. The pipes, buried in the road about two feet deep, broke regularly causing interesting geysers and sink holes. Mr. Garcia patched the pipes while they were still under pressure so service would not be cut off. This involved digging down to the pipe by hand, installing a bolt-on collar, back-filling and patching the blacktop. He had a gas powered portable pump to keep the hole as dry as possible as he worked. It was always a great show, particularly when the hole was on the top of the pipe. Mr. Garcia donned a yellow slicker and sou'wester in his futile attempts to stay dry. After fixing a particularly voluminous geyser in front of our house one winter shortly after we moved in, mother invited Mr. Garcia into the house to dry out and warm up. Over glasses of red wine they started a lasting friendship based on their shared interest in chickens. They would babble on for what seemed like hours. Mother liked to speak Spanish and Mr. Garcia enjoyed conversation in his native tongue. They both understood chickens, Jesus raising them for profit, mother keeping laying hens. Mother and I visited Mr. Garcia's home to purchase spring chicks every year. Before the war Mr. Garcia was a migrant farm laborer from Tiajuana. He enlisted in the US Army, fought in the Pacific and established US citizenship. On his modest utility salary, with a little help from his chickens, he was able to provide his own style "American Dream" for his homemaking wife and four children.

These were some of the diverse people of our neighborhood. They were the software — they made it tick; but the collection of old, remodeled, and new houses; big and small, was the unique fabric that accommodated the great variety of lifestyles. The whole unplanned mess would be quite illegal today. When built, no permits were sought or needed. By today's standards most of the houses were building code and zoning disasters. For the most part they were sited, framed, plumbed, wired, roofed and added to, by owner-amateurs. The wood-frame houses, like the people, were unpretentious, sometimes poorly proportioned, proudly eccentric and surprisingly functional.

Most of the original lots were very small. The larger, more regular lots were created when the old golf course was subdivided in 1944. The new development could most easily be distinguished from the old by the absence of the spectacular mature tree cover in the older parts of the community. Red oak, white oak, bay and eucalyptus giants gave the feeling of living in a forest. The roads were steep, narrow and winding— perfect for walking. The relatively high density put all the necessities within reach by foot; this was particularly important for youngsters growing up. The Community Store, Emerald Lake, the "Boulder", the "Big Hill" and the houses of friends were walk-able. "We shape our buildings and then they shape us" is a loose paraphrase of a Churchill quote that some say he stole from Shakespeare or Vetruvius. Wherever the thought comes from, it is indeed too bad our old illegal melange of a neighborhood could not be replicated today. In all of its eccentricity and diversity it would be a great place to live. It was Neo-traditional urban design without high paid consultants, before Neo-traditional urban design was invented. One reason that "diversity" is in such demand these days is that it is so hard to find in ordinary life. I visited the old neighborhood several years ago and was very disappointed. It had been discovered and rebuilt under the yoke of regulations and affluence. Literally rebuilt, the old houses were purchased for their sites, torn down, and replaced with ostentatious mini-mansions. In the place of converted summer homes, I found big new expensive fake Spanish colonial houses too large for their sites. The mature trees that shaded the land and contributed so much to the character of the neighborhood had been cut down to provide garages and paving for the SUVs of the upwardly mobile. Fortunately, the Lake remains much the same.

The benefits derived from the lack of planning for the Emerald Lake neighborhood were gloriously augmented by accidents of topography. Two are worth mentioning. The "Boulder" as we called it, is a sandstone formation depicted on the USGS map as Henley Rock. It is situated on a high point in the foothills about a half mile from Hampton Glen. From its 50 foot summit there is a very good view of Redwood City and San Francisco Bay beyond. On the 4th of July the neighborhood families would crowd the summit to view the fireworks and enjoy an evening libation. The steep surrounding five acres of "badlands" made up of boulders and scrub brush could not be developed, so it became tax sale orphaned land. Neighborhood families, particularly the children, adopted the "badlands" for a natural park. Concealed in the brush and rocks were caves carved by the ancient action of water upon the soft sedimentary sand stone. To gain the summit of the "Boulder" one climbed up notches carved in the rock. A couple of places fissures had to be jumped. On the top, neighborhood kids carved their initials for posterity. I checked on mine several years ago. They are still faintly visible with my then girlfriend Judy's after 50 years.

The "Boulder" offered our generation of Emerald Lake kids an exciting place for hide-and-seek, cowboys, and steal the flag (sometimes in the dark), all without serious injury except for one rattlesnake bite, a broken collar bone and memorable close calls. One time we were playing cowboys when one of the "enemy" tried to sneak up on our bastion on top of the rock by clinging tenuously to the rounded rock crown just out of sight. When we spotted him he began to slowly slip away, his fingernails scratching across the rock. I extended the barrel of my BB gun to him while my friend held my legs. He grabbed the barrel just in time, pulling himself up the gun until I could grab his hand. We all grew up some that day, learning a lesson about taking dumb chances. None of us told our mothers of this close call. My mother continued to confidently send us to the "Boulder" to get us out of her hair without the slightest apparent fear we might hurt ourselves. If any of us did hurt ourselves we knew mother would say it was our own dumb fault. Contrast that to neighborhood parks today, where 30% of the cost of equipment is the manufacture's expense of defending against lawsuits from claimed injuries. I think we had more fun, and learned more.

Another natural feature of our neighborhood was what we called the "Big Hill". This too was an un-developable orphan track of land. It was a very steep grassy hillside located 150 yards from our house. Perhaps altogether 3 acres, this bit of precipitous open space served the kids of our neighborhood very well. When the grass dried out in the Spring it was perfect for sliding on flattened cardboard boxes at considerable speed, the western equivalent of eastern kids sledding in the snow. However, before the grass dried our favorite game was sod fighting. When a bunch of grass was pulled out a ball of soft earth remained attached to the roots. This would be compacted in our fists for the business end of the sod missile. Without too much effort the missiles could be hurled 100 feet. Usually we played with five or six on a side. Once hit, the person left the field. It took 10 or 15 minutes of battle for all the contestants from both sides to be hit. The battle stopped. We then sat on the hill and relived the great battle. These were friendly fights. One could take a nasty hit occasionally on the head, resulting in a bump. There was one time when the sod fight turned nasty.

A gang of innovative city kids staying with the Crockers attacked our gang with improved missiles. It almost cost me an eye. They broke bottles and imbedded glass in the soft earth balls. I caught one on the bridge of the nose that split my nose open. I left the field bleeding profusely. My step-father assured me he saw much worse on Tarawa as he grasped me in a head lock to stop my flinching from his efforts to stem the bleeding. Actually, the pain was slight compared to the dramatic show of blood. He quickly patched me up. For the next 20 years I was frequently asked how I got the nasty scar on the bridge of my nose. Five decades later, other more prominent creases and imperfection on my face have ended the questions about my scar from the "Big Hill".

The hill was also a good place to test-glide model airplanes that most of the boys in the neighborhood built. The steep slope guaranteed a long flight and a gentle landing in tall grass, that is unless the model flew straight. Then it would crash land on the unforgiving blacktop road, or even worse on the roof of Dr. Gobar's house across the street. Dr. Gobar chased me and my friend Jerry all the way to my house when he found us on his roof after his afternoon rounds at Hillcrest Hospital. He must have been in a bad mood or thought we were burglars. Mother offered him a glass of wine as they discussed our misdeeds. The good doctor took us to task for breaking a trellis in making our ascent. Mother suggested he leave a ladder out for future aerial rescues. The doctor could not argue with her logic and said he would leave a ladder along the side of his house for future use. So introduced, mother added the attractive, single Dr. Gobar to her Christmas party list.

Patch died under Dr. Gobar's house. Patch was a medium sized, flea bitten, non-descript brown mongrel dog. We named him for the white patch on his left ear and eye. He led a troubled life panhandling off the families in our neighborhood. He was dumped out of a car on the

Emerald Lake dam, probably by his first owner who found little use for him after he grew out of the cute puppy stage. For several years he romped and played with neighborhood kids following them home in the hopes of a bit to eat. We took him into our house on wintry rainy nights when he appeared at the door wet, lonesome, cold, and hungry. Mother was happy to feed him and let him sleep with our cat and dog in the kitchen, but she resisted our efforts to make Patch a permanent member of the Hampton household. Patch was sweet tempered. He loved to play with us even in his malnourished and mangy condition. Unfortunately, nobody really wanted Patch. Everyone knew if he were reported to the county Animal Control Officer he would be euthanized or used in medical research, prospects horrible enough to save him from this fate. For three years he scrounged, played, and forlornly waited for some family to love him in spite of his deteriorating condition.

On the fateful day Patch played with us on the "Big Hill" until late in the afternoon. We were walking home up a steep part of the road, several kids on each side. Patch took a notion to cross from one side to the other just as Mr. Martel floored his old Chevy to get a run on the hill. Patch didn't make it. From a few feet away I saw the car roll over Patch, first the front wheels then the rear. Mr. Martel stopped. Patch got up shivering, looked at me with glazed brown eyes, then threw up. He turned and wobbled down toward Dr. Gobar's house where he found the uncovered foundation vent that provided access to the crawl space and disappeared. Mr. Martel told us to stay away from Patch because badly wounded animals can instinctively attack. We ran home, told mother what happened, and she immediately called the county Animal Control Officer. He arrived at our house in about half an hour. We ran back to Dr. Gobar's house, the officer following us in his pick-up truck. The officer wiggled into the crawl space with a flashlight and a small black bag. A few moments later he backed out pulling Patches' body by the hind legs. As he lifted the limp mass of our former playmate into the truck the officer told us he had to put Patch to sleep.

Whenever I see people walking on a road with a unleashed dog my mind flashes to 1950, and the instant the wheels rolled over Patch. That look Patch gave me before he went to that dark place, a look that seemed to say I am now even less lovable, but my nature ordains that I still love you. I wonder what normally decent people say about me when I stop my car and beg them to leash their dogs. "There goes another cranky old man", I expect.

The Emerald Lake neighborhood had no public parks. In the summer the grounds and lake of the Emerald Lake Country Club were our park. After the Fall clean up at the end of September, the Lake was partially drained for flood protection. The Club gates were locked until the next spring. It was our good fortune to have the "Boulder" and the "Big Hill".

EMERALD LAKE COUNTRY CLUB

Even though the Emerald Lake Country Club was a shadow of its former self, after the war it continued to be the focus of neighborhood life. The club was not very exclusive in the true "country club" tradition. Any family willing to pay $100 for the season could join without further adieu. Individual memberships were offered for $27 per year. Special arrangements for membership were made for those without funds; the usual means being work in lieu of dues. Several of my young friends took advantage of this form of membership. When the Hobrechts visited Hampton Glen they paid a 50 cents per person guest fee to swim in Emerald Lake. Kids under 12 were free. Altogether there were about 35 family memberships and 50 individual memberships.

The old Emerald Lake club house sat majestically on a hill overlooking the lake. It was sold to become a private residence in 1946 to keep the club solvent. Herb Gardener bought it. He worked with David Packard and Bob Hewlett in a Palo Alto garage, trying to get a computer company going. The sole remaining property of the club was the lake surface itself and a narrow strip of land between the road that curved around the irregular lake shore. The only part of the road that was straight was the 100 yard long portion that ran on the top of the earth-filled dam. In the old days the main beach was located in front of the clubhouse, which served both the lake and the golf course on the north shore. When hard times forced the club to sell the golf course and later the club house, the main beach, dressing rooms and life guard shack were moved across the lake where there was more room between the lake and circumfrential road. The start of the annual cross-the-lake swim was the last remaining use of the old beach area. I can remember lining up, ankle deep in sandy mud with 12 other free-style racers, trying to suppress pre-race nerves while gazing out 200 yards to the finish line, a barely visible rope supported by football size white wooden floats on the other side of the lake.

If Alexis De Tauquville appeared at Emerald Lake some 120 years after his lauded tour of the US in the 1830's, he would recognize the same volunteer self sufficiency he so fondly documented in his book "Democracy in America". Emerald Lake Country Club had no staff. All work, except for the paid summer life guard and the kid who cleaned the locker rooms, was accomplished by volunteers. The mild California climate provided a four month swimming season. The rest of the year club members improved the facilities and performed required maintenance. The work was organized and directed by Charles Belton, the club's elected President and Chief Executive Officer, a portly Caterpillar Tractor salesman when not on lake business. The volunteer work was accomplished cheerfully. All the members, young and old, had a stake in the results. Two special projects of the club's volunteers come to mind, one successful, the other not.

Teen Beach—In the 1950's the "baby boom" was in full swing. There were little kids everywhere, four of them my mother's. They were particularly noisome to the lake teenagers, who like my sister and myself, were born in that small depression cohort just before the war. The little kids seemed to always be underfoot; and worst of all, un-nervingly honest observers of the teen condition. They undermined our awkward attempts to grow up with at least a little dignity intact. In sharing limited beach space with the kiddies, we were always under the scrutiny of adults who were there to mind the legions of toddlers. It seemed that no teenager could ever reach adulthood under these impossible circumstances. Something had to be done!

One evening at my house, after a uproarious game of hearts with lots of friendly cheating , six teenagers hatched a plot to remove themselves once and for all from the shackles of toddler and parental oppression at Emerald Lake. The solution was to build a teen beach. As we discussed the idea several potential sites were considered; most were rejected. The two locational criteria that evolved as paramount were: 1) the beach could not be observed from the main beach or life guard shack, and 2) access had to be controlled. Imagine the chaos if a couple of stray six or seven year olds pursued by parents stumbled onto a beach where teenagers were self-consciously holding hands with the opposite sex. These concerns left us with but one choice. The prospective teen beach must be located behind the women's dressing room on an unimproved 80 foot strip of lakefront whose isolated and unimproved condition was the exclusive hangout of an ex heavy weight prize fighter who had been enjoying it just the way it was since 1925. We would have to deal with John Williams.

John was a founding member of the Emerald Lake Country Club in 1923. In his early career he earned his living in the ring. He was a "contender" in the 20's and early 30's. We heard that he was quite conspicuous on the San Francisco social scene. My Uncle Saint Claire remembered that John Williams was a big tipper. As a kid Uncle Saint worked the locker room desk at the Olympic Club where "Big" John worked out. In 1950 boxing was long behind big John and so were the old days at the lake. All that remained was his little solitary refuge on the lake front where he set up his beach chair each weekend in the summer, and his permanent spot in the boat house for his varnished wood canoe. In 1928 he purchased the canoe; tried it once, didn't like it, and hung it from the rafters in the boat house. For 30 years no one questioned its right to be there or its owner's intentions.

Big John was a creature of habit. Every summer weekend he made the trip from his apartment in San Francisco down the Peninsula. Except for the few times he brought a lady friend, he arrived alone in his yellow Cadillac convertible, top down. He parked in the exact same place each weekend. He set up his beach chair in the same spot, facing the same way, on the same old tattered beach blanket. He lumbered into the water at exactly the same place three times a day. He swam the same course with a slow deliberate Australian crawl, breathing each stroke. In the water he followed an invisible grove in the surface he etched in 30 years of repetition. He passed the time reading "The Wall Street Journal" and hard cover books. Very few people ever spoke to him, leaving him the respectful distance he seemed to want.

The first step was approaching "Big" John. None of us teens had ever spoken to him. He did his thing; we did ours. The project required not only communicating with him, but ultimately securing his collaboration. It was decided that three of us would approach "Big" John, none of us individually having the nerve to initiate the contact; each of us secretly thinking one of the others would make the pitch. "Big" John had to be on our side if we had any hope of getting President Belton's approval. We figured that we would need about $200 of supplies from the club for wood, sand and timber. We would supply the labor.

We found John in his usual place, reclining his sagging bulk in perfect orientation to the sun, his face in a book. The three of us invaded his peaceful space, standing there on the edge of his blanket, just staring. He looked up over his reading glasses saying nothing. I got pokes in the ribs and said "hello". Then, as if some linguistic dam had burst I spilled out the whole pleadings. When I lacked momentarily for words my fellow diplomats enthusiastically chimed in. He remained stone like, not moving or speaking. When we finished there was an excruciating pause. He looked at us; we at him. Then, when the passage of another second would have us all running from the spot, his face cracked wide open into a smile. This was the first sign that his computer was on and he was open to our arguments. He spoke like he swam, very slowly. He liked to use big words—at least big for us. He said he understood our need for privacy "commensurate" with our status in life. When he said "commensurate" we still weren't sure whether he was for us, or against us. As it turned out he was for us. We overlooked John's big words since it was his problem that he had to deal every day with boring adults in his stock brokerage business that demanded important words. He asked us if we considered him an adult. I said; "absolutely not". More to the point we assured him that he would have full privileges on the teen beach when it was constructed. "Big" John helped us draft a letter to President Belton expressing the dire need for a teen beach as soon as possible, and pleading for $200 for construction materials. The letter assured President Belton that the new beach would greatly enhance the club's value to its members by providing a place to concentrate disruptive teenagers away from the adult areas of the beach and especially to keep toddlers safe from being crushed by careless ball tossing teenagers. I typed the letter on our family's old Royal portable set up on "Big" John's beach blanket under his watchful eyes. He signed the letter along with my two henchmen.

After due consideration, President Belton sent a letter to our new found Godfather, "Big" John, agreeing to our request. He further stated that our money request was turned down by the Board since there was no money. He concluded on the hopeful note saying he believed the money could be raised in the Fall from proceeds coming from the fund raising annual Emerald Lake Country Club Ball. This was June, school was out. How could the old lake politician be so insensitive, we thought. Our new hero, "Big" John stepped in and provided the $200. We immediately made him an honorary teenager for life!

I made a list of materials with the help of my stepfather. He also fetched the supplies in his jeep truck. We were in business; sort of. First we had to decide who was an official teenager; there were some 12 and 13 year olds that wanted to join the work crew in the hopes of being allowed onto the teen beach when it was finished. We convened a summit at my house to settle this delicate question and organize the work. Since many of the teens were 15-17, and they intended to do a great deal of the work, the decision was that if your age didn't have "teen" in it you were not a teen! This was something of a victory for the younger teens, since several sixteen-plus teens argued that a teen was hardly a fully qualified teen without a California drivers license. However, a look at the amount of earth and sand that had to be moved led to the practicality of inclusion.

The work was hard. The area to be cleared and leveled with pick and shovel was about 12 feet wide and 35 feet long—the width dictated by the circle necessary for teens to lay on a large blanket to play cards. The length was established by the space for the circle, a buffer zone, and "Big" John's special sand patch. Board retaining edges had to be constructed to hold the sand, forming a teen sandbox as one unkind parent observed. Then there was the matter of entering the water. A small dock over the muddy shore and through the thick tulles would be needed to get out to water deep enough for diving and swimming. We borrowed a fence post ram to drive 4X4 posts into the mud out about 15 feet. We built a light 2X4 frame and deck three feet wide. All of these things were designed and constructed by the 14 teenagers of Emerald Lake Country Club in the summer of 1953. The generous and unacknowledged help and advice from a parent or two could not undercut the great singular pride we had in our accomplishment!

In late August we had a beach party to launch our independence. We borrowed a grill, scared up hamburger, buns, potato chips and Hawaiian Punch mix for the big event. The grill overheated, the hamburgers burned, the buns got sandy, and the punch was lukewarm. This lack of perfection was barely noticed as we were dedicated to having a good time; and we did! Jim, the lifeguard, who normally would not be welcomed on teen beach, was the invited guest of honor.

This was Jim's second year as Lifeguard. He attended Stanford University part time, not enough credit hours to earn a deferment from the draft. At 20, unmarried, not a full time student and in good health his Selective Service number went into the draft pool lottery every six months. About 30% of those eligible would be drafted by lottery. He took a chance; the summers seemed endless; he survived four lotteries. His luck ran out in the July 1953 lottery. The Draft Board ordered him to active duty September 15th. In 5 weeks he would report for boot camp at Fort Ord in Monterey; by Winter he would be in Korea in the UN sponsored peace keeping force. My battle scared stepfather said Jim was lucky because the shooting part of the Korean war ended that July. This was good luck? Our image of Jim was seeing him jumping out of his wire-wheeled 1932 Ford V-8 coup in swim suit and sneakers ready for work. It was hard for us to imagine our Jim in an Army great coat, rifle in hand, snow frosting his helmet, hunkering down in a muddy trench a world away. The grim images on black and white TV seemed fantasy, not reality. We only knew Jim in the California summer, a tanned authoritative Adonis with a whistle around his neck. Emerald Lake folks, young and old, thought he was the best Lifeguard ever! An entourage of little kids attended him, sitting in the sand around his elevated chair, or if he moved, following him like gnats. With difficulty he separated himself from his attendants and showed up late at the party. Big John made a special Hawaiian Punch toast to Jim, wishing him luck in the Army. That afternoon we were full of food, our youthful selves, camaraderie for Jim and Big John, pride in our accomplishment and secure in the California afternoon sun.

The last time I saw Jim, the life guard, was on Montgomery Street in San Francisco three years later. It was 1956, the year I graduated from high school. I had a part-time job chauffeuring for a rice merchant, Mr.

Green. His office was on Montgomery Street in the "City's" financial district. When Mr. Green had finished working China Town taking rice orders, I drove him, and his wife, Rosamond, to the Green Company office on Montgomery Street. Here Mr. Green checked on his boxcars full of Texas long grain, usually somewhere in Arizona, and placed his new orders. If it was past 5:00 PM, Mr. Green sent me to the Foster's Cafeteria 2 blocks down Montgomery Street for dinner. It was while I walked to my breaded veal cutlet that I spotted Jim, the lifeguard. While totally out of context, we still recognized each other instantly. A three piece pin stripe suit stretched over his large muscular frame. We shook hands. He said he survived the bitter Korean weather; finished Stanford; got married and was currently a stock broker for Dean Witter. I felt myself shrinking in size and retreating back in time to the foot of his lifeguard chair! He asked me what I was doing. I told him I was still just a student, finding part-time work where I could. Jim surely led a charmed life I thought, as I dug into my breaded veal cutlet and mashed potatoes!

We didn't forget our patron and honorary teen, "Big" John. On his birthday, which was just one week after the dedication party, we had another party especially for him. I personally baked a chocolate cake from the finest cake mix available at the Community Store. The budget would not support acquiring 55 candles, nor would the cake surface accommodate such a spectacle. Instead we put one big candle in the center signifying that the honoree was number one with us. Helen, my sister, mixed up an big pitcher of Cool Aid to wash down the gooey slightly undercooked cake. On that special late summer day it seemed we would be teenagers forever, that our beloved "Big" John would be with us forever and there would always be a teen beach in our lives. I remember suppressing a fleeting thought that soon school would abruptly break the spell of summer at Emerald Lake. It did, but the teen beach and its denizens would reincarnate at Emerald Lake for several more summers. Then, inevitably we grew up; our core group began to dissipate. Some went off to university, some started jobs, some moved away.

Boxing was on my mind in the Spring of 1966. I lived in London then. Muhammad Ali came across the Atlantic to defend his heavy-weight title against Henry Cooper, the British National Heavyweight Champion. Ali won in a sixth round TKO. A few days after the fight I received a surprise letter from a former teen beach denizen. The subject was "Big" John, our teen beach heavyweight. He said he saw John Williams' obituary in the San Francisco Chronicle and thought I might like to have a copy, which he enclosed. It was an impressive full column write-up headed by an old ring photo. Much was made of John's ath-letic career in boxing. It even mentioned his association with Emerald Lake Country Club! At the end it said John Williams left no kin. I felt like honorary kin, because of the freshness of his memory. The obituary forgot to mention that "Big" John was an honorary teenager for life. Who would know and who would care? Probably, only those teens on the beach at Emerald Lake those 4 summers in the early 50's. And of them, to my knowledge, not one of the original 14 beach teens attended his funeral. When "Big" John died I was the 28 year old project director in charge of designing one of the British New Towns. I was married, had one son with another on the way and stressfully overworked. Life was for looking forward, not backward, to of all places, teenage roots. The 14 had all grown far away from shared teen years by then. If we all appeared in a room together in 1966 it would be questionable whether we would even initially recognize each other. Yet, on reflection, those precious summers on teen beach are part of us. For me, "Big" John, teenager for life, will always be there in my memories lounging in his beach chair on that tattered blanket, finned yellow Caddie parked nearby as usual.

Not all the projects approved by President Belton came out as success-fully as teen beach. The club leadership seemed to have an unquenchable thirst for recapturing the past grandeur of the club and a collateral unre-alistic optimism. In fact, many projects, particularly those with the strong political support of just a few vocal club members, ended up revealing insights into human nature and economic circumstances heretofore unappreciated by the club's establishment. A case in point is the Emerald Lake Country Club Aquacade.

In 1952 a very attractive lady moved to the Lake with her husband and their young daughter. They rented a house on the road that ringed the lake. From their elevated porch they could see the large main beach. Madeline had the distinction of swimming in the giant Aquacade spectacle staged for the 1939 San Francisco World's Fair. The fair celebrated technology, and particularly the opening of the San Francisco/Oakland Bay bridge; a marvel of engineering. The Fair was held on a manmade portion of Treasure Island located mid bay. This is where suspension cable design meets cantilever design; long spans over deep water on the San Francisco side required a cable suspension bridge like the Golden Gate Bridge several miles away at the "gate". On the Oakland side a cantilevered design was preferred since spans could be shorter. The natural island was extended to the north with fill from bridge construction. Madeline, along with 240 other swimmers, performed in a huge pool constructed specially for the Aquacade. After the fair the other swimmers went back to regular work; except Ester Williams, who went into the movies and Madeline, who began a career as a swim coach and Aquacade instructor.

My mother thought Madeline was beautiful, like Ester Williams. This surely accounts for some of the splash she made on the club's social scene. It was not long before she attracted President Belton's attention. She had the instincts of a fine cutting horse when it came to breaking a man free at a cocktail party for an intimate tete-a-tete. Soon the Board of Directors of the Emerald Lake Country Club had before them a proposal for an Emerald Lake Aquacade that would restore the club to its former eminence and provide sorely needed physical activity for the club's young women, who it might be added, were totally unaware of their lack of exercise. The proposal had President Belton's full support. The only thing the club would have to provide was a raft from which to start the aquacade. Madeline's said her husband, with the help of four or five club members, could easily build a suitable raft. The fact that her husband, a master carpenter, never built anything that had to float did not surface. The Board approved a budget of $250 for building materials for the raft. To the man, the Board volunteered to help build the raft. The women Board members where a bit skeptical, but voted for the scheme anyway, providing sufficient "rope". There was no time to waste. The debut of the Aquacade would be on the occasion of the club's annual July 4th festival that included swimming races, diving contests, and a sumptuous barbecue. July 4th was only 3 months away.

At first Madeline thought she would be able to make a modest living teaching local girls to Aquacade. She even had the grandiose notion that Emerald Lake could be the San Francisco Peninsula Aquacade teaching center. An ad was placed in the Redwood City Tribune announcing the time and place for the lessons. No one showed up! My mother and a few other kind hearted ladies of the club offered their daughters for lessons. That is how my sister became the grouchy Ester Williams of Emerald Lake Country Club Aquacade team. There were eventually 12 girls taking instruction. The routines were practiced on the beach. Madeline's enthusiasm and faith in great results charmed many of her students. She projected her vision of scores, maybe even hundreds of highly syncopated bathing beauties moving rhythmically to beautiful amplified music in a huge crystal-clear pool with a waterfall at one end. The reality was a lumpy beach, murky lake water, a scratchy 78 portable record player, 12 skinny flat chested preteen girls, and a group of by-standing irreverent boys who had nothing better to do than to harass the classes.

Madeline's optimism and vision, perhaps self delusion, seemed to run in the family. Her husband, Bill, truly believed he could build what Madeline envisioned for the aquacade raft. The raft needed to be about 30 feet long, 3 feet wide, and 3 feet above the water. The girls would use it as a diving platform, a place to begin the Aquacade. Madeline would direct the action from a row boat nearby. Materials were ordered and construction started. The raft would be built next to the boat house within sight of the practice beach. Mutual visual reaffirmation seemed necessary to keep the faith. My stepfather, whose normal keen sense of practicality was intimidated by Bill's solid reputation as a master carpenter, did his duty and worked cheerfully with the other volunteers. The design was never committed to paper. It resided only in Bill's mind and seemed to change a fair amount as the project moved forward. In Bill's mind, wood floated very well. Whenever buoyancy was mentioned he pointed out the club's wooden row boat. He was a bit stubborn and learned by experimentation. He did not notice that the hole in the water made by the row boat's hull was the source of floatation, not the wood itself.

The raft had a structural system closely resembling standard wall studs and floor joists. The depth of the structure was 4 feet. Bill figured that a foot of wood framing underwater would float the raft about right. One of the club volunteers, an airline pilot, said he saw some docks on one of his trips that had oil drums for floats that seemed to work very well. My stepfather convinced Bill that putting oil drums under the raft would be a good safety measure. Bill reluctantly agreed only after the men discovered how heavy the raft had become when they turned it over. It took two trips to the city dump on the bay shore in my stepfather's pick-up truck to retrieve ten 55 gallon drums. Items like the drums, that were too good for the land fill, were sorted into piles for sale. The drums went for 50 cents apiece. The drums were laboriously sanded and painted, then placed between the structural members on the bottom of the raft. They were secured by a 2X2s with nails into the studs. The whole raft was painted white the weekend before the 4th. For the top deck Bill had the men mix sand in the paint for good footing. He himself painted marks every two feet to position the swimmers as Madeline specified. The work of the rehearsal sessions intensified as Madeline and her girls saw the raft being constructed before their very eyes—all this work for "their" aquacade. The raft's physical presence convinced the girls, and even the most skeptical club members, that

Emerald Lake would have at last a splendid aquacade. A reporter from the *Redwood City Tribune* was invited to cover the momentous event.

The big day came. The girls were ready as they could be with mostly dry land practice. The raft was ready to launch. It took all the male members that could be found to bring the heavy raft to the water's edge. The reporter snapped a photo of the straining men as it was being carried. The Aquacade was scheduled immediately after the diving contest, which was the last event before the barbecue. President Belton approached the microphone, his dark blue blazer with an embroidered gold seal stretched to its limits over his low slung pot belly. Few spectators realized the seal was not the club's official seal. It was on the blazer when Belton bought it from a thrift shop in 1951 when he ascended to the Presidency. He thought it looked smart. And he did look very presidential from the blazer up. Below, his baggy brown swim suit and skinny legs seemed a less convincing presidential foundation. There was little question that the President was savoring this moment, and what he was about to say. He majestically cleared his voice, said "testing" two or three times and commenced the launching ceremonies.

Madeline and Bill were brought forward to receive the appreciation of the members for propelling the club into a new exciting program. The reporter snapped another shot of them with President Belton. They modestly accepted the slight ovation offered from the crowd of about 150 that seemed to be ready for lunch. The applause would have been more enthusiastic if the gathering were not downwind from the cooking hamburgers. Ignoring his own growling stomach President Belton ordered the launch.

The men, 10 to a side, lifted the raft forcing smiles across their reddening faces as the reporter asked them to hold it while he focused his camera for a potential front page shot. Much scuffling later they struggled the raft off the beach into the shallow water. The plan was to walk the raft out until it floated proudly for all to admire. The club rowboat propelled by the lifeguard stood by to tow the raft out 100 feet where it would be anchored with two concrete blocks on each end. My step father knew they were in trouble pretty quickly when it took all their strength to keep the raft upright as it gained buoyancy. Madeline, sensing trouble cranked up the portable record player full blast. The scratchy sounds of Harry Owens and the Royal Hawaiians echoed over the green water. When the men in the deepest water had to let go the other men lost control. The laws of physics took over. The raft slowly rolled over exposing the beautifully painted white oil drums. The drums began to lift the raft until the 2X2's started to pull away from the studs. The drums popped out almost in syncopation to "Lovely Hula Hands". The lifeguard in the rowboat pursued the drums as they drifted away in many directions. The raft seemed comfortable lying on its side with six inches of white boards above the water. The men towed it toward the beach till it grounded.

Madeline, not to be defeated by the sinking of the aquacade TITANIC hurried the girls into the water. She would launch the Emerald Lake Aquacade from the beach; never been done before, or probably since! My sister and the rest of the girls waded out and began to swim in rhythm to the Royal Hawaiians rendition of "Hilo Hattie". From the shore about all one could see was 12 white swimming caps, 24 thrashing arms, and Madeline, treading water, shouting instructions. The swimmers did seem to stroke together from time to time, and once submerged into the opaque water to surface feet first in a circle. More of the audience would have stayed were it not for the pungent smell of cooking hamburgers that lured them and our representative from the press away, one by one, to the barbecue pit. President Belton, who had never launched a sinking before, seemed less grand; particularly when he took off his blazer and waded into the water to help the lifeguard retrieve barrels.

Madeline and Bill moved away the next winter. Emerald Lakers, the adults and children alike, grieved slightly that they were not the "right stuff" for performance level aquacade, and that the lake was too murky.

The Board, under President Belton's administration, declared the experiment a great $250 success. The ladies on the Board had some good ideas on how to cut the Club's loss. The next summer the barrels were reused to float the rope boundaries of the outer swim area. The raft was dismantled; its wood used to strengthen the shaky high dive platform. My sister and her cohorts went back to their normal lives of growing up without aquacade. After he enjoyed a big juicy hamburger and creamy potato salad offered on-the-house by President Belton, the Redwood City Tribune reporter left and was never seen again around the lake, and gratefully there was no story.

Emerald Lake and Hampton Glen made growing up easy. We were exposed to a great range of people, environments, and institutions, all with their warts and wonders showing. We learned that things were not always what they seemed. We learned to be resourceful and self-reliant. We learned to respect the dignity of the individual. And we learned to work, not to waste time, and to laugh at our own failures.

While Emerald Lake was a great place to grow up, it was nevertheless a real treat to get away to the "City" from time to time. My Aunt Amanda, my father's closest sister, was single and still lived in the house grandfather Barker built in San Francisco. In addition to getting away from our normal routines, my sister Helen and I knew that when we visited Aunt Amanda she would spoil us to the hilt. Mother also knew this. She accepted the spoiling and encouraged these visits, I think out of recognition that we would benefit from occasional special treatment that was not possible in a household crowded with four much younger Hampton children.

CHAPTER VII

VISITING AUNTIE

OFF TO SAN FRANCISCO

Helen and I eagerly pressed our noses against the rain streaked front window hoping to see Auntie's car. The rain pounded on the roof and gurgled in the down spout by the window as if it were happy to be on its way to Emerald Lake. Helen was 10, (see photo 13) and I was 12, that dreary early spring day in 1950. The bad weather could not dampen our spirits! Auntie would be here at 2:00 PM and we were ready. Mother packed us each a suitcase full of our best clothes—small suitcases. I had on my leather cowboy jacket my father gave me two Christmases ago. It had hairy brown and white cow hide insets on the front that smelled like ripe road kill when wet. I knew better, but I couldn't resist going out into the road in front of the house to listen for the sound of Auntie's car. The rain beaded and ran off my head, repelled by a thick coating of Wildroot Cream Oil that pasted my blond hair to my scull in comb-tooth strips . When I came back into the living room I brought the smell of death. The cat and dog ran for cover. The jacket was huge two years ago. Now it was hard to zip up. Mother planned to properly bury it after this trip. Helen had on a black wool coat that fit, new black patent leather pumps, and white ankle socks. She always dressed better than I did. Our cheeks reflected light like fleshy marble. Mother insisted we burnish our faces with a coarse wash cloth after lunch. We were two tow-headed country kids ready as we could be for a visit to the big city with our favorite aunt.

Photo 13—Helen Barker, age 11. (1950)

Mother sensed our impatience. She said that the rain had probably slowed Auntie. Her drive down the Peninsula from San Francisco normally took an hour and fifteen minutes. The Bayshore Highway was very treacherous in the rain, two slippery lanes in each direction with no barrier in the center. The speed limit was 65 mph, but most people drove 70. The name "Bloody Bayshore" was well earned. Head on crashes at closing speeds of 140 mph made this highway the most dangerous in the country. Staying in the 12 foot lanes, separated by only four inches of white paint was never easy. The most treacherous stretch lay between the southern tip of the main runway of the San Francisco International Airport and Coyote Point, five miles to the south. Here cars were regularly buffeted by 30 mph cross winds off San Francisco Bay. The only alternative route was El Camino Real, the old king's highway. It ran up the center of the Peninsula through a string of seven towns in the 20 miles between San Francisco and Redwood City. Traversing each town required negotiating five to ten unsynchronized arterial stop signals. The frequent stops and the uniform 35 mile per hour speed limit enforced by vigilant, fine hungry cops slowed the trip to over two hours. Mother, always sanguine, reminded us that Auntie was skillful at piloting her 1939 Hudson. She said that as far as she knew, Auntie had never been defeated by bad weather.

At 2:10 p.m. the bulbous blue four-door sedan lumbered around the corner and pulled up in front of the house. We ran to the front door and flung it open. Standing under the portico, we saw the front door of the Hudson slowly swing open. Out into the rain jumped Jacque. He took a quick look around, ambled over to the front steps, totally ignoring Helen and me, and cockily urinated on a potted azalea. Auntie followed popping open her umbrella on her dash for shelter. Jacque was Auntie's small white French Poodle. She loved the dog! The rest of humanity that had any contact with the animal found nothing worth liking. It snapped, barked, and underneath its bravado was a cowardly manipulative bully. Entering the house Jacque stayed very close to Auntie, recalling in his dog brain that we had a big family dog that on a previous visit bit his ear after he nipped first when introduced. Mother threw our back-pedaling dog out the back door into the rain when she heard Auntie's car. Jacque liked to pick fights when he had Auntie's protection close at hand. Auntie and mother greeted warmly. Aunt Amanda caught my sister and I up in her arms and hugged us. Jacque growled sullenly as he sniffed the still warm spot on the sofa just abandoned by our wary Siamese cat that now was perched safely on top of the refrigerator in the kitchen looking relaxed, but attentive in the expectation of the action to begin.

Amanda was my father's closest sister. Everyone called her Auntie as if she were the only real aunt in a family that actually had dozens of biologically entitled aunties. The appellation signified great love and affection for this woman who elevated the title to the zenith of family esteem. (see photo #14) After our father died, she took a special interest in Helen and me. In 1950 she was a youthful 49 year old single woman who had a great zest for life. She lived in the old family home at 438 Clement Street in San Francisco's Richmond District, where as a five year old girl she survived the great 1906 San Francisco earthquake. It was an enormous treat to be with Auntie in San Francisco. She took us to new and wonderful places and generously give us presents. Easter break from Mount Carmel Grammar School in Redwood City was our opportunity to get away from nuns, younger siblings, suburban life, and to be spoiled for three days, never mind Jacque.

Photo 14—Joe Barker (author's grandfather) and Auntie (author's aunt Amanda) holding author. (1938)

The ride was fun. We sat pressed together on the mohair bench style front seat; Helen in the middle, Jacque on Auntie's lap occasionally growling, and me by the right door. The last time we visited Auntie, one of us rode in the back seat. This caused so much squabbling between us that Auntie wisely concluded being crowded up front was preferable to the bickering. It rained all the way to "The City" as San Francisco was called by practically everybody in our family, except our East Bay relatives who seemed to think that Oakland was a city and that San

Franciscans were snobs. Rural San Jose only vaguely existed in our minds because of some ill-fated investment grandfather Hobrecht made in a prune orchard. City meant the center of urban life. To us it more especially meant the Zoo, Fisherman's Wharf, Stow Lake, cable cars, Golden Gate Park, and Auntie's loving attention. Oakland or San Jose were no competition.

Auntie kept her 11 year old Hudson in show room condition. The glossy simulated wood dash curved and bulged in amazing ways real wood could not. Imitation materials were very stylish in 1939. What stamped sheet metal did for the dash plastic chemistry did for the control knobs. A row of simulated ivory knobs told the Hudson what to do with nary a loss of tusk. Above the knobs chrome framed rectangular gages spanned the distance from the round art-deco speedometer on the left behind the steering wheel to a clock on the glove box door on the right. Except for the calibrations, the speedometer and the clock were the exact same modern design, self-consciously stylish and hard to read. The top speed on the speedometer was an astounding 120 miles per hour! The soothing tick of the clock could be heard when the engine was not running. Auntie adjusted the vacuum supplied to the wiper motors with a fake ivory knob protruding where the two part windshield made a "V" shape on top of the dash. It was no use. When Auntie accelerated the windshield wipers stopped mid-wipe; when she throttled back they went hyper trying to make up for all the missed wipes. Helen and I were in such a ready state to have a great time, that as mundane as it was, keeping the Hudson's windshield clear was hilarious. Near Brisbane Auntie hit 75 while Helen and I cheered! Everyone drove fast past Brisbane to minimize breathing in the putrid air coming from the San Francisco land fill that was on a tidal flat, immediately in front of Brisbane, an otherwise scenic hillside town. That day we were in double jeopardy! It was also low tide exposing the bay mud flats on the other side of the highway. With the rotting garbage on our left and the sewage steeped mud flats on our right we were trapped in olfactory hell. The overpowering stench was eye-watering. Rolling up the windows did no good. Speed was the only way to minimize the discomfort. The Hudson roared on in the rain delivering us safely through the gauntlet. Our spirits were high! We laughed.

Hudsons were a family tradition because of Krieger. Mother drove a '36 Hudson Terraplane. Uncle Saint Claire drove his third Hudson, a low slung '48 Hudson Super Six. Auntie drove her vintage '39 Hudson Deluxe. Krieger and Son, Inc. sold and serviced Hudsons on California Street just two blocks from Auntie's house. His showroom, shop, and display lot was part of a subdivided estate. The old carriage house had been converted to his showroom, the barn to his shop. He sold only the number of cars he and his son could service. When we arrived in the "City" Auntie pulled into Krieger's for gas. Krieger himself came out in the rain in his grease monkey smock and greeted Auntie warmly. His gray hair squirted out from under his oil soaked leather mechanics scull cap. He asked brightly; "Are these Cecil's kids"? Auntie said that we were her brother Cecil's children. He greeted us with a big smile and a "aren't they fine looking children". They both momentarily grieved about my father's untimely death. Then Krieger asked: "Is the car running OK"? Auntie said the car was running like a Swiss watch. Krieger said; "good"! He was in no mood to fix another Hudson that gloomy afternoon.

Krieger sold gas the old fashioned way, from a enormous, elevated glass vile with horizontal marks for gallons and quarter gallons. Auntie usually asked for 20 gallons of premium ethyl. Krieger hand pumped this amount up from the underground tank into the glass vile. Each full stroke on the long handled pump lifted a half gallon, enough fuel to propel the Hudson six more miles. Helen and I closely watched the vile fill. When the 20 gallon mark was reached, Krieger continued to pump slightly beyond the mark. Krieger was not one to shortchange his customers. He jammed the metal tipped rubber hose connected to the bottom of the vile into the Hudson's filler pipe, and opened the valve. We could hear the orange liquid gurgling into the cavernous tank as we watched the ethyl drain, line by line, from the vile. Krieger distrusted automatic gas pumps. The only evidence of the correct amount of fuel was a spinning gage that could be wrong. The old glass vile system was slow and foolproof, like Krieger and his son. At 27 cents a gallon, premium gas was not cheap! Auntie handed Krieger six dollar bills. He dug into his smock, counted out 60 cents, and passed the change to Auntie. He sincerely thanked her for her business and wished us well in our visit. We would gas-up again at Krieger's before our return home.

Like other Richmond District merchants, Krieger maintained a personal relationship with his customers. He got pleasure serving their needs, by knowing their needs, and if in the process he could make a living, so much the better. Likewise, his customers were interested in his well being. They needed him. This personal relationship bred loyalty to the old neighborhood businesses, even after people moved away. Barkers in a 50 mile radius from San Rafael to San Carlos drove Krieger Hudsons for over 20 years, until Krieger was sadly stripped of his dealership for insufficient sales in 1952. There was no good reason for Barkers to buy Hudsons from the slick new dealer on Van Ness Avenue on San Francisco's auto row. The ostentatious showroom, tiny service department, and impersonal staff alienated the Barkers. And that wasn't all! Hudson Motors, usually technologically innovative, produced its last innovative vehicle in 1948 with the underslung Super Six. Hudson marketing could not hide the fact that cosmetics had replaced engineering and quality. Perhaps Krieger saw this and simply could not sell more Hudsons to his customers in good conscience. The last Hudson was built in 1954. The last Hudson in the Barker family was my uncle's lowriding 1948 Super Six. In 1955 he traded it in on a Buick Century V-8, the same high powered model used by the California Highway Patrol.

438 CLEMENT STREET

Auntie's house was a marvel of adaptation. Located at mid-block, 438 Clement Street was a commercial and residential agglomeration— an encrustation of a Victorian house sitting on a standard 25' city lot. Two stores with striped awnings, plate glass display windows, and recessed entrances, took up most of the sidewalk level. On the second floor two large bay windows protruded out over the sidewalk providing views up and down Clement Street. The third level was an extension of the old Victorian gable roof. A row of 3 double hung windows provided light to the apartment in the gable. To the right of the stores was a small recessed entrance alcove for the living units above, providing a three foot by three foot sheltered space out of the busy foot traffic of the side- walk to juggle keys and fetch mail. The entry landing, one step up from the slightly sloping sidewalk, was paved with tiny tiles in an Egyptian motif, for no good reason other than that some earlier Barker thought Egyptian was a good idea at the time. "Amanda Barker" read the first name slot on one of the three brass mail boxes countersunk into the orange-brown "Permastone" walls. High design this was not!

The entrance alcoves and the store fronts of most of the buildings on Clement Street were trimmed with an orange-brown "Permastone". A team of slick sales people took the neighborhood by storm in 1947. Their specialty was covering real wood and stucco with an unconvinc- ing concretized fake stone. They guaranteed the simulated stone would last a lifetime and its modest cost would be paid back many times over by higher rents and lower maintenance. Auntie was sold. They were right on the first count. The second count, who knows? The material's ugliness matched its durability. The lifetimes of all the original pur- chasers, most of them lengthy, expired well before the fake stone grudg- ingly showed any sign of wear, Auntie included. Pity! On the positive side, the material provided a certain visual unity to the streetscape and reminded the customers that 1947 was a year that bound them together as a "Permastone" community.

Auntie found a parking space in front of 438 Clement Street in a one hour zone, designated by a green painted curb. Auntie said it would be no problem to stay longer because the local police officer knew her and her Hudson. Parking meters didn't appear on Clement Street until 1956. We piled out onto the busy sidewalk. Jacque sniffed the discolored lower tiers of Permastone for messages. He returned his calls with an arrogant practiced finesse. Helen and I also knew the routine of checking in on arrival. This included visiting each of Auntie's tenants in the stores.

The larger store was the shoe man. Displayed in the window were Built Rite shoes, new Stride Rite heels, metal taps, and polishes. You could see the men working through the plate glass window; looking up the men waved to recognized customers when they passed on the street. We entered passing by the battered glass-paneled door held open by a wooden wedge. From the smell of leather, contact cement, and Shinola you knew that this was a place where important things got done! The completed work was displayed on a high shelf, row upon row of paper wrapped shoes with bright yellow tags, packages of stored-up pleasure awaiting their owner's opening. That first puff of leather and polish smell when the packages were opened had to be as pleasurable as opening a fresh can of coffee. Auntie reintroduced us to Anthony, the proprietor. He wore a stained green shop coat loosely tied around his ample waist. He grinned and extended a black gnarled hand. I shook it. Helen smiled. He warmly greeted us in a thick Italian accent. Once Auntie reminded him that Helen and I were Cecil's children, he shouted in Italian over the roar of the machinery to his helper conveying the news. The helper turned away from a long row of machines whirling along the wall behind the counter and toothlessly smiled at us. Anthony and his helper handled virtually all of the neighborhood shoe repair. As we talked he resumed stitching a new tanned leather sole on a man's wing-tipped blucher on an amazingly powerful green sewing machine. I looked down at my scuffed Tom McCann oxfords with Neo-lite rubber soles that cruelly betrayed my status as just another kid. I fantasized that someday I would have real leather soles.

The smaller store belonged to Bill the jeweler. His window displayed Ingersoll, Timex, Gruen, Waltham, and Westclocks watches, Speidel watch bands, and dead flies on faded green velvet. Marketing was definitely not his forte! The store was quiet except for the tick-tock of the brass pendulum on the Regulator clock mounted on the wall behind the counter. Bill, paunchy, in his mid 50's, worked in a tan apron partially covering his white shirt and rabbinical tie. A black yarmulke adhered to the back of his bald head. As we entered he looked up over the counter from the watch he was repairing without raising his head. He flipped down the magnifying lenses that were attached to his gold framed half-glasses to see us normal size. Bill never looked up. He seemed to have become used to seeing the world over his half-frames, chin on chest. He smiled and said he was pleased to see us again. Auntie gave Bill a good deal on the store and the attic apartment. He asked me about the Westclocks pocket watch Auntie bought from him for my Christmas present. He offered to set it and adjust it if needed. Unfortunately, it would never need adjustment again. Mother washed it when I forgot to take it out of my jeans pocket. I mumbled. The store was pretty shabby. Nevertheless Bill did a good business in watch repair, obvious from the dozens of tagged watches hanging from peg board hooks behind him. During our short visit, Bill compulsively checked the time on his own gold wristwatch against the Regulator several times. Time seemed to be very important to Bill in the technical abstract of measuring its passing, but not in reality. He worked very slowly and always had time to chat. Auntie said he frequently lost track of time, particularly when the rent was due. Helen and I thought that Bill was sweet on Auntie and teased her unmercifully about what life could be with Bill, dead flies and clocks in every room!

Clement Street in 1950, as it is today, was a bustling commercial strip 12 blocks long running from Arguello Street to Park Presidio Boulevard, in the Richmond District. It's hard to imagine that the colorful continuous rows of shops and restaurants on Clement Street, block after block, entomb Victorian gingerbread detached single family houses. Addition after addition, first starting with shops on the street property line, then extensions to the side property lines, and finally expanded upper floors encapsulated the original rows of Victorian houses on Clement Street. In Auntie's house the high interior ceilings with ornate crown moldings, antique fire places, sliding paneled pocket doors, and peculiar floor plan hint at the houses' heritage. On that humid, overcast day April 19, 1906 Auntie was with grandmother Barker in this very house. She remembered being in the kitchen while pots, pans, plates, and glasses tumbled from cabinets and shelves. Furniture bounced about the room. The house survived the earthquake, and more importantly the great fire that burned most of San Francisco. Grandmother Barker from then on was fearful of humid, overcast days. She knew from terrible experience what earthquake weather was. We joked with Auntie about imminent earthquakes when it was overcast, arrogantly relying on our recently learned notion that weather had nothing to do with earthquakes.

Auntie found the right key from a brass ring holding a dozen or more jingling keys. She opened the heavy oak door, its beveled glass panels rattling under the silk shear stretched on the inside. "Home again" she said! Raucous street noises followed us into the small foyer, bouncing off the hard wall surfaces. She quickly closed the door instantly sealing off the noisy street life outside. The new world of Auntie's quiet inner sanctum was before us. In one corner of the foyer a brass umbrella stand sprouted a colorful assortment of "brawlies". Several leashes for Jacque hung from a coat stand. Auntie kept the stairwell spotlessly clean. Walls, ceiling, floor, and stairs were painted glossy white. Helen and I ran up the stairs being careful to stay on the black rubber treads, our footsteps and chatter echoing our excitement: Jacque, first to reach the mid point landing, stopped to disdainfully survey his pursuers. He knew he had never been beaten to the top. As we reached the landing he bounded up the final steps for yet again another triumph for dog-hood. The landing at the top was carpeted, part of the upstairs central hall of the vestigial house. To the right toward the rear was an apartment Auntie rented to two Chinese nurses. To the left, toward the front of the house, was the door to Auntie's apartment and a door to the attic apartment rented by Bill the jeweler. In its first 50 years the Victorian single family house grandfather Barker built had become 2 stores and 3 apartments. In its second 50 years it did not further encrust. By 1950 it had gone as far as any reasonable building code would allow, especially for flammable wood frame construction. The "Permastone" marked the time the tide of growth stopped, the high water mark.

Auntie's apartment was a treat all by itself. The two main attractions were the black and white TV, it would be two years until we had a TV at home, and a player piano Auntie bought especially for our enjoyment, she neither played the piano nor enjoyed piano music. Being excited and "wound-up" my sister and I shattered any hope Auntie might have of any peace for the next three days. I turned on the 10" TV full blast and momentarily watched bits of an old cowboy movie. The picture was speckled with "snow". When a trolley car clanged by outside the cowboys became diagonalized and buzzed off the screen to the right. My sister experimented with the player piano. It turned out to be far more entertaining than the TV. Once all the controls were mastered and the rolls played, we invented a game, "Guess the Tune". We played the rolls backwards at varying tempos. My sister and I are now among the few in the world that can identify Joplin's "Maple Leaf Rag" at half tempo backwards—a useless skill that is best left modestly concealed and forgotten. As we moved onto classical music, Auntie was in the small, compact kitchen making dinner. The kitchen had a stove/refrigerator combination. Where the oven would normally be in a regular stove, under the burner top, there was a small refrigerator. We knew dinner would be good. Auntie was a great cook! That is to say she cooked what we thought was great, hamburgers with a side of macaroni salad from the deli on the corner, and brownies from the bakery up the street. We washed down our meal with several bottles of Coke, a luxury never seen at home. Mother believed Coke rotted teeth, made kids hyper with caffeine, and insulted the consumer's intelligence by costing too much. Auntie had no such hang-ups! I must admit that I always found it difficult to go to sleep at Auntie's. It could have been the caffeine, the excitement, or the rumblings of the trolleys late into the night.

Helen and I slept on sofa beds in the front sitting rooms. We each had a bay window overlooking Clement Street. Passing trolleys rattled the big double hung windows well into the night. As usual, I found it hard to go to sleep, consoling myself by imagining the fun we would have the next day. Then it was suddenly morning. Waking up in San Francisco was a feast for the senses! Sounds and smells tantalized. Nothing like this in the "country". We only had clean air and chickens. I woke to the clanging bell of a Muni streetcar. I could hear the whine of the straining traction motor applying power to steel wheels unhappy about climbing the slight hill in front of Auntie's. Next I heard the distant groans of fog horns reverberating in from the Golden Gate as the fog retreated. My nose became operational picking up the smell of fresh baked bread, cookies, and donuts from the bakery next door. It could only be another great day in "The City"! The storm of yesterday had passed. Sun streamed in through the windows. Soon we could not stand the anticipation anymore and ran to Auntie's bed room in the middle of the house. It was located on a light well created by an indentation in her building and a reflecting indentation in her neighbors building. It was darker and quieter than the front rooms. She slept in a fluffy feather bed with Jacque. He snapped at us as we tried to arouse Auntie. I realize now that she was playing opossum and thoroughly enjoying our desperate attempts to awaken her. She finally showed signs of life, choreographed to crescendos of our pleadings. Simpson's we would say over and over. Eventually, Auntie would pull the covers from over her eyes and say, "OK Simpson's".

We dressed and folded the bedding. Everything went into the big compartments in the sofa beds. I tried more than once to stash Jacque in the compartment, but he wouldn't be fooled by the old dog in the sofa bed trick. The toilet room we used was off the hallway. The walls and floor were tiled a dark bilious green. The toilet itself was also the same green color imparting a green tint to the water and anything else in the bowl. I had never seen anything like it! It made going to the bathroom luxurious. Soon we were ready to leave.

SIMPSON'S

Auntie usually had breakfast at Simpson's before going to work. She was the popular receptionist at a nearby doctor's office. Simpson's, a brick faced art-deco restaurant/diner on Geary Street 12 blocks from Auntie's house, had become a neighborhood gathering place. The regulars had the look of a westernized Norman Rockwell illustration idealizing the American way of life. My sister and I salivated at the prospect of gobbling down fresh-baked sweet rolls dripping in butter and icing.

Auntie parked the Hudson on one of the avenue side streets. Jacque gave us all a dirty look as we left him sulking in the drivers seat. We walked around the corner, and entered. The smell of fresh-baked pastries and coffee smacked us in the face as we left the windy street. Auntie greeted and waved to several patrons in booths. We headed for the counter. The usual crowd was there, even though it was Saturday. We found three stools together in the center of the counter. On the left perched Fred, regaled in his fancy tennis sweater and white shorts. Fred, fit and 50, was in his prime as the local club tennis champion. He liked Auntie. They exchanged flirtatious pleasantries. On the right was Dr.

Hare, the local dentist. His office hung over the corner of 6th and Clement in a Victorian turret. From his chair you could look up and down Clement Street and 6th Avenue. He was eccentric, but considered a good dentist. He was treating Auntie for pyorrhea. Once he replaced a filling of mine that stuck in a stale gum ball I was chewing. Auntie's warnings unheeded, I could not resist that bright red gum ball from a rusty vending machine in the park. My penny indulgence cost Auntie five bucks and Dr. Hare an hour of his Sunday afternoon. Auntie never returned us to our mother damaged. This morning Dr. Hare wore muddy jeans and a San Francisco 49'ers sweat shirt. He had been digging in the Presidio for Emperor Norton's buried treasure.

The fat middle-aged waitress greeted us with a big ceramic smile showing off some of Dr. Hare's fine denture work. Without any instruction she placed a brimming cup of coffee on the counter in front of Auntie. The cup was massive, made from thick tan pottery. She asked; "Are these Cecil's children"? Auntie said we were. The waitress knew who my dad was and that he died recently. Auntie and the waitress commiserated briefly. After the relationships were straightened out the waitress presented a large metal tray of pastries. Helen and I made selections. I took one that had lots of frosting and a custard filling. Helen chose a bear claw. Auntie picked a Danish with nuts. In a slight gesture to health Auntie ordered tumblers of fresh squeezed orange juice for each of us. The waitress cut oranges in half and squeezed them in a machine in front of our eyes! This was really living! At home we drank canned unsweetened bitter grapefruit juice mother bought by the case. This was such a special treat! There were no diners like this where we lived; even if there were, mother would never take us out to breakfast. In the "City" having breakfast at a slick diner was what one did! I relished city life.

Fred asked Auntie what our plans were for the day. She said we were going to Stow Lake in Golden Gate Park. Fred asked us if we played tennis. I said yes in the spirit of being full-of-myself, far from home, and intoxicated by city life where everything that could be imagined was possible. Auntie seemed to bring out the fantasy in me. In reality I don't think that I had ever held a tennis racket, let alone played the game. My sister and I may have tossed a tennis ball once. In my mind with a little imagination this was center-court tennis. Fred asked if we had our tennis gear with us. Unfortunately, we left the mythical gear at home next to the nonexistent tennis courts. Fred said he had some old equipment in the trunk of his car that we could have since he recently replaced his rackets. Being a delusional tennis celebrity out of town with an embarrassment of equipment, I accepted. Fred facetiously made it clear that he was in no way insulting my game with the offer of used equipment. Smiling, Auntie assured him that the offer of his old gear was not offensive in any way. He asked Auntie to save his seat. He said, "I'll be right back".

Dr. Hare was grumbling. While Fred was playing tennis he had been out for two hours digging in the Presidio for treasure with only a sore back to show for it. The San Francisco morning paper, the *Chronicle*, was sponsoring a treasure hunt for Emperor Norton's buried treasure. Each morning a new clue was in the paper. This morning the clue appeared in a special box under the headline "Truman Asks Statehood for Hawaii and Alaska." The *Chronicle* had a way of mixing in news with promotions and counter-crowd interests. Simpson's breakfast crowd was sure the treasure was in the Presidio based on the clues of the past week. While almost everyone had an opinion on where the treasure was located, of the regulars, only Dr. Hare actually did any digging. Auntie thought they were all egging him on. Dr. Hare asked what I thought. I quickly re calibrated my imagination from tennis player to treasure hunter. This might be an opportunity to extend my non existent reputation to a new field, I thought. Anything was possible in the "City"! Auntie and Helen could always be counted on to encourage my delusions so their enjoyment of the inevitable deflation would be all the more pleasurable.

The waitress pulled out the clues from the counter copies of the *Chronicle* for the previous week. I read them with Auntie and Helen kibitzing. Auntie told us about the Emperor. He was the self-declared Emperor of San Francisco and Protector of Mexico and the Farrallone Islands. Myth had it that Norton buried a vast fortune in gold somewhere in San Francisco. His real name was Joshua Norton. In 1850, at age 30, he brought $40,000, a sizable fortune at the time, from his native England to invest in booming San Francisco "Gold Rush" real estate. He built up a half million dollar fortune buying and selling commercial properties, mostly on Montgomery Street. He became overconfident. He decided to move his assets into the booming world rice market. He failed in several attempts to "corner" the market. Eventually he lost every cent, going mad in the process. He began dressing like Napoleon. He degenerated into a tragic character of pomp and circumstance supported by several wealthy San Francisco businessmen for their amusement and their contribution to San Francisco's reputation for eccentricity. Auntie said Norton actually believed he was Emperor. The comforting thought crossed my mind that my tennis game and treasure hunting prowess would not seem peculiar to the Emperor.

Dr. Hare said that during public events Emperor Norton would be given an honored place at the head table next to the Mayor. He lived with two dogs, Bummer and Lazarus, mostly on the streets around Union Square. He pan-handled tourists and made impromptu speeches on municipal matters, like the excess of pigeons and police insensitivity. On opening nights at the theater and opera there were always three reserved seats in the front row for Norton and his royal canine entourage, courtesy of the same business men. Emperor Norton died in 1880 with no heir to the throne. Five thousand San Franciscans turned out for his funeral. The *Chronicle* hoped to increase slipping circulation by sponsoring a contest to find a planted Norton treasure. "The treasure must be buried somewhere in the landscaping in Union Square" I offered. Dr. Hare was skeptical. He leaned toward my sister's idea that a good place to dig was at Ocean Beach. In the end it really didn't matter. Shortly after our visit the contest was canceled because of pressure from property owners objecting to the pox of holes being dug all over the city.

Fred returned with two Spalding Llama tennis rackets in wooden presses and a corrugated box full of gray partially bald tennis balls. The rackets were worn down to the strings on the crown. Otherwise they looked good to me. The balls were soft and well broken in. But these were the best balls I had ever seen! The ones around our house were brought home by the dog and had already satisfied his need for a chew. I imagined being on central court hitting huge forehand ground strokes inches over the net. Fred seemed to read my mind. He suggested that we might want to practice at the squash courts in the park so the balls wouldn't go too far. We thanked Fred, tucked our new rackets under our arms, and left Simpson's eager for a game. Auntie said we could go to the squash courts after Stow Lake.

Each time we visited Auntie we would go to Simpson's at least once. We saw more neighborhood characters each time; like the man with the Salvador Dali mustache who owned the florist shop on Clement Street one block up from Auntie's. He sold cute little painted turtles from a sidewalk terrarium by the entrance to his shop. Auntie indulged our desire for personal reptilian pets after pathetic pleading. Helen and I sadly learned that the turtles always died two weeks after they were purchased, no matter how well we cared for them. We met the druggist who reeked of Lifebuoy deodorant soap, just like his store. The drug store was across the street from Auntie's. To draw in customers he had a free scale near the door standing over 7 feet high. When loaded, chromed gears slowly activated weights behind a glass covered chamber to give the customer a pseudo-scientific visual sense of gravity upon his mass. We could never get Auntie on the scale. Jacque weighed 13 pounds. One morning we had breakfast with gregarious Father Gallagher who ran Star of the Sea Parish and looked after Auntie's soul. Priests in Roman collars always intimidated me until I sat next to Father Gallagher while he ate a jelly donut dribbling powdered sugar on his black shirt and black trousers just like me. I didn't realize what a leveling influence a jelly donut could be. A Simpson's breakfast never disappointed in cuisine or company.

STOW LAKE

In 1866 Frederick Law Olmsted, the father of the field of landscape architecture in America and the designer of New York's Central Park, was asked by the San Francisco Lands Commission for his advice on the practicality of creating a major park on the sand dunes in the middle of the city. After inspecting the proposed site he pronounced the project hopeless and returned to New York. His views were ignored. The Commission hired William Hammond Hall, a retired Army engineer to design a park and to figure out how to grow a landscape on the barren, sandy, wasteland. In spite of meager funding, he did! In 1886 he hired his successor, "Uncle John" McLaren. Mclaren, a superb gardener, spent the next 60 years constructing most of the park. He lived in a cut sandstone house at the entrance to the park, not far from the Hobrecht house. He died in 1943, still in office, at age 96. One of his greatest achievements was the renowned ornamental Stow Lake shown in Hall's original plan. When he started the 20 acre site was nothing but bleak sand dunes. By 1950 the lake and its surrounding gardens were a showplace for the art of landscape architecture. Scenic paths laced though gardens bursting with blooming flowers and exotic foliage. Rustic bridges spanned small inlets and connected several islands in the meandering freeform lake. Red and white carp lurked just below the surface among the crags and rocks looking for handouts from strollers. The tour de force was the man-made waterfall built on an island with a foot-path underneath the cascade. All of these splendors paled in my mind to the one special feature I liked about Stow Lake. I got to drive a sleek electric speed boat! The brightly painted plywood boats looked fast, like Chris Craft runabouts. Actually, the motor powered by two car batteries, would just about produce enough speed to gain on a paddling duck. A visit to Auntie's would not be complete without a visit to Stow Lake.

The 10 acre lake provided interesting navigation problems. There were several islands, dead end bays, and shoals. It would take over an hour to motor around the whole lake. When we got out into the middle of the lake Auntie and Helen wanted to get off on Alford Island to take a closer look at the waterfall. The path on the island ascended the top of the 30 foot falls for a nice view of the lake. The path also wound down into a subterranean passage under the falls. Normally I would like to explore such an interesting landscape, however, the prospect of a lighter and faster boat tipped the balance in favor of chasing swans and ducks. There was one other passenger that added weight. I motored around a small island out of sight and deposited Jacque on a big rock surrounded by water. He reluctantly jumped off the boat when he realized that he was onboard without his protective mistress. I knew the dog hated water! He also may have sensed the rising water under the leaky boat's floorboards; the outer ones floated when the boat heeled. The lightened boat went faster, but not fast enough to catch even a distracted duck. I kept the three speed switch set to "fast". The boat gradually lost what little speed it had as the batteries ran down. The chase was over.

When I returned to pick up Auntie and Helen, I pretended not to noticed that Jacque was missing. Helen and I tried to convince Auntie that Jacque was at home. After a few minutes we knew the gag was over. I motored slowly back to the rock. No Jacque. Auntie got worried. We searched the area with no luck. Helen speculated that one of the giant carp nabbed him when he made a desperate attempt to swim for safety. It grabbed him by his churning legs, pulling him under. Two gulps and he was gone! My theory was that he antagonized a big killer swan. With no Auntie for protection he got gobbled up. The more Auntie worried the more grisly our descriptions of Jacque's probable fate became.

We motored slowly back to the rental dock as our batteries went dead. There was Jacque tied to a piling, being his usual obnoxious self, barking at the dock boy who saved him from his watery exile. The dock boy discovered Jacque during one of his scheduled tours of the lake to retrieve boats with dead batteries. Auntie was very happy! Jacque jumped into her arms, surveyed the audience that was straining to feel positive about his rescue, and growled menacingly. Auntie gave the dock boy $5.00 for his valor. She overpaid!

A BAD HAIRCUT

Jacque wasn't the only one that was the brunt of a cruel prank. Sunday after church, I was in a good mood. Auntie always took us to Father Gallagher's quick 9:00 a.m. mass at Star of the Sea. Father Gallagher had a way of concentrating religion—in and out in 30 minutes. Suburan religion by comparison, was slow and boring. After mass we went across the street to the Flying Saucer for breakfast. I liked the Saucer almost as much as Simpson's. We sat at the counter, front row seats for a culinary spectacle. The Saucer's theatrical owner/fry cook was the best in the business. His gastronomical ballet dazzled customers and passers-by who stopped to see him in action through the diner's steamy front window. Instead of tights and dancer's tunic, he wore a greasy white smock and tall white chef's hat. Gracefully working three grills simultaneously, he cooked eggs to order, browned hashers, fried bacon and ham, flipped perfectly done pancakes, and on the side ran a double waffle machine and 8 slice toaster. He cooked 15 to 20 breakfasts at a time. The waitress took our order on a small form and placed it in a slot on the stainless steel hood in front of the cook. He grabbed it. Read it. Memorized it. Then placed it in a new position in the slot. The action was so fast and complicated I couldn't identify our order in process, although Helen and I speculated on which sausages we would get. We ate off large plates laden with creamy scrambled eggs, hot hash browns, and greasy sausage. Like a race car fueled with high test gas, I was powered up for another great day in the "City". Little did I know that I would end the day humiliated with a terrible disfigurement.

After breakfast we stopped at a flea market in the Pan Handle of Golden Gate Park. A well-dressed man standing on the back of a low flat-bed truck was pitching knives, scissors, and electric clippers. He showed the small audience the sharpness of the knives by thinly slicing tomatoes on a small table slanted to offer a good view. He told jokes while he demonstrated his goods. There was a certain cadence to his presentation that was beguiling, even hypnotizing to my innocent brain. Helen and I never saw a pitch man before. We were enjoying the show despite having absolutely no interest in the man's wares. The seamless monologue of hucksterism flowed, as the man imperceptibly maintained a shrewd side to side surveillance of the crowd. It wasn't long before he noticed Jacque on the leash through the legs of the small group gathered around the back of the truck. He artfully switched his pitch from tomato cutting to dog clipping. He reached into a box behind him without turning around. Like a blind man who knows where things are by feel, he pulled out a dog clipper all the while smoothly pitching the audience. He zeroed in on Auntie, his piercing eyes burning right through her retina into her brain with the message, buy, buy, buy; now, now, now; if you love your dog. Auntie, knowing a hard sell when she saw one, grabbed us to leave when Helen suggested that Auntie might save a lot of money and aggravation by cutting Jacque's coat herself. Jacque hated to be cut. He was fast becoming canine non grata at the few dog grooming shops around. He snapped and bit the hands that groomed him. If it weren't for Auntie's generous tips the shops would be perpetually too booked to fit him in. The prospect of clipping Jacque down to size intrigued me. Auntie, forever skeptical about schemes that would allegedly benefit Jacque from people acquainted with him, was eventually persuaded to buy the clippers, more out of indulging Helen than agreeing with the idea of home dog care. She bought deluxe animal clippers with attachments and instruction book. The man on the truck leaned over and took Auntie's money. As he stuffed the bills into his pocket he complimented Auntie on her sharp eye for a bargain. Then in a reassuring voice, as he handed over the clippers, he said: " It's as easy as one, two, three".

When we got back to Auntie's apartment Helen pointed her finger at my head and said that my hair was longer than Jacque's. In all fairness, she said, sounding suspiciously like the truck pitch man, it was her brother that needed a haircut more than Jacque. Auntie agreed. But it was Sunday and there were no barber shops open. Helen, always creative, suggested they could do me a great favor and give me a haircut. She said people hair, particularly straight hair like mine, was much easier to cut than curly dog hair like Jacque's. She proclaimed that my case would be good practice. After the Stow Lake affair Auntie could not be faulted for some interest in the idea of practicing on me. Helen said she watched mother cut my hair many times with her old hand operated clippers. It would be so much easier with the big power clippers to get the right effect. Since my mother always cut my hair I had no idea what a bad haircut could be like. I was simply not hair conscious. The thought of the special attention from my favorite Aunt as she lovingly did my hair beguiled me into agreeing to the experiment.

I should have known that I was in big trouble when Helen said that the only equipment needed in addition to the clipper was a large bowl. Auntie remembered seeing a movie starring the Three Stooges where a bowl was used as a guide for haircutting. In order to build my confidence they sat me on a stool, draped a towel around my shoulders barber style, and in sugar coated tones reassured me of their expertise. Jacque looked on with cynical interest.

Auntie placed the bowl on my head and began running the powerful clippers around its lip as a guide. I watched chunks of blond hair hit the floor. She removed the bowl to study the results. Sure enough after a few minutes I looked like Mo. Helen and Auntie burst into laughter at Auntie's handiwork. I was becoming uncomfortable despite their soothing comments made between hysterical fits of laughter. Helen told Auntie that she could improve the cut with some tapering which she saw our mother do many times. Helen went to work. Unfortunately it was hard to start a taper above the ears. Soon amid howling laughter the job was done. I asked for a mirror. Auntie fetched one from her dresser, handed it to me, and said perhaps more tapering would help.

What I saw horrified me! There was no hair below the ears. Above the ears there was stubble with exposed skin in streaks converging in a tuft at the top. Helen admired her work as original and innovative. I howled! Auntie offered to cut some more—I fled the chair. Jacque, who ordinarily would be enjoying my distress, remained cautiously subdued gripped by dog instincts that he could be next. Now what to do? Auntie promised to take me to the barber on 6th Avenue first thing Monday. Forever optimistic, she said he could fix me up like new. In the meantime she searched the house for a hat to hide the carnage. The closest thing to a man's or boy's hat she could find was an old Shriner's fez left by one of her former gentleman friends. I looked at the red tasseled truncated cone incredulously. I put it on my head. A bit large, it rested on my ears. But it was the only choice of headgear until Monday.

That evening Auntie took us to the Star of the Sea parish carnival. I began to have a good time, playing the games of chance and skill that were arrayed in the parish hall. The food was good—foot long hot dogs, potato salad, and ice cream. When Auntie introduced us to friends nobody mentioned the fez on my head. They all knew that I was not a Knight Templar, but were delicate enough not to ask about the hat; perhaps secretly speculating that it covered a bad case of ring-worm that was epidemic in many public schools at the time. I almost forgot it was there until the tassel dropped into my ice cream. Then the ultimate of all embarrassments happened. I won a prize. Father Gallagher asked the young man in the fez to come forward and receive a two pound box of

Blums. I tried to resist, plums I thought. I wailed to Auntie "I hate plums"! Helen and Auntie pushed me forward. When I got to the stage Father shook my hand so vigorously that the fez rocked for and aft on my fulcrum ears until it plummeted forward to the floor. The onlookers sat in stunned silence at my exposed deformity. My face turned the color of the Fez. Helen and Auntie, three rows back, started the perfunctory applause. It didn't mask their eye-watering laughter. I took the Blums and fled the auditorium—Auntie and Helen trailing behind. When we got to the car I found that Blums was not plums. It was two pounds of delicious chocolate candies. Self pity turned into self indulgence as I attempted to chocolate my sorrows away; with some measure of success. We ate most of the box that evening. In a magnanimous gesture of one who finds himself bound to another creature by mutual cruel sport, I gave four pieces to Jacque. He ate them with relish with absolutely no ill effects.

On Monday morning I put on the fez as we headed up Clement Street to the barber. It was a busy place with three barber chairs, all filled. Along the wall opposite the high barber chairs, three shaggy headed men waited, firmly planted in a row of tubular chrome framed chairs with red plastic seats and backs. Between every two chairs a small table held a selection of newspapers and men's magazines. The glass case under the front counter displayed straight razors, strops, shaving mugs and creams, hair creams, masculine lotions, and Trojan rubber goods I was too young to know about. This was definitely a man's shop. Auntie boldly entered with Helen and me in tow. Pete the owner worked the chair by the door. He greeted us. Auntie explained the situation, snatching the fez off my head so Pete could see. Pete, said he better handle this job himself. I waited anxiously under the fez next to a man carefully studying the centerfold of a girlie magazine. Auntie grabbed a *Popular Science* and said, "read". My turn came. I climbed up in the chair. It was in the window. The barber cautiously removed the fez, like taking a stuck bandage off a gangrenous wound. I knew passers-by on the sidewalk were shielding their eyes from the hideousness. Pete, trying to relieve the tension with a sick joke, said, "What kind of dog chewed on your head"? Helen and Auntie burst into laughter. The other customers joined in. I turned beet red and shriveled down in the high chair, unable to escape their stares nor my image repeated into infinity in the opposing wall mirrors. Pete said the lack of hair made his job difficult and that his only recourse was to shave my head so it all looked the same. Auntie agreed, probably wondering what my mother would think. In less than a minute the job was done. Pete then dashed out the door and came back with an Eskimo Pie, coffee flavored. He gave it to me in consolation. In spite of his good intentions, to this day I intensely dislike coffee ice cream.

The next four weeks were unbearable. My neighborhood friends and school mates teased me, but surprisingly mother seemed to hardly notice my bowling ball slick head. Helen, always helpful, did not overlook an opportunity to call attention to my head among those less observant. My hair grew back at a glacial pace; first a little fuzz, then stubble, then baby hair. Just when I thought my hair was growing out enough to be normal again someone would indelicately ask: "What happened to your head"? Having had the world's worst haircut, I now have little sympathy for people who agonize in useless vanity over minor imperfection in their "do". On the positive side, the experience taught me to detach myself from the immediate situation, to see the humor, even if I was the brunt. Auntie was a model. She found humor in her own life when things went wrong and was not reluctant to help others find the humor in their own predicaments. She had me weakly laughing at myself when first confronting mother. On subsequent visits to Auntie's we always got a big laugh out of the haircut episode. Auntie never did use the clippers on Jacque.

FISHERMAN'S WHARF

We took the Hyde Street cable car over Russian Hill to the turntable on Beach Street near Fisherman's Wharf. Cable cars are exciting! Uncle Saint Claire, my godfather, was a grip man on the Geary Street line in his youth. Forever a joker, he tried to scare me by telling me stories of run away cable cars blasting through buildings right into San Francisco Bay. Everyone knows the cars are securely locked to the slow moving cable so they can't go over 12 mile per hour, even down the steepest hill, like the part of Powell Street that runs down to Union Square. Nevertheless, as the cars teeter over the edge of each cross street and begin their steep descent a gnawing doubt can cross the mind, particularly if implanted by your godfather. We liked to sit on the outside benches up front where we could see ahead, and by looking over our shoulders, observe the grip man at work behind us. The grip man's job requires strength and agility. There are only three controls: six foot long levers for cable gripping, large peddles for braking, and the bell. The gripper, wooden brake pads, cable slot, and rails are visible through several rectangular openings in the cable car floor. It takes some imagination and faith to be secure in the belief that the grip man has actually attached the 20 ton car to the cable by sheer human muscle power and mechanical advantage. To brake, oak blocks are forced down on the rails by the human might of the grip man in front jumping with his full weight on cast iron pedals. The Brakeman, in back, does the same. The brakes are mainly used to hold the car still on level ground, not being powerful enough to stop the car on a steep hill. The third control is no control at all, but very important. It is the big bell. The grip man sounds the bell approaching all intersections and when any traffic threatens the cars preordained track. Each grip man prides himself on bell-ringing technique. From gentle warning to sheer terror of eminent collision, the pattern, rhythm, volume, and beat tells all. Kids and grip men have a natural affinity.

Part of the excitement of cable car riding is mounting and dismounting the moving car. To get on before the crowd it is necessary to jump onto the running boards, then up one step to the outside benches. Experienced riders do this with alacrity. Up to 30 riders can stand on the large wooden running boards. When viewed from the front, a fully loaded cable car looks like it might topple over, the narrow track insufficient to keep the whole contraption upright. The 19th century engineers seemed to have figured it out right since even my Uncle Saint lacked stories of cable cars tipping over. Helen and I did OK at jumping on and off. Auntie, carrying Jacque in her arms, was a little slower. Adults on the side benches gave kids seats if there was not enough room. Men always gave seats to ladies. San Francisco etiquette of the time always provided us with great seats!

Fisherman's Wharf was still a "fisherman's wharf" in 1950. Twenty colorful flush decked "one lung" Monterey style fishing boats were permanently berthed at the wharf. Each afternoon they would return on the tide from sea with their catch. The boats tied up to floating slips 15 feet below the wharf level. The high wharf provided a great viewing platform. Helen and I ran ahead of Auntie from incoming boat to incoming boat, checking out the catch. A fat man wrapped in a white apron hoisted the catch off each boat with a block and tackle dangling from a swiveling boom. He dumped the fish, some still wiggling in a metal bucket for weighing. A separate bucket held the big Dungeness crabs that refused to stop fighting until iced or boiled. Scales on gallows were strategically located along the dock. A second man on the pier, the buyer, weighed the catch and shouted down his offer to the captain. All the negotiating was in Italian, in colorful language as the bright as the boats. While the captain dickered the crew washed down the boat with high pressure hoses. Once weighed the fish and crabs were placed on wobbly wooden carts with rusty metal wheels and pushed to the nearby restaurants and street vendors. Some of the larger fish were filleted on the pier on special long wooden tables. The table ends cantilevered out over the water where the fish heads and guts were scraped off. Screeching combative seagulls thrashed the air over the tables, occasionally trying to snatch a meal from the table itself. An Italian epithet and the flash of the fillet knife temporarily dissuaded the precocious seagulls, who seemed to have very short memories. Most hovered trying to take the leftovers before they hit the water where barking harbor seals lurked among the pilings for their share of the bounty.

The Wharf's street market was another world. Dungeness crabs and jumbo shrimp boiled in massive stainless steel caldrons lining the sidewalks. The swirling steam could be so thick visibility became zero. People and cars would just disappear until the wind swirled the steam in another direction. Both sides of the sidewalk had displays of the catch of the day—squid, abalone, shark, clams, eel, bass, capazonie, live crabs and shrimp—for the eyes, the gastronomic bounty of the Pacific Ocean artistically arranged on beds of shaved ice; for the nose, exotic aromas of steaming seafood. Fixed awnings extended from the buildings to street line creating the impression of walking in a tunnel. The confined space compressed the smell of baking sour dough bread and steaming sea food. This got the stomach's attention. Auntie took us to Alioto's for lunch. We settled in a padded booth with a view of the wharf through blue tinted plate glass windows. Before us, fancy dishes, glasses, and silver, were extravagantly displayed on a real white table cloth.

I ordered crab Louis salad. A very large plate came heaped with big chunks of crab meat, with a separate pitcher of Louis dressing on the side. The waiter brought a hot-from-the-oven loaf of sliced sourdough bread on a board covered by a cloth napkin. I dug my knife into a pottery crock of salted butter, then smeared a thick coating on the bread. The warm sourdough melted and soaked up the butter. The first bite was heaven. At home we normally spread greasy margarine on tasteless day-old Wonderbread. The only seafood we ate we caught. My step father and I occasionally fished the reefs of Half Moon Bay. The fish we caught were a special Half Moon Bay species that were 90% sharp bones. Our cat along with several other cats from the neighborhood enjoyed eating the heads on our patio as mother cooked her famous, make that dreaded, fish stew. If I were not introduced to seafood al la Fisherman's Wharf with Auntie I would never have known how good seafood could really be!

After lunch we walked—the first stop, the art-deco San Francisco Maritime Museum, located on the bay just west of The Wharf, and below the Ghirardelli Chocolate Factory. Here in a building that mimicked the superstructure of a steamship, I studied the fantastic collection of ship's models, some as long as 10 feet. Mast sections, figure heads, and anchors from the great clippers that brought the miners to the "Gold Rush" were all there to touch. The visit was always too brief for me. Helen and Auntie, not sharing my enthusiasm for sea adventure, headed for the door. I reluctantly followed.

A long breakwater extends in an arc from the museum out into the Bay creating a small harbor, called Aquatic Park. Whitecaps were beginning to trace across the bay. We walked out to the end of the breakwater passing several old fishermen tending their lines on the Bay side of the breakwater. The surf was rising, occasionally sending icy spray over the parapet. Small bug-eyed bait fish swam in buckets at the fishermen's feet, looking unconcerned. A fisherman in a pea coat, collar braced against the strengthening wind, tipped his watch cap to me. He probably thought I was a prodigy 32nd degree Mason. The view was exquisite! Panning, we could see the Golden Gate Bridge, Alcatraz, Angel Island, the Bay Bridge, and Berkeley. There were seals and what looked like men swimming in the protected water of the harbor. After closely watching I could see five or six swimmers. Auntie pointed and said, "Look there, the Olympic Swim Club"! It sat squat on the harbor in an old shack. It was famous for its great swimmers, like my godfather, Uncle Saint Claire. The swimmers practiced in the 54 degree waters of the harbor for their swims across the Golden Gate. Uncle Saint swam the Gate as a young man in the 30's. Helen reminded me of the time he tried to teach me how to swim in San Francisco Bay with poor results. The story, now family legend, was a reliable source of amusement when recalled. Helen and Auntie got a big laugh out of imagining Uncle Saint throwing me into the Bay off a boat. They had a knack for descriptive prose at my expense! I reminded them that I was now quite a good swimmer having taught myself in Emerald Lake. Somehow the reality was dwarfed by the images they conjured up. Through their teasing I developed a sympathy for anyone that became the brunt of teasing and ironically the ability to tease back without remorse.

It was getting late. On our way up Beach Street to where it crosses Hyde Street, the cable car stop, we passed the Ghirardelli Chocolate Factory. A stiff, fog laced wind blew off the Bay. We were getting cold. The chocolate factory had a retail store under its bulky tower. We ducked in for a hot chocolate. The shop was steamy warm; the smell of chocolate overwhelmed. As we sipped the foamy hot chocolate, Auntie suggested we take some chocolate home for the family. She knew Helen and I were flat broke, not even a jingle in our pockets. She purchased a two pound box. When it was being wrapped she pushed a card in front of us to sign. It said: "To Mother with all our love". Big spenders that we were, Helen and I signed.

As we arrived at Hyde Street a cable car coasted onto the turn table. The grip man and conductor jumped off and started to push the car around. Helen and I eagerly joined other waiting passengers, lending what force we could to the turning car. The Conductor rewarded us by helping us onto seats up front. On the ride up Russian Hill the cityscape unfolded before us. The East Bay glistened in the afternoon sun. Behind us the fog closed in through the Gate. A sad twinge gripped me as I realized that we would soon be leaving Auntie and the "City".

GOING HOME

Going home after visiting Auntie was never fun. We had a loving family, a comfortable house, good teachers, lots of friends, and the serious business of growing up to do. The growing up part was the hardest. We were leaving a fantasy world for a real world. Heading north the Hudson was full of cheer and anticipation. Heading south the Hudson was ordinary transportation. In the world Auntie created for us we were never judged, criticized, punished, or thought of as anything less than marvelous. Our mother knew better. She believed that Helen and I were raw material needing shaping by discipline, competition, and hard work. She wanted us to "make something of ourselves". In heading-home self pity, I thought all adults, except Auntie and maybe Uncle Ed, were perpetually on duty to tell us what that meant. Auntie, goodness incarnate, thought we were just perfect as we were any time we visited. This miraculously continued through our difficult teen years. She never failed to overlook all character and physical flaws. I suppose Jacque and I were proof that she could overlook even the most repulsive shortcoming of any kind in man, child, or beast. God bless dear departed Aunt Amanda and all the other "Aunties" of the world, passed, present, and future!

CHAPTER VIII

WORKING AND GETTING AROUND

THE COMMUNITY STORE

Mother found me my first real job in 1952. I was 14. Mother felt that my blooming puberty required nothing less than 24 hours of non sexual activity each day. "The idle mind is the devil's workshop," she would say. Her devil's workshop extended beyond the mind to all parts of the anatomy. Her goal was to have me on a tight schedule, without free time. Unfortunately, there were no traditional kid jobs, like mowing lawns or delivering newspapers in our Emerald Lake neighborhood. In the steep and heavily wooded yards, slope and lack of sun combined to extinguish any hope of a suburban type lawn. Newspapers were delivered by a man in a car over terrain too precipitous for a newspaper laden bicycle. My keen-eyed mother noticed that the Community Store had no kid flunky to carry out boxes of groceries for customers. She was a regular customer at the Community Store. She knew Bennie, the owner and operator. He had a reputation of being very careful with a buck. One day while checking out she pointed out to Bennie that he was using highly paid skilled stock clerks at $1.75 per hour to do the menial work of carrying out customers' groceries when a young kid might do the work for a dollar less an hour. In fact, she said, she knew just such a young unemployed person. She looked at me. Bennie could not refute her logic. He offered me 75 cents an hour; mother accepted before I had a chance to negotiate.

My classmate and friend Earl, who lived on the flatlands below the Emerald Lake dam, was making 60 cents an hour sweeping up in a small grocery store near his house. Before I had any gainful employment, he boasted to me he was earning a penny a minute. Translated into purchasing power it meant that one hour of work would buy a "junior" movie ticket, or in 150 hours of work a new 26 inch balloon tire Schwinn bike. I was green with envy! Mother's intercession on my behalf with Bennie was another awesome coup for her motherhood. I was delighted to start my working career at 75 cents an hour, much to the chagrin of Earl, who thought I was overpaid.

The Community Store was not imposing or large. It started as a house that was expanded on the sides and in the back as business grew. It was located at a major crossroads. Today it would be considered a "convenience" store in size, but since the closest real supermarket was 8 miles away it attracted most of the local grocery business. Bennie, 4-F due to poor eyesight, made money during the war supplying the county jail with groceries out of a big panel truck, enough to make a down payment on the Community Store. The former owner wanted to retire in 1947. Little did he know that 1947 would be the beginning of a business boom for the store. Timing is everything! Bennie was a sharp business man. He was becoming prosperous as the population in the Emerald Lake district grew due to new construction and summer home conversions to full time residences. He drove a new Oldsmobile Rocket "88". Not bad for a hard working high school drop out!

I started on weekends. The store was busiest then. The first time I put on a white grocer's apron I felt proud; proud to be a working somebody, proud to have a Social Security card, and proud to be growing up! Carrying out boxes loaded with groceries to customers' cars was my primary responsibility. No tips were expected or allowed. The customers assumed their groceries would be placed in their cars. They also assumed the car door would be opened and closed for them. And finally, they expected to be thanked politely for their business. Bennie told me to always address the customer by their last name, proceeded by Mr. or Mrs. even if I knew them outside work. The last thing a customer was to hear as they prepared to drive off was, "Thank-you Mrs. Jones for your business". I had other chores when the check out stands were quiet. But, if I was in earshot when one of the two checkout clerks yelled "Going out!" I would drop whatever else I might be doing and walk briskly to the checkout stand and cheerfully greet the customer by name—Bennie's orders. Bulging boxes would be waiting for me to carry. The clerks had a neat way of increasing the size of a box by tipping up and securing the top flaps with string after groceries filled the bottom. The loaded boxes must have been quite heavy; at 14 I didn't notice. In less busy times I was often assigned to the hot, noisy bottle room, a locked, high-fenced side yard where all returned bottles were dumped, and where a large rack of refrigeration units provided cooling for the butcher's walk-in meat locker, the cold food cabinets, and the frozen food cases. The motors and pumps cycled and recycled coolant through radiators in a cacophony of compression and expansion, all the while shedding immense quantities of heat. The temperature in the bottle room was rarely below 100 degrees.

Returnable bottles of varied brands and sizes were collected at the check-out stands in cardboard boxes. Customers received 2 cents for each small returned bottle and 3 cents for a large returned bottle, enough of an incentive to guarantee the return of virtually all bottles. When several boxes accumulated I hauled them out to the bottle room for sorting. Once a week the vendors made a delivery of new stock, and picked up their returned bottles in proprietary wooden cases. It was my job to see that all bottles were returned to their original wooden cases, and stacked neatly so the vendors could snatch them with a hand truck. Returnable glass bottles in those days were quite substantial, on average being refilled 40 times before succumbing to scratches and chips. At 2 and 3 cents apiece, Bennie let me know I was being trusted with expensive and potentially fragile stock! Bennie told me there was no room for error. The wooden cases were designed to fit precisely into exposed racks on the side of the vendor's truck. He said if just one bottle got out of place, say a Pepsi bottle for a Coke bottle, it could create havoc on the bottler's production line and bring disgrace to the offending store. Bennie had a way of making the mundane dramatic and my responsibilities very clear. Another less pressure-full duty I had at the Community Store was burning the trash, mostly cardboard and paper, twice a day behind the store and sweeping up, inside and out.

In my first year of punching the time clock I was raking in $12.00 a week! This was big money when a movie cost less than a dollar and a hamburger, shake, and fries about the same. My transportation costs were near zero. I walked the 2 miles to the store or rode my bike. My performance did not go unnoticed. Russ, the fat wise-cracking Italian butcher, asked Bennie if my hours could be extended to assist him. The growing meat business was very profitable at the Community Store. Russes' most memorable line when a customer was thinking about buying red meat was, "Madam, our beef is as tender as budder". Soon I was working 10 hours on the weekends and 2 hours each day after school. Working for the butcher was remunerative, but unpleasant. When the butcher shop closed (5:00 PM, union rules) I cleaned the meat grinder, band saw, display cases, and butcher blocks. Cleaning the display case was particularly disgusting. It required washing the green plastic trimmers and metal display pans in a big double sink until my hands puckered. Later I crawled into the bottom of the display case and scrubbed the area underneath the display racks, trying unsuccessfully to keep my head out of the splatter of stinking meat and fish juices. During the holidays I put in extra time cleaning chickens and making brine for the corned beef. I liked Russ. He enjoyed joking around. He called me "chief". To get my attention, or just be silly, he would occasionally throw chicken guts at me. When I returned the fire he stopped.

He called Carl, the store's produce man, 'banana head". He did have a long somber face, like Laurel's, Hardy's partner. The worst part of it was that Carl eventually responded to 'banana head" in the store. Despite all this they seemed to be good friends, reading the dirty magazines together after they were delivered each month. They would grab several magazines before they were put on the display rack hustling back to the butcher shop to enjoy manly titillation. Carl's eyes popping whispered, "That's a good one" or "Look at those knockers"! Russ responded saying, "Take a peek at this, is that hair"? They shooed me away, nevertheless occasionally I got a good look, not knowing exactly what to look for. When I was burning the trash once I found two dog-eared unsold girly magazines. Recalling Carl's and Russes' comments I began to look for the right parts to notice on the half-smiling ladies posing in modest pre bikini bathing suits. When Bennie was around he got mad at Russ and Carl for pawing the stock.

By the summer of 1953 I was working 28 hours a week pulling in $21.00 of spendable cash. Unfortunately, when high school started in the Fall I had to give up the weekday work. School work, the 2 hour round-trip train commute to get to Serra High School in San Mateo, and being a teenager was too demanding on my time. I continued to work at the Community Store on weekends. Bennie increased my pay to $1.00 per hour when I turned 15. This pleased me greatly. I was saving for a car.

The next summer I returned to weekday and weekend work and acquired another lucrative job as well. This job I found on my own initiative, although mother was always a lurking presence. Each weekend morning at 7 AM I cleaned the locker rooms at Emerald Lake County Club before I showed up at the Community Store at 8:30 AM. The lifeguard was expected to clean the locker rooms during the week. I negotiated my compensation directly with President Belton himself. He thought the job would take 2 hours. I agreed. He offered $1.50 per hour, or $3.00 per cleaning. I accepted. What President Belton did not know is that I had in mind a breakthrough technique for cleaning the locker rooms. Actually it was quite simple. I removed all paper goods then blasted the room clean with a high pressure water hose. To complete the job I dried off the paper goods containers and mirrors with a towel, replaced the paper goods, and sprinkled disinfectant liberally on fixtures and floor. Some said the locker rooms were never so spotless. I did the job in an hour for a cool three bucks!

When I turned 16 in the winter of 1954 my savings were adequate to purchase car insurance. Insurance was the biggest financial barrier to auto mobility. My insurance would add $114 to the cost of my mother's policy. My mother made it plain that she was not interested in financially supporting my quest to have a car. To her, a bicycle was an adequate means of transportation that had the added benefit of burning off noisome testosterone. She didn't understand that a 16 year old California male without a car was like a cowboy without a horse. A serendipitous insult to Auntie's Hudson unexpectedly put me in the driver's seat.

For my 16th birthday Auntie gave me her 1939 Hudson when she was advised by the Nash dealer that it was worthless. She tried to turn it in on a new Nash Rambler. Auntie, irate over the insult to her beloved Hudson, got even by giving the car to me and buying a Plymouth. Mother's reservations disappeared when she considered the shear convenience of her oldest child as chauffeur for his younger siblings. At that time we all were attending Catholic schools; which meant no school bus transportation for such privileged students. The old Hudson became a school bus with me as driver. Each morning the first stop was Mt. Carmel elementary school in Redwood City where my 3 half brothers and sister attended. The second stop was Notre Dame Academy in Belmont, my sister Helen's high school. Finally, the last stop was Serra High School in San Mateo, my school. My friends called the whale backed four door Hudson, the Blue Bomb. The 30 mile round trip spared mother so much grief that she kicked in gas money when I ran short.

The next summer, my 17th, I quit my job at the Community Store, kept the cleaning job at Emerald Lake, and started a new job as a chauffeur for a Jewish rice merchant. On my last day at the Community Store, Carl, the produce man, I never called him "banana head", took me aside and thanked me for my work. Over the years he said he noticed that I worked hard, would do any job with good humor, and came in on time. He said that in the future, if I ever needed work, he would find me a job in the grocery business. I believed him! The sincerity of that kind offer in 1954 has come to mind several times in my career when I thought my efforts were unappreciated.

MR. GREEN'S CHAUFFEUR

Mr. Arthur Green sold rice, mostly Texas long grain, to Chinese restaurants in China Town in San Francisco. He lived near Emerald Lake with his wife Rosamond. In the late 20's they bought a summer house on the lake like other San Franciscans looking for an escape from the summer fog. In 1950 the Greens moved to Emerald Lake full time. Arthur Green, then 75, with an ailing heart, decided to work from his home. Mr. Green was a big rumpled man with a sagging body draped in a baggy three piece suit. For 50 years he sold Texas and California rice in Northern California. At an age when most men would be retired or dead, Mr. Green kept on selling rice to his favorite long-time customers, the Chinese. Rosamond, his wife, a pert 70 year old non-driver, noticed that Arthur's driving was getting erratic. He drove to San Francisco twice each week. She worried about him crashing on the Bayshore Highway, or possibly dropping dead from a heart attack while plying his trade on the steep China Town streets. While Mr. Green would not admit there was anything wrong with his driving, he was very well aware of the angina that gripped his chest when he walked uphill. He had to admit that even when he parked in the most convenient garage, his angina acted up as he trudged up and down the steep hills of China Town to do business. He concluded that it made sense to hire a kid to follow him from business to business, double parking on the jammed street out front. It was Mr. Green's angina pain that opened up a new opportunity for me.

I responded to a "job available" notice Mr. Green posted on the Emerald Lake bulletin board. Being the only applicant, and the fact that I was available and could drive landed me the job. During the first summer with Mr. Green I drove to San Francisco 3 times a week. When school started Mr. Green changed his routine so I could continue to chauffeur for him on weekends. This turned out very well since the Chinese shopkeepers didn't pay much attention to work-weeks; they seemed to work all the time. Typically, I'd double park the Pontiac straight 8, or keep it circulating, as Mr. Green made his rounds and took orders. When I miraculously found a parking space, Mr. Green would ask me to go underground and check out the basement storerooms that laced old China Town to see what rice was on hand and who the competition might be. This sensitive mission could be challenging. I accidentally ran onto more than one high stakes mahjong game and escaped by being fleet of foot and knowledgeable of Chinatown's labyrinth of interconnected basements and back alleys. One time Mr. Wing Duck, a regular Green customer for 40 years, got me out of a jam by letting me flee through his kitchen. Mr. Green liked the Chinese, taking great pleasure in doing business with them. The feeling was mutual.

On Chinese New Year Mr. Green gave his customers Marilyn Monroe pin-up calendars. They gave him firecrackers which wound up in my hands. It greatly amused me when I overheard Mr. Green negotiating an order in a mix of English and Chinese. He had been doing business with the same customers so long that he developed a vocabulary mix of Cantonese and English that covered the range of possible transactions. To make his point Mr. Green told me he could call upon a Cantonese or English profanity to suit the customers sensibilities. His customers responded in kind. In addition to words, facial expression and hand gestures were essential tools of communication in completing a deal. Both sides enjoyed using their full array of bargaining tools. It was an art form. In a way I believe Mr. Green loved his customers, and they loved him. Doing business for 40 years created a bond, a mutual respect, a sense of trust, and a genuine fondness. Mr. Green was not unchallenged by upstart rice salesmen. When they went head-to-head, Mr. Green usually came away with the order and a touch of angina.

Rosamond always came with us, riding in the back seat. She never left the car, except when we went to the company office on Montgomery Street to check out were Mr. Green's rail cars were with his Texas long grain rice. The old lady and I spent many hours sitting in the car waiting for Mr. Green. She turned out to be a great story teller—a chronicler of San Francisco of the 20's and 30's. She let me know that she and Arthur were among San Francisco's social movers when they were young. They lived together on Telegraph Hill for 20 years before marrying. "Very Bohemian", she winked. She told me stories of high speed, high stakes buggy racing on Ocean Beach at midnight, gin parties in speak-easyies, dashes down to Mexico in Arthur's Stutz Bearcat, and overnight big band, black tie, dance parties on luxurious side paddle steamers cruising up the Sacramento River. The Greens had no children or relatives that I knew of. Rosamond told me stories as if she was sharing them with her son. When I had an exam coming up and needed to study, she quizzed me from the books I'd bring along. She frequently helped me with "word power" and physics equations.

Both the Greens took medicine directly from cloth covered bottles. Each time Mr. Green came back to the car he'd turn around to the back seat and toast to Mrs. Green's good health. Two long swigs of medicine was the normal dosage. Mrs. Green replied in kind. Arthur kept two cloth-covered bottles in the glove compartment. Rosamond kept hers in a magazine pouch attached to the back of the front seat. Mrs. Green explained that they both needed frequent stimulation for their bad circulation. Doctor's orders. It seemed strange to me to see medicine in sack covered bottles, but it worked. In the afternoon they were usually feeling quite well!

The Greens were kind to me. They paid me $2.00 an hour, provided meals at Foster's Cafeteria, and where mercifully uncritical of my driving. On the way home I drove the solid, road hugging Pontiac 85 miles per hour on Bayshore Highway. In my 2 year service to the Green's I didn't get a ticket or have an accident. Call me lucky! The work day ended with me parking the Pontiac in front of the Green's house where Mr. Green concluded the business of the day by paying me. Mr. Green ceremoniously removed five's and ones from his bulging breast pocket wallet. He closely inspected each bill as he slowly counted the money, seeming a bit sad to part with any of it. Nevertheless, Mr. Green was not cheap. More likely his failing vision slowed the counting in the dim light inside the car. Walking home, 14 bucks wealthier, with a new story or two about old San Francisco social life, and a few more word definitions ready for my English teacher, I felt pretty proud. I stayed with the Greens until Mr. Green died of a stroke in 1956, the same year I finished high school. For a while I took Rosamond shopping and to other appointments. This didn't last long. Her failing health and broken heart soon put her into a nursing home. She complacently died a few month later. I learned two things from my association with the Greens; that they lived full lives enjoying the richness of their times, from horse and buggy to jet travel; and that I had a lot to learn to make the best of my lifetime, whatever span of years it would be.

A COUP AND A "REPO"

When I was a Junior in High School (1955) my Uncle Jim Rezos offered me a 1934 Willys coup for $10.00. Uncle Jim loved automobiles so much that he would do almost anything to save a car from the wrecker, particularly a car he fancied as interesting. He was like a dog lover saving a homeless dog from being put to "sleep." When his sister said she was going to junk her old Willys for the going rate of $10, Uncle Jim gave her $10 on the spot and began to look for a new home for the car. Later I found out that Uncle Jim wanted a new Willys 20 years earlier, but couldn't afford one. Now he had one with no place to put it. Uncle Jim was widely respected in the family as a first rate auto mechanic, although this was not his regular occupation. In his regular job he serviced commercial water accounts for the San Francisco Water Department. He was a man who knew a good car when he saw one. With this in mind I said, "sure" to his offer, thinking it would be handy to have a spare car since my 1939 Hudson had over 100,000 miles on it.

The next weekend Uncle Jim drove the Willys down from San Francisco, leaving a trail of blue smoke the length of Bay Shore Highway. Aunt Marion followed in their spiffy boat-like Chrysler New Yorker. When I first saw the Willys I wondered what Uncle Jim saw in it. It was rather strange looking. The radiator grill looked like a large urinal with Willys written on it in slanting chrome script. Its bullet headlights were mounted on top of its protruding fenders like mechanical eyeballs. It had two forward opening doors, a rumble seat, four oil burning cylinders, mechanical brakes, yellow wire wheels, and ripped brown mohair seats. Like a salesman in a Cadillac showroom, Uncle Jim proudly pointed out the cars features. Only in this case we were looking at a junker with 90,000 miles on it. He explained in a tone reserved for mechanic's asides that the spark plugs would need cleaning every 100 miles to remove the carbon buildup from oil burning, an inconvenience for those mechanically inept—but not for a young mechanically inclined nephew. On the less positive side, Uncle Jim admitted the car needed a new battery, which might have been a real drawback for a flatlander he said. But where I lived in a hilly area, and having so many friends it would be no problem. He said only a fool would pay $17 for a new battery for a car that was only worth $10. For me the solution was using the car only when it could be parked on a hill at my destination or when I had several beefy friends along to push start it. The car had only two real serious flaws. Its mechanical brakes were connected to the pedal with steel rods rather than hydraulics, making it impossible to get them adjusted properly. No matter how carefully I adjusted the turnbuckles on the steel rods, the bald left front tire skidded when I tried to stop quickly. The other more annoying flaw, was the dashboard oil leak. When the car got up to speed, oil dripped out of the oil pressure gage onto the legs of the right seat passenger. An oily gunny sack was acceptable protection for my male friends. Girls would not ride in the car, period. The leak persisted until I unsentimentally junked both the Willys and Hudson a year later, but not before I ran the car for 4,000 enjoyable miles.

In the Fall of 1956 the Hudson needed a new transmission and the Willy's tires were worn through to the cord. I junked the pair for $20.00. For my first two years of driving, up until I graduated from high school, my total capital investment in cars was $10.00; not bad for 2 years and 25,000 miles of transportation. To be fair, parts cost about $40.00 over the same period. The Hudson needed a new clutch, a junkyard "new" rear end, and some valves to keep it going. A side benefit of owning these old cars was a free hands-on education in auto repair, and the new and used parts business. For example, an opportunity to learn something about the junkyard business unexpectedly presented itself when the differential gears ("the rear end") of my Hudson ground themselves into metal shavings on El Camino Real at the midpoint of an afternoon school run. A professional repair would cost $200. This was totally beyond my means and far exceeded the value of the car. The solution was finding a replacement part at a junkyard and fixing the car myself. The next weekend a friend and I headed for the big junkyard on Old County Road in San Carlos.

The junkman, sitting behind a grimy desk pointed a black greasy finger in the direction of a wrecked 1939 Hudson some 100 yards off. He said it was running when it was junked. A good sign! We found the forsaken

Hudson where it was driven in and parked three years earlier, only now it was surrounded by a luxurious growth of thorny weeds. We hacked away the weeds, jacked up the back end, removed the wheels and axles, dropped the drive shaft, and two hours later pulled out the planetary gears. We presented the greasy pile of gears to the junkman. He looked over the gears admiring their like new condition. "6 bucks" he said. My jaw dropped! I said I was thinking maybe 3 bucks. He said new gears would cost $125 if they could be found at all. I paid in 6 greasy dollar bills. On the way home my friend and I considered the economics of the junk business, concluding that any business that could buy a car for $10 and sell just a small bit of it for $6 was the business to be in. We speculated that when we had completed our MBA's at Stanford we might become partners in the wrecked car business.

My insurance tab for my first 2 years of driving totaled $220, gas about $535, bringing my cost per mile to less than four cents. So much for cheap early transportation. The reverse status of driving one car that supported mushroom growth in the back seat when it rained, the Hudson, and one that dripped hot oil onto the passenger's legs, the Willys, lost its youthful attraction. The Hudson and Willys served their purpose well. Now as a senior in high school, I needed transportation more commensurate (as big John would say) with my higher station in life, so I turned to Doc. Doc, our next-door neighbor, found me a suitable "new" car in the Wells Fargo Bank Repossession Department.

The repo car was going to cost me some real money; but we're talking about a pretty stylish vehicle, a boxy 1952 DeSoto two door. Doc said that I could have the blue beauty for $260.00—not bad for a four year old car with 35,000 miles on it. It had a 300 cubic inch V-8, a four speed semi-automatic fluid drive transmission, a push button AM radio, a few dents, and a criminal record. Doc said it wasn't perfect, but at the price he said it should provide loads of cheap transportation. Among its imperfections were 2 bullet holes in the trunk lid. Doc explained it was used in an armed robbery. The trunk could not be opened without a crowbar. As-is meant as-is. The car came directly from the police lot under its own power to the alley behind the bank where it sat forlornly in the Bank's loading zone. At least it started and ran! Sounded like a great deal to me! I rode to work with Doc to bring the car home. I was very eager to find out what was in the trunk, maybe a dead body? No, it didn't stink. Maybe suitcases full of money? No such luck. Using a crowbar that became part of the car's essential equipment, I pried open the trunk. It contained 2 cloth sacks filled with model airplane engines, apparently overlooked by the cops when they pried the trunk open—perhaps loot too minor to secure for evidence or just overlooked. So I acquired a toothy grilled DeSoto and 27 model airplane engines for $260.00. Imperfect though its pedigree was, after many hours of scrubbings and polishing, I finally had a car that was built after World War II, that girls would ride in, and that had more than ample power at stoplights.

FIRE AND FURNACES

The summer of my senior year I found a job as a firefighter for the San Mateo County Fire Department. It opened my eyes to another world, living with professional career firemen at the Hillcrest Station, 25 miles from home. It was the first time I lived away from home. I felt privileged to be with a macho bunch of real men, doing dangerous work. There was a brotherhood among the men. They did ordinary things the manly way, even if it was inconvenient. Take shaving for example. In the morning, after my first night at the station, I went into the bathroom to shower and shave. What a sight! Eight sinks in a row, a naked man at each sink, either stropping a gleaming tempered steel straight razor or shaving his grizzled beard with one. I stood there with my puny Ronson electric shaver with no plug in sight. All the real firemen used imported straight razors with bone handles. The last time I saw this kind of shaving was when I stayed with my Uncle Saint in San

Rafael and watched old Uncle Jack do his cowboy face. I took a shower and decided that I didn't need a shave after all.

Whenever there were no fires the men trained and maintained the equipment. There were drills on structural fire fighting that included ladder climbing with heavy wreathing hoses, nozzle control of high pressure water, donning and using breathing apparatus, and smoke control. That whole summer we actually fought only 3 structural fires, one in a rural church that got pretty exciting as we tossed out burning debris that contained lots of coins. The neighborhood kids scrambled for the change as the pastor vainly tried to fight them off. It seems the pastor hid the collections in highly flammable bedding. Our usual fire calls were for brush and forest fires since we were a county unit, not a city department. Our equipment was mostly four and six wheel drive Army surplus vehicles. The fire Warden flew the station's ex WW II spotter plane off a dirt strip adjacent to the station. He supervised our fire suppression efforts from the air by shouting out the side window of the plane at very low altitude. The men thought this was very unnecessary and dangerous. However, the men cut the Warden some slack knowing he liked to fly and couldn't afford a plane on his salary.

There were 3 rookies that summer. Each of us was assigned a buddy from the ranks of the seasoned firefighters. These veterans would be our roommates, mentors, guardian angels, and moral supporters. My buddy was Pete, who had no regular roommate. He had recently returned from a tuberculosis sanitarium where he was cured for the second time. The men weren't too keen on bunking in the same room with Pete who coughed a lot. I didn't have a choice. He turned out to be the best buddy of the lot. The first day he showed me exactly how to put my fire pants over my fire boots next to my bunk so I could jump right into the boots and pants at the same time when a fire call came. It was this kind of mentoring that really paid off. He introduced me personally to the station cook, a irascible retired Filipino Navy man, who was our only contact with the outside world during our two week duty period.

The Hillcrest Station was quite isolated in the coastal foothills 15 miles from the nearest settlement. Sarg, as we called him, went to the store every other day. If any fireman wanted something, Sarg would get it as long as you were on Sarg's good side. Pete told me this required a demeanor of exaggerated respect, copious praise for the cooking, and a pack of cigarettes each week. Sarg smoked Camels. To have the right currency available I bought a carton of Camels even though I didn't smoke, except occasionally to impress girls with my maturity on a date. At the time I failed to appreciate that coughing and turning green proved quite the opposite. One evening Sarg got so mad at one of the firefighters who didn't like his dinner that he went to the kitchen, fetched a clever, and chased the man out of the building shouting something in Filipino. The Warden had to intervene. He promised Sarg that the firefighter would control his tongue and show more respect in the future. In the process I learned that cooks were harder to find than firefighters.

Each summer one part-time rookie would be selected to be trained as an equipment operator. The one who could best drive the 1927 White fire truck would be chosen. This was a tough test. The open truck had a six speed main transmission, a four speed Brownie auxiliary transmission, and a two speed rear axle—48 possible gear combinations. The idea was to drive the truck smoothly, double clutching through all the gears going uphill and down. The biggest challenge was keeping the truck under control going down hill since the primitive brakes simply could not stop the heavy vehicle. One time we were rolling along out of gear at about 10 miles per hour. I stood on the pedal with all my strength, back braced against the seat. The truck grudgingly stopped in about 100 feet. The critical skill was the synchronization of engine speed with the gear speed so a shift could be made, a lower gear slowed you down, a higher gear let you go faster. My experience driving the old Willys, where double clutching was necessary on its non-synchronous transmission, paid off. In the end, the honor was bestowed upon the rookie Pete was least terrified to ride with, me. Pete himself knew how to drive the truck, but his small size, his physical lack of strength, and his weak lungs side-lined him.

Driving the old White could be exciting! Outward bound on a fire call the old White ran away with us going down the long 2 mile grade into Belmont. As I was shifting up at the top of the hill the engine died, with it went the breaking and the ability to get the machine in gear. Pete radioed the station informing the dispatcher of our predicament as we picked up speed and I vainly tried to restart the engine. Our dispatcher informed the Belmont police that an out-of-control fire truck was heading straight for town. The cops blocked off the major cross streets on our route. When we hit 60 mph Pete turned on the siren and flashing lights. I could see the panic stricken faces of the 2 rookie fire-fighters hanging on the back in the rear view mirror as the 500 gallons of water in the tank accelerated us to warp speed. At 8.1 pounds per gallon, that was over 4,000 pounds of water. As we lurched over cross streets their feet became airborne, slamming back down onto the running board in the troughs. Pete and I suspected that crossing El Camino Real's 6 lanes and the Southern Pacific tracks just beyond would be the most exciting part of our coaster ride. What if a train appeared on the busy line? We got lucky! Like a fine sports car the old White stayed on the ground crossing El Camino Real, but when we hit the tracks it went airborne at about 80 mile per hour, seemed like 200 miles per hour!

Fortunately, the long incline of the Bayshore Freeway overpass a mile down the road slowed us enough so I could steer for the shoulder and stop in the soft earth. We all sat there in semi-shock for a while. Pete bummed a cigarette from one of the rookies. The radio crackled to life getting our attention. The dispatcher said he had a solution for us. He instructed Pete to climb onto the side of the truck and start the V-8 pump engine behind the driver's seat. He said the pump engine was connected to the truck's vacuum system, according to the 1927 manual that the Warden was flipping through. He said this might get us some breaking capability if the replacement pump engine installed last year was connected the same way as the original. The dispatcher then informed us that the call we were on was determined to be a false alarm. He told us to turn off the flashing lights and siren and resume normal speed. When the cops pulled up they found four guys in fire hats laughing hysterically.

The real bonus of being an equipment operator was staking out. This meant that we didn't have to do station work. When there was a severe threat of forest fire the Warden would post us up on Sky Line Drive during the day, so if fire should break out our response time would be reduced. Our perch on top of the mountain was about 20 miles from the station. The vehicle used for this task was a surplus WW II Studabaker diesel tanker. It was built to carry fuel oil, now it carried 2,500 gallons, or 21,000 pounds of water. The red paint, a small 65 HP pump engine mounted on the back, and hose racks welded to the top of the elliptical tank could not disguise the 18 wheeler's military heritage. This truck was even tougher to drive than the 1927 White pumper because of the immense weight of the water that either wanted to stay where it was or keep going, usually contrary to the driver's wishes.

I drove. Pete sat next to me in the cab. As usual, two rookies hung on the back. We growled slowly up the Skyline grade. As we ascended I was already worrying about coming back down. The worst part would be the steep grade just before the Crystal Springs Lake Causeway. Here the road narrowed and curved sharply to line up with the lake crossing. A missed gear change at this curve would mean excessive speed and maybe a plunge into the lake. Fortunately this never happened. When we arrived at the top, I pulled the rig into a large turn-out so that we could depart in either direction if called. Pete stayed in the cab making a initial radio check. His job on stakeout was to cover the radio. The guys and I climbed up on top of the hose racks where the view was spectacular. We looked for "smokes". By this time, all the WW II fire towers that had been constructed up and down the coastal mountains to counter the threat of fires caused by Japanese incendiary balloon bombs, were unmanned.

Our high platform on top of the truck now served as a substitute fire tower at times of high forest fire risk. If a "smoke" was spotted I would take a bearing, estimate its distance, and radio the dispatcher. The Assistant Warden would scramble into his Dodge Power Wagon, mini fire truck, and head for the scene. The few times we actually spotted a "smoke" it turned out to be an overzealous camper's fire. Usually, we "killed time" playing cards and reading magazines.

The idea of "killing time" was new to me, since it seemed that I never had enough of it. Mother saw to that. However, in the fire fighting business I learned that time could be excessive at one moment, only to be at a great premium the next. Pete was the best at "killing time" due to his long career in fire fighting and his periodic convalescing in tuberculosis sanitariums. His only duty on these stake outs was to tend the radio and mentor me. Every hour he would report in to the station, a requirement the Warden imposed to make sure the stake out crew was not sleeping or away from the truck. When not performing these duties, Pete read dirty magazines. Our fire station's and Pete's personal collection of girlie magazines was extensive. I thought I knew the field from Russ, the butcher at the Community Store. Was I naive! The fire fighting business in those macho days demanded the finest pornographic library possible. The Hillcrest collection was the pride of the station. Our only competition was our substation in La Honda.

Once while on stake out we received a call from our dispatcher to be back-up at the La Honda station because all their trucks were called away to fight a stubborn brush fire. When we arrived at the station 15 miles away, Pete huddled with the La Honda station cook, the only one there, who was also the honorary station librarian. Later Pete bragged to me that he swapped some of our station's dog eared second copies for six new titles that recently came from Mexico, where the most explicitly perverse sexual photography was published. Naturally, I was impressed! Under Pete's mentoring my literary horizons where expanded and my time killing capabilities greatly improved; all without a sense of guilt! I think Pete is now in heaven enjoying the ultimate challenge, "killing time" for eternity.

The next summer after I graduated from high school in the quest to earn more money for college I sold door-to-door furnace cleanings for Holland Furnace Company. This was an education in handling rejection, in perseverance, and in the service industry. In one day I would canvass one or two neighborhoods, maybe 250 houses altogether. Out of these "cold calls" on average I would sell six or seven furnace cleanings, including sales from evening call backs. The next week when the huge vacuum bag truck came through the neighborhood making a racket, I might get another sale or two. For each $24.95 sale I would keep $7.50; there was no salary. The harder I worked the more I could make. But it was tough. Soon I learned to size up the people who came to the door. It became easier and easier to sniff out a sale from a waste of time. Some school friends of mine tried selling for Holland when they saw all the "easy" money I was making, $125 in a good week. This was twice the income of my peers in regular hourly jobs. Saving for college meant we all needed to earn as much money as we could. Unfortunately, the easy money was more elusive than the unwary expected, they were usually defeated by taking rejection personally, and lacked instinctive salesmanship. My friend Jerry for example, the popular heavy weight school boxing champion, actually shed a tear while sitting in my car late one afternoon after a totally unproductive neighborhood canvas. It was not for lack of trying on that hot summer day that did him in. He never experienced a personal failure before on that scale. It hit him like a solid blow to the solar plexus.

If it is true that one learns more from defeat than success; selling door-to-door is a unique, and often brutal learning opportunity. To walk up to the front door of total strangers, interrupt them in what they are doing, and then proceed to sell them a service they didn't know they needed, or in many cases, didn't know existed, takes courage, self confidence, good manners, and persistence. Totally defeated some long days,

I made 300 calls without a sale. The next day I would be back out on the street in my Holland smock, maybe shaken, but not conquered, to work another 200 homes. On occasion I would be accosted with hostility, not the normal suspicion. A few neighborhoods were mine fields. Profanity and physical threats blasted out doorways from people who thought they had been cheated by the Holland Company, putting me in full retreat. My most prized sales were those where I turned initial hostility into a $7.50 commission. I also met some very nice people, and probably just missed meeting others who peeped out, but wouldn't answer the door bell. Pity, their loss, I thought in a contrived effort to stay cheerful and optimistic. After door-to-door selling, no one had to convince me of the value of a professional education at university.

This job also opened my eyes to the concept of overhead. Before I earned a cent, I was out $15.00. The $15.00 covered a $5.00 peddler's license from the local cops and a white Holland smock, a uniform for door-to-door canvassing sold exclusively by the company. To comply with the local peddling ordinance I had to be "booked" by the local police. After rolling my fingerprints, taking a mug shot, and searching my criminal record I was issued a Peddlers License. The Desk Sergeant said I could use the license in my sales pitch to show that I was a cut above the usual criminal unlicensed door-to-door salesmen. Obviously the Sergeant didn't like door-to-door salespeople, but he knew I was legit. In those days a door-to-door salesmen ranked in popularity about where telemarketers, lawyers, and politicians do today. A week later I sold his wife a furnace cleaning, the Sergeant's house just happened to be in the neighborhood I was working that day! Perhaps if I had been selling $150.00 vacuum cleaners, not a measly $24.95 furnace cleaning, the license may have come in handy. As it was, I never used any of the many peddler's licenses I eventually acquired as sales tools.

Another overhead was $6.40 of gas a week for my thirsty DeSoto. The car was a necessity for the daily visit to the office in San Mateo to turn in my orders, to get to the target neighborhoods, and to make call backs in the evenings when necessary. The car also served as my site office and restaurant. At lunch time I ate the sandwiches I packed in the morning, listened to the noon news on the car radio (a family tradition), and did my paperwork. That summer of 1956 the UK surrendered the Suez Canal to the Egyptians, Congress authorized the 41,000 mile interstate highway system, the ANDREA DORIA sank in a collision with STOCK-HOLM, Eisenhower and Nixon were renominated for second terms, white mobs violently opposed school integration in the South, and Jack Kennedy was passed over for Stevenson's vice-presidential running mate in favor of the more promising Estes Kefauver. The changing world reported on the radio outside my cocoon in the '52 DeSoto barely penetrated my brain that was otherwise occupied by contemplating which blocks of houses to canvass next.

Some family friends who were acquainted with the Holland Company told mother that the company unfairly exploited young men to sell for them knowing full-well that most would be unsuccessful. True, the company invested virtually nothing in their amateur sales force. My first time in the Holland office, immediately after my "inter-view", they showed me a film strip of a smiling, Holland smocked man selling a furnace cleaning to a well dressed housewife at the front door of a Hollywood perfect suburban home. So much for training. The next day I acquired my peddler's license, made three calls with an experi-enced door-to-door Holland man to perfect my pitch, and started. Really, anyone could work door-to-door for them. Several of my friends lasted less than a week. When they asked for their money back for the hardly used smocks, the reply was, "sorry". This led me to suspect that the company was in the smock business as well as the furnace business. I realized, even while I worked for Holland that the company was not perfect. However, the company proved to be an opportunity for me to grow up some more, make good money, and see another view of life. I still recall with pride a one time recognition I received in the monthly company newspaper, *The Firepot*. A photograph taken of me in my smock, standing in front of the office, gawking self-consciously into the lens, appeared on the second page. The caption read; "Michael Barker, Top salesman in San Mateo".

These early work experiences taught me that there was honor in work, any work, that reward was in proportion to effort, and that work brought independence and self-confidence. I realized that if all else failed, I could always seek employment in the grocery business or in door-to-door sales.

CHAPTER IX

SCHOOLS

STAYING BACK

On a cold Saturday afternoon in January 1943 the tragedy happened. By world standards of tragedy, it was of little account. The war raging in Europe and the Pacific produced tragedy at a high octane frequency that was a constant oppressive force in American life. But all that tragedy was "over there", and seldom comprehensible to me, a five year old in the first grade. (see photo 15) I lived locally, very locally. The Saturday tragedy was one I could grasp. It was the most destructive fire the San Carlos Fire Department ever had to fight. In our suburban town of 2,500 people it was the Sunday banner headline—"Fire Leaves Ten Families Homeless!" The fire raced through a two story cheaply constructed 10 unit apartment building on the poor side of town, leaving all the tenants homeless, their misery compounded by the loss of all their worldly possessions. I heard the sirens of the fire trucks and the fire horn off in the distance. I heard the story on the radio. I heard about the fire listening to a telephone conversation between my mother and one of her friends. I heard about the fire when a neighbor visited. It was terrible, and so very close and real to me, a first grader. Housing was scarce. Building materials were going to the war effort. It was said that one of the ladies who was burned out recently lost her husband on the beach at Salerno. Now she was homeless, husbandless, and pregnant. These poor people; what would they do?

Photo 15—Michael Barker at age 5. (1943)

On Monday our teacher called us to the regular Monday morning "show and tell". One kid found a warty green frog and showed it around in a mason jar. Another kid told a story about going bowling for the first time and getting a strike. Another kid told about his father who came home from war that weekend with a souvenir Japanese canteen which he passed around. When my turn came I drew a blank. All I could think about was the horrible fire. My imagination took over as my tongue tried to keep up. I told the story of how I barely escaped the flames, running for my life with my mother and sister. The teacher and my classmates listened with breathless attention. So rewarded, I couldn't stop embellishing the story to maximize the pleasure of the audience, probably a genetic trait I inherited from my show business father. I described in vivid detail how our old family dog caught on fire and had to be "put-to-sleep"—we never had a dog, but I always wanted one. The teacher solemnly asked: "Did you lose everything"? I said, "yes" in a whisper, guilt beginning to dry out my throat and choke my words. The barely audible reply must have been taken as evidence of my suffering, not the first twinge of remorse for blatantly lying or the fear of the inevitable crush of reality. Our teacher, Miss Chase, took over. My story, that I hoped would be forgotten after show-and-tell, became public property. The pitiful story transformed me from a nondescript first grade blob into an instant class celebrity. Miss Chase asked the class to take up a collection from their homes for my poor homeless grieving family. Later, the word spread to other teachers and classes. For the rest of the day I was the beneficiary of doting attention, an instant hero of pity.

When I got home mother asked if anything special happened at school. I replied "nothing special". I clung to the self deceptive hope that the morning's show-and-tell episode would fade away. On Tuesday the space around the teacher's desk filled up with bags and boxes of clothes, household goods, and canned food. Teachers from other rooms brought in donations from their classes, in a school-wide display of mass sympathy. The teachers and the students seemed very pleased with themselves for their generosity. I was such a good cause! Pride was swelling in the breasts of my classmates and teacher for their goodness. At this point even if I wanted to come clean, it just couldn't be done out of respect for the feelings of these selfless people. What would happen next, I wondered, as events ominously took on their own dynamic.

As the school day wound down I savored the last of my honorary status. The principal, a corpulent middle aged man dressed in a suit with shoulder to shoulder lapels, stopped by the classroom. On seeing the large collection he profusely thanked Miss Chase and the students for recognizing a great need, and without hesitation, generously stepping in to relieve human suffering. He looked at me, his eyes filling with the same pride that infected the whole benevolent school community. He asked Miss Chase to have the class move the bags and boxes to the front vestibule so that my mother could fetch them right away, charity would not be delayed in such a tragic case. He told Miss Chase that he would phone my mother immediately. Desperation took hold of me. The fox was finally cornered by the hounds. I blurted out that the phone burned as well as the family car. A quizzical look came over the principal's face. His nose twitched. He smelled a "rat. " The odor of guilt vaporized off my sweating body. Caught like a fly on fly-paper, my glue like sweat stuck my back to the chair. "Show and tell" was over!

The principal did call my mother that evening to express the school's condolences, just in case the story was true, and asked her to pick up the collection for our needy family. Mother expressed appreciation for the unnecessary thoughtfulness, and then went on to explain that the fire was two miles from our house. She said that we were all quite well and that there must be some mistake, she looked over to me with an expression that was a cross between anger and amusement. The words "vivid imagination" popped up several times in the conversation.

In the end it turned out better than I expected. Mother's sense of humor was confirmed. The collection was rerouted to a needy family that had actually been victims of the fire, a collection they would never have received without an advocate in the first grade classroom. Miss Chase, the principal, and my mother came to the conclusion that it would be better for me to repeat the first grade so that I could mature to the point of having an improved understanding of the difference between reality and fantasy. This was fine with me for two reasons.

First, I would be changing schools anyway, so a grade repeat would not be a social stigmata. A new precedent setting California Style neighborhood school (the classrooms opened onto outdoor covered walkways, not interior halls) was just completed one block from our house after a slow three year construction process due to material shortages. Secondly, I would be the same age as my new classmates—mother started me in school a year early due to her erroneous belief that her firstborn was brilliant and mature, neither of which proved to be true, although I looked pretty convincing in a sport jacket. (see photo 15) I repeated the first grade at the new sprawling single story White Oak School. Unfortunately, I was not quite able to totally escape my past. Three of my former first grade classmates also transferred to White Oak. Except for a few taunts, these new second graders had little time to waste embarrassing a lowly second time first grader. On the other hand, Miss Chase was appointed Principal at White Oak, putting her in a position to forewarn my new teacher, thereby squelching any extravagant thoughts I might have at show-and-tell.

I spent three unmemorable years at White Oak School, during which time the war ended, mother remarried, and I had a baby half-sister. In 1948 our family left suburban San Carlos for Emerald Lake and the "country" lifestyle. I was nine. Mother enrolled me in the 4th grade at Lincoln School in Redwood City.

MISS FLOWERS

Young boys, by nature and maybe partially by nurture, need physical competitiveness to establish the "pecking order" in peer groups. This particularly applies to students that come into an existing functioning classroom from another school. Girls determine a "pecking order" without violence, at least I never saw this happen in my school years. It seems girls have evolved beyond what I observed in our hen house, and boys have not. Whenever new hens, usually pullets, are added to the hen social structure a terrible competition starts with head pecking until the new comers either die or take their proper place in the social order. Chickens never seem to have learned the Golden Rule. The very pullets that were almost killed when they entered chicken society would themselves remorselessly peck away with the same fury at subsequent newcomers. Order was established with no quarter. Conclusion: boys are more like chickens than girls. Since I changed schools many times I had my share of "pecking order" rituals. Lincoln School in Redwood City in 1948 (4th grade) and Mount Carmel School in 1949 (5th through 8th grade) were my hen houses.

After staying back in the first grade I went from one of the smallest boys in my class to being about average. This was a great advantage in changing schools, since small size attracted bullies. Other differences that attracted bullies were awkwardness, clothing that appeared unusual, strange shoes, physical deformities, and self confidence. That was me all right. I was skinny and awkward. My mother selected my clothing and shoes totally oblivious to school peer pressure, a certain invitation to trouble. The physical deformity was a mole on my cheek. While my mole was never attacked directly, as it might have been on a chicken, it was a constant reminder that I was different. Finally, I had the undeserved confidence of a first born. The trouble started when we moved to Redwood City and I transferred into the 4th grade at Lincoln public school. Mother actually wanted me to go to the parochial school, but there was no space for me. Therefore the move required assimilation at not one, but two new hen houses, first at Lincoln, then at Mount Carmel the following year. My sister was more fortunate and entered Mount Carmel parochial school at the 3rd grade level. Outside of the "pecking order" my Lincoln School experience was super.

My new teacher was Miss Flowers, a really sweet career teacher, the kind of lady that represents everything right about public education. She was patient, kind, skillful, persistent, dedicated, and loving. At the same time she seemed totally oblivious to the hen house terror I was going through, except the one time she noticed my shirt was torn after lunch recess. I told her rough house yard play was the source of my ruffled appearance. She accepted this explanation and continued the multiplication table drills. Here I had barely escaped with my life from recess, was anticipating a threatened attack after school by the same kids, and now in the in-between time had to learn the 7's table.

Fortunately, my friend Mac , was a welcomed ally. He was also part of the problem. I met Mac the first day of school at the bus stop on the Emerald Lake dam. He was a big strong kid. He looked like a 6th grader, but actually was in the 4th grade with me. We had a lot in common. We both stayed back in school, Mac twice. We came from the same semi-rural neighborhood, and we were different. Mac's family moved to Redwood City the previous year from Utah. He had a slight stutter, wore heavy Utah clothing, and didn't like the class bullies. The year before I arrived Mac settled with the bullies by punching Jerry, one of the leaders, in the mouth when he made fun of his speech. One punch and his size established the pecking order. In a way he was really outside of the order—a special case. He was never accepted in the order, but rather given a place of fearful respect adjacent to it. Now we were friends. The same kids that went after him wanted me. He intervened. I remember him saying, "pick anyone of the bullies and I will give him a bloody nose for you." He was part of the problem because his intercessions delayed, not prevented, the required personal confrontation that was necessary between me and the bullies. His protection worked fine until he got sick with the flu and missed a week of school. That was the same week Miss Flowers started us on the 7's.

After school I rushed to the place where the school bus would pick me up. The bus was late. The bullies lived in the immediate neighborhood and walked to school. They knew each other since first grade. To them, bussed-in kids were outsiders. The school and its surroundings were their territory. To be challenged by them meant that if you dealt with the challenge, you might be accepted into the order, might even get an invitation to play at one of their houses. In a peculiar way the fight ahead was an honor. If kids were just too strange, as one or two of the kids were, they might be totally ignored. The stakes were high. If I lost I would be subject to torment every day. Spit balls in the back of the head, name calling, being pushed around at recess, never being chosen for a team in pick-up ball, and physical intimidation whenever they had a mind to, was the fate of losers. Perhaps the hardest to bear consequence of being a loser was the practical joke. It would always be on you. I had seen it before. Stink desk was typical, where animal excrement and sometime dead animals themselves would be placed in your desk, the perpetrator confident of no reprisal.

The first rock winged over my head; the second caught me on the arm. There they were throwing rocks and yelling insults from the sidewalk across the street. I returned fire with broken blacktop from the playground edge. I turned to pick up more ammo when the school bus came around the corner taking a hit on the hood lobbed from across the street. Mousie, the bus driver stopped; immediately saw me with a fresh handful of blacktop chips, and not knowing where the projectile had come from, thought me the culprit. The bullies ran. I stayed and faced the music. Mousie, the bus driver, normally a very nice gentle guy, bounded out of the bus temper up. He grabbed me by the arm. His vice-like grip was on the thinnest part of my arm below the shoulder. It hurt. What a grip! Clenching the bus steering wheel all those years to the tune of screaming kids, built up his forearms to gorilla power. I limply came along as he hauled me to the Principal's office. We barged into the office, Mousie shouting that I had just hit the bus with a rock. I told what really happened. I said that it couldn't have been me since I was throwing bits of blacktop, not rocks, a crucial detail that only seemed to incriminate me further with the Principal. I told how my tormentors across the street, whose names I couldn't remember, ran away. The Principal calmed Mousie. Shortly, Mousie went back to the bus to drive his route without me. This was real trouble. The bus was the only way to get the five miles home to Emerald Lake. The Principal sat me down on a steel folding chair in the outer office while he called my mother.

Mother showed up an hour later with my sister, and half-brother and half-sister, both still in diapers. She had to load all her children into the Willys jeep station wagon since there was nobody to mind them during this needless, time consuming, and unwarranted trip. She intended that this be a lesson for all involved. Carrying one child, dragging the other by the hand, and issuing constant commands to my sister to keep up, she strode into the Principal's office and demanded an explanation. The Principal realized that he made a tactical error. He could see that my mother wasn't intimidated by his summons. Quite the contrary, she was upset before he even had the opportunity to present his case against me. Before he spoke she made it clear that whatever her son might have done, was no reason to keep him off the bus home, in effect punishing her for my misdemeanor. The clash of the authority titans in my life promised to be a spectacle of Olympian proportion. It turned out to be disappointingly anticlimactic. The Principal seemed to shrink behind his desk. It was as if invisible gremlins were slowly lowering the height adjustment on his desk chair. Mother stood, looming. The confrontation ended in agreement that rock and blacktop throwing was an unacceptable behavior. When we got home I explained what had happened. Mother understood and was sympathetic. Then she sentenced me to three weeks of doing the family dinner dishes. I protested the severity of the sentence! She said this punishment was for the problem I caused her. She said that it was my responsibility to deal with the bullies so as not to inconvenience the whole family, which meant her. Case closed.

The next morning I got on the bus at the Emerald Lake dam. Mousie took no special notice of me. That was good. When we arrived at the school I went directly to the classroom, unmolested. Jerry the most aggressive bully came over to my desk. He said he would get me at lunch recess. Miss Flowers greeted the class as usual. In the meantime I tried to get my mind off lunch by concentrating on the 7's and Palmer Method writing drills. Later in the morning sweet Miss Flowers called me to her desk. She said the Principal told her about my bad rock throwing habits. I felt like telling her that I could have gotten the driver's window if I had a mind to, that is if I really threw the rock. However, from experience I learned that contriteness was more important than accuracy in this case. She said my misbehavior reflected on her and the whole class. She said she would keep a special eye on me. I gratefully accepted her surveillance in anticipation of Jerry's lunch-time attack, although I expected little protection from her.

The bell rang. Time for lunch. We usually ate our lunch on benches in the play yard under the ubiquitous California sunshine. There were no government subsidized cafeteria school lunches in those days. Each kid's mother packed a lunch into a colorful metal lunch pail. The top had a cavity for a thermos of milk. The inner glass vacuum part of mine was broken. I ate the peanut and butter jelly sandwich, the apple, and the five Hydrox cookies by myself in peace. The bully crowd walked home for lunch since they all lived within four blocks of school. The teacher on duty in the yard organized a kick ball game. This was a lot of fun. It was like baseball, only the soccer-sized ball was kicked instead of being hit with a bat. The teacher asked two of the larger girls to be captains. The captains chose teams. I was chosen early, a real honor. The bullies appeared shortly after we began play. I played 2nd base. Jerry went over to my lunch box that I had left on the bench, picked it up, threw it on the ground breaking it open, and then looked at me while the other three bullies jeered. When my team got three outs we left the field for our turn at bat. I walked over to pick up my lunch pail. As I bent over Jerry pushed me. Unfortunately for him, I grabbed him by the shirt, got him off balance, and pushed him over the bench. He landed on broken pavement skinning his elbow. The 4th grade windows overlooked this particular part of the play yard. As I glanced up there was Miss Flowers looking out the window, keeping an eye on me. Jerry ran to the yard duty teacher. She took him to the school nurse. Having been to the nurse before myself I knew my lunch box would be amply revenged. School nurses had a knack for inflicting maximum pain in treating minor scrapes and cuts. The usual treatment for a skinned elbow or knee was a painful iodine scrub of the open wound itself. Jerry's treatment was bound to hurt more than the original injury.

When the bell rang I didn't want to go back into the classroom. The kick ball game was too much fun, also Miss Flowers face in the window haunted me. Sure enough, a few minutes after class began I was called out by the Principal and scolded for my rough housing on the playground that caused a very nice boy personal injury. He told me I would have to apologize to Jerry for this misbehavior. I gulped and said I would. Why not? I was the 4th grade's rock throwing bully. The Principal would have ordinarily called the transgressor's mother, but in this case, he made an exception, having gotten acquainted with my mother the day before. It all turned out OK in the end. The neighborhood bullies didn't bother me the rest of the school year due to my undeserved reputation and Mac's return. Miss Flowers learned to see my good side. She taught me with gusto. I was one of the few kids that actually enjoyed the Palmer Method script writing drills. The next year I left public school and transferred into Mount Carmel at the 5th grade level.

MOUNT CARMEL SCHOOL

Mount Carmel School, was started in 1885 by four sisters of Notre Dame de Namur. Rumor had it that one of the founders still lived in the convent! When I arrived in 1949, Father Cavanaugh, the Pastor of Mount Carmel Church, was in charge of the parish, including the school. He was a kindly, white haired old priest. He dutifully handed out the report cards every six weeks, class by class. The students, 40 to a class, were called alphabetically from their alphabetically arranged rows, boys on one side, girls on the other. Father entered the classroom escorted by Mother Superior. He sat down at the teacher's desk, authoritative in his Roman collar and black cassock. Mother Superior and the classroom Sister stood behind him, one on each side. The teacher's desks in all the classrooms were elevated on a platform for symbolic and practical reasons. Symbolically, the desk was the center of power and authority, like the judge's bench in a courtroom. Practically, the elevated position afforded clear sight lines to all the student's desks. An authoritarian eyeball dissuaded deviant behavior, greatly reducing discipline problems and helping student's focus their attention on their work assignment. When Father sat at the desk, his presence and power rivaled that of the Pope in Rome. He theatrically read the grades aloud, always trying to say something positive about each student. If a student's grades were failing in some subjects, he would focus his comments on the passing grades, and perhaps say a few supportive words on a solid record of attendance, deportment, and if he had to, scrape the bottom of the barrel, religious development. No one ever got less than a "C" in religious development. Doing so might suggest the Sister's themselves had been less than zealous in religious instruction. While Mother Superior and the Sisters always showed Father Cavanaugh great deference, the form far exceeded the substance in day-to-day operations. We all knew that despotic Mother Superior and her nuns were in charge of our school life.

The relationship between Father Cavanaugh and the nuns was formal and diplomatic, similar to the relationship between great powers that might inhabit the same continent. The disposition of the power was reflected in the architecture of the place. The Mount Carmel church, school, rectory, and convent occupied a full Redwood City block, each function dominating one corner, with the rectory and convent maximally separated on diagonal corners. The school yard occupied the hollow in the block's center. The two story Spanish Colonial school, that loosely matched the other structures on the site in architectural style, contained eight grades in eight classrooms. With 40 kids in each class, the total maximum enrollment totaled 320 students. The convent housed a teaching nun for each grade and the Mother Superior. The rectory housed three priests, the Pastor, the Assistant Pastor, and a young priest, an intern of sorts. The church itself was quite modern. It had a large "crying room" on the side of the alter, its double glazing separating the prodigious infant Baby Boom Catholics in progress from the congregation in the nave. The church could seat about 400. The priests and nuns, in numbers ecclesiastically luxurious by today's standards, offered a highly structured educational and religious environment. The large classes required strict discipline, perhaps more easily attained in those days when the parochial school culture and its supporting community was solidified by shared values. The diversity common today did not encumber a clear view of what each component of the community should be. The priests, sisters, students, and in an extended sense, the parents were part of the "system."

The school day started with an 8:00 am assembly in the school yard. Uniformed students formed two lines in alphabetical order for each class, boys in one, girls in the other. When the 16 lines were perfect, role call was taken by each teacher, the proper response to ones name was; "present Sister". As Sisters walked down each line uniforms were inspected. Items like improperly tied girls scarves and unpolished boys shoes were noted for later action, perhaps a note to the parent. The assembly was snapped to attention by Mother Superior with her amplified wooden clicker. The Star Spangled Banner was played on a squeaky loud speaker, leading into the Pledge of Allegiance that was recited in unison to the prompts of Mother Superior. Her voice rose with emotion when she came to the "under God" phrase. This completed, a prayer was offered by the young intern Priest , usually asking us to pray for a Communist country where Catholics were being persecuted. Poland and Russia received the greatest amount of prayers. The Amen was the signal for the "Stars and Stripes Forever" march. Starting with the 1st graders the entire student body marched to the classrooms. The alphabetical ordered lines at assembly merely had to march to the proper classroom, segment by row, and sit—no pushing, shoving, or reordering of positions was tolerated. The clicker signaled the class to sit. Each nun had a clicker that was used for commands like these. A click was the command to execute a pre taught maneuver, like stand, sit, genuflect, and kneel. A rapid succession of clicks meant come to order this instant or else.

Some of the clickers were plain, some were decorated with carvings. A basic clicker was a tapered turned wooden shaft about 7" long with a higher ring in the center. A tounge-depressor like stick that could be flicked with the thumb was attached by rubber bands thus making the clicking sound necessary for commanding without words. What could be routinized was. The transfer of knowledge would not be short-changed by time wasted on maintaining class order. In extreme cases the clicker could be used across the knuckles of boys to get their attention or as a prod to keep lines moving and straight. Girls never required clicker contact. My explanation was that nuns, under all that black cloth, were still females and were not about to treat their own kind like boys whose nature, they believed, demanded corporal instruction. The orderliness and discipline at Mount Carmel was a shock to me after Miss Flowers and the disorderly public school. Five through eight appeared to be a tough sentence when I first transferred. But I adapted, and even learned spelling, writing, mathematics, and catechism under the tyranny of the clicker!

Silence, or not talking in my case, was the hardest essential component for order. Silence, did not mean talking less or more quietly, as in public school. It meant silence! When I kept my naturally active mouth shut I soon discovered it was possible to learn something. Perhaps the nuns were on to something. In public school we were treated as creative little creatures that needed to self express. Too much squelching of creativity would hurt the learning process. We chatted in class and passed notes. The standard of order was relaxed. In Catholic school it seemed that we were treated as reluctant vessels into which a cargo of knowledge and spiritual values could be loaded only if silence and order pertained. This was not just another modern theory in the shifting sands of education theory. It was the nun's lives! In their own lives the good Sisters maintained silence in the convent, except during meal times. They spent time every day in silent meditation, in search of spirituality. Theirs was a culture of discipline, reflection and silence. The standards they imposed on their classes were modest compared to their own regimented lives. Therefore, talking when not called upon, and note passing in the classroom were swiftly punished by banishment to the cloakroom, extra home work, staying after school, reduced marks in deportment, and parental counseling. In extreme or chronic cases, Mother Superior would be called in to raise the stakes. Threats of suspension and expulsion were her arsenal to get the students', and their parents', attention to address behavior problems. The school simply could not function without order in the classroom. Lack of order was seen as a disservice to the students who came for an education. In four years my class had two expulsions for behavior problems. The empty desks were quickly filled and the former non-conforming classmates soon forgotten.

Routine abounded. Fire drills took place once a month. When the alarm sounded the classes marched out of the school, reversing the rigid process of starting the school day. The lines formed in the courtyard, alphabetically, by sex and grade. Role was quickly taken and the students returned to the classroom. No talking was allowed during the drills, so all commands, mostly by clicker, could be easily heard. In September 1949, just as the school year started, it was confirmed that the Soviet Union had the atomic bomb. Every other month from then on the fire drill would be combined with the atomic bomb drill. One wall of the classroom was virtually all glass. We were told that when the godless Communist Russians dropped an atomic bomb on us flying glass and the bright flash could be very dangerous. Naturally, Mother

Superior had a countermeasure. When Sister clicked we crawled under our desks and tightly closed our eyes, no peeking! We had confidence that Mother Superior could predict the exact timing of the explosion so as not to take too much time from regular instruction. The lack of a foolproof countermeasure to a clicker wielded by a Sister of Notre Dame would eventually doom the "Evil Empire".

Another manifestation of order, the school dress code, required all students to wear a standard uniform. Clothing as a means of self expression didn't exist except for free dress day. Twice a year, just before Christmas and Easter vacations, a free dress day would be declared. This day would coincide with a school event like the Christmas pageant to which parents would be invited in the afternoon. The excitement was particularly noticeable among the girls, who jabbered about what they would wear. The boys already mostly knew what hand-me-downs they would wear. The spectacle of the whole school in civvies of choice was like a school-wide reprieve from oppression. The girls above the 5th grade were a real sight! They wore dresses. They were transformed from the uniformed blobs they normally were. They looked like females with waists, breasts, and other female parts I was beginning to notice. The boys wore slacks, neck ties, and sport jackets, mostly ill-fitting, either hand-me-downs or acquired for a past religious ritual and now too tight. Free dress didn't improve their appearance much. The girls looked like young ladies in growing up clothes. The boys looked like Halloween kids masquerading as miniature sartorially compromised adults. Nevertheless, the parents seemed proud of their boys and girls, and were very glad to be attending such important functions with their little adults. If the school year went well, a third non-liturgical free-dress day might be granted by Mother Superior the last day of school, in a flight of ecclesiastical spring fever. The relief from the uniform was a reward for good behavior and the nuns' subtle way of saying our captivity at Mount Carmel was temporary.

The sense of order gained by uniforms was appreciated all the more in its fleeting relief. Unfortunately, the nuns themselves never enjoyed free-dress. In all the years at Mount Carmel I never saw a nun clad in anything but full habit, even on very hot days! On the other hand, the parish priests would often be seen on the playground shooting baskets in sweats. Added to the nun's vows of poverty, chastity, and obedience must have been a forth vow, habitation, that is the wearing of the habit like a second holy skin, rain or shine, hot or cold, at school or church, without relief. The black robe, a starched proscenium of white cloth over the head, a white starched bib on which a crucifix dangled, and a huge rosary binding the waist as a belt defined nun-hood. I remember conversations with other boys at recess speculating on what nuns might wear to bed. Our adolescent curiosity imagined Sisters turning over in bed impaling themselves on the sharp points of the crucifix or entangling themselves in beads. Order in the classroom, order in dress, and order in routine did not totally free our minds from disorderly thoughts.

On the first Monday of my third week at Mount Carmel the pecking order was established. With the rigid discipline of the school, it would seem difficult for bullies to terrorize other kids, but they could and did, after school. It seems that "pantzing" was the torment of choice at Sequoia, the local public high school. Some called it harmless hazing. Like chickens, the aggressive boys in the upper grades thought that it might be fun at Mount Carmel, although they themselves would likely be victims of it if they went on to Sequoia. Some 7th graders noticed that I was the new kid from Lincoln school and targeted me. After school, four of them followed me into the boy's bathroom, and threatened me with a pantzing. A pantzing was merely the forceful removal of some one's trousers, leaving the victim with the embarrassing task of getting home without. For me, getting the five miles home without the bottom to my uniform was less daunting than facing mother pant-less after she recently purchased the uniform for me at great expense. The situation demanded nothing less than a concerted effort to hold onto my britches. The 7th graders intention was to embarrass me and put me in my place, not harm me. My stepfather taught me a few simple judo holds that saved the day, or more accurately the pants. As the preliminary pushing and shoving started, I selected the boy who seemed to be the most vocal. I grabbed him two fisted by the left arm rotating under his armpit to a position behind his back, his arm pinned painfully up on his shoulder blades. He leaned forward to escape the pain while I maneuvered his head into the closest urinal. The other boys still pushed and shoved. Head down in the yellow liquid he screamed to the others to back off, and to me to let him go. It was like having a tiger by the tail. Any of these boys could probably beat the heck out of me if they had a mind to. Fortunately for me they didn't. After securing promises of letting me be, I released my grip. Mother asked if anything exciting happened at school. I said, no, just the usual.

One of the dreaded monthly duties of a Catholic school kid was to relieve a guilty conscience in the Sacrament of Confession. In between confessions the nuns worked very hard to develop a keen sense of guilt in every one of us. Sister Theresa, my teacher, spoke with high praise of one of her former students from the farming community of Watsonville, who felt so guilty and in need of penance, that he would walk on his knees to communion after a confession. At this stage in my life I was almost totally guiltless, a condition that demanded remedy. But how? My unstoppable puberty and the churches' dogmas on sex provided the answer. Sister Theresa revealed that one could not have sex, or even think about sex, until adult marriage, and maybe not even then. Before the 5th grade I didn't think about sex. In the 5th grade puberty and Sister Theresa changed my life. She said thinking about sex before marriage produces a confessable amount of sin. Girls began to look interesting. Sinful unsatisfied curiosity produced a constant confessable amount of guilt. I dutifully, and I must say courageously, confessed to old Father Cavanaugh in the dark secrecy of the confessional. I was so ashamed of my guilt that when it was my turn to confess, I entered the dark box lurking in a position so Father couldn't see my face. Sometimes I would attempt to disguise my voice to mask my identity; I felt so ashamed. Nevertheless, I always confessed to Father Cavanaugh. After trying the other parish priests, I found that he gave the least penance and advice.

Thank God for the secrecy of the confessional, without it godly father Cavanaugh might recognize me as the school yard sex fiend, sinning profusely in one field only. For variety, and to show that I could sin more generally, I confessed venial sins such as sneaking candy during the Lenten fast, drinking water before receiving communion on Sunday morning, or showing up late for church. Up through the 8th grade, my confessions were pretty ordinary, that is until the time I denied the faith.

Usually I rode my bike to school. When it had a flat tire or was otherwise unserviceable I either caught a ride from a neighbor or hitchhiked. This particular late afternoon I was hitch-hiking home when I was picked up by two strange Catholic bating men. As I climbed into the back seat of the big sedan the driver asked me if I was one of those "cat-lickers". There I sat in the back of the car, almost a prisoner in a Catholic school uniform, telling these strangers that I was not a "cat-licker". They let me out about half way home at the Community Store, where they turned off. Getting out of the car seemed like an escape, with a price; guilt for mortally sinning. I thought of Saint Peter, the disciple and first Pope, denying Jesus three times on the eve of His Crucifixion. That was me all right, a weak kneed betrayer of the Catholic Faith. Not one to waste guilt when I found it, and in need of finding non sexual sin for variety, I proceeded to confess this denial to Father Cavanaugh a week later, along with my sexual misdeeds. I feared that the denial of faith could draw a full Rosary penance. Penance was said at the alter after confession, a Rosary would tip off the whole class to the seriousness of my sins—the ultimate embarrassment. When I finished I was much relieved when Father Cavanaugh gave me my usual three Hail Mary penance. As I was leaving he said, "Michael, you should not accept another ride in that car". I almost fell to the floor. He knew who I was all these years of confessions. How could I face him in the school yard. He knew that I was a sexual sinner, a lax Catholic, and a betrayer of the Faith. Yet he never failed to greet me with kindness and apparent pleasure. It could have been that he himself had sinned once, and he knew how I felt. No, that was too far fetched!

When I graduated in June of 1952, my academic and moral development was judged to be sufficient to meet the competitive standards of Serra High School. The rigid discipline, large class size, and strict catholic school culture didn't stop me from absorbing a basic understanding of mathematics, English, geography, and European history. In fact the peculiarities of parochial school education may have saved me from my undisciplined self, at least in the school setting. Out of school, the guilt training was not as successful as the nuns had hoped. Where the academic content seemed to stick, the guilt training was largely forgotten as I spent the next four high school years blatantly trying to learn more about the opposite sex, admittedly with little success. Maybe that was the point!

Father Cavanaugh presented the diploma with his blessing, good wishes, and a wink. Looking back, I think he took the sex and guilt game a lot less seriously than the good sisters. If Mother Superior's 15th century concept of the Faith pertained, I would still be kneeling at the alter rail saying rosaries. If my penance ever exceeded the hours in my lifetime I could have obtained a plenary indulgence by a concentrated period of self imposed temporal punishment (usually prayers, fasting, and daily mass attendance) accompanied by remorsefulness. If I lived in the 15th century my family could have purchased an indulgence for me from the church. Fortunately, in 1562 the church discontinued this practice 45 years after Martin Luther pointed out selling indulgences was a blatant conflict of interest. Mother Superior was still catching up! In the end, selecting the right confessor proved to be the key in making religion tolerable. Never more than three "Hail Marys" and a kind word from a wise, old, and very holy priest did the job!

SERRA HIGH

We showed up on the steps of Serra High School in the Fall of 1952. We came from all over the San Francisco Peninsula, by bus and train. The class of '56 must have presented a ragged spectacle before the teaching priests as we marched in, but probably no worse than so many other earlier classes. The faculty of Serra High were charged with making men out of us, the adolescent putty offered up by the nuns of the feeder parochial schools. With only four years to work with, there was no time to lose. The all male environment, the strict class structure, and remote location (my commute was 18 miles) deflated most of the once proud former 8th graders. Any loftiness, earned or otherwise, due to having progressed 8 years to the pinnacle of elementariness, in academic achievement and physical size, vanished that first day of classes. The former 8th graders were now humbled at the bottom of a new institution, and knew it! The size of the high school juniors and seniors was impressive. They were men, at least in dimension. They had cars and girlfriends! The entering freshmen didn't drive, shave, smoke, do girls, or drink beer. There was so much to learn!

The 12 priests and 2 lay teachers saw it all before. In the welcoming assembly of the student body, freshmen sat in front, seniors in back, sophomores and juniors in between. The faculty, except for a few who patrolled the isles, were on stage. The priests wore black floor length cassocks and the traditional Roman collar. There was an air of unity, authority, and purpose in their demeanor. They seemed to possess a singular and communal sense of power. I never had seen so many priests in one place before. Sitting in the front row I smiled, like one might smile at the doctor before an inevitable tetanus injection. I could see that these men were not going to be our friends by the way they clinically surveyed our bright apprehensive faces. The prospect of educating us as we moved through hormone driven adolescence to physical maturity didn't seem to daunt them. Perhaps they drew some comfort knowing that we were prepared by dedicated nuns, were in the top 50% of our classes, and were the sons of parents willing to make the monetary and convenience sacrifices to see that we were properly educated in a private Catholic school.

The Dean of Men, Father Maher, looking like a bulldog in a smock, paced the stage while addressing the assembly. His remarks seemed particularly directed to those in the front seats. He developed the theme of academic guilt. This contrasted with personal behavioral guilt that we were so extensively instructed in by the sisters of Notre Dame. He placed the responsibility on us for successfully mastering the subjects we would be offered at Serra. In other words it was our responsibility to make something out of ourselves. Academic failure could only come about by lack of personal effort, since we were all capable of learning, or we wouldn't have been accepted to study at Serra in the first place. The Dean went on to explain that we would be placed in classes according to the results of our IQ tests. The homerooms were divided into A, B, and C. The A group were the smartest and would get the toughest assignments. The B group were average, and while they might be mixed into some A classes, their usual workload would be of average college prep difficulty. The C group were those students who would have to work very hard to master the minimum college prep curriculum. Everyone wanted to go to Berkeley or Santa Clara, Stanford while close by, was thought too expensive and exclusive for Serra students. All students were expected to feel very guilty if they fell behind their peer group, since this could only happen by lack of effort. Having heard that the A's were expected to master both Latin and Greek, I was greatly relieved to find that I was assigned to the B homeroom, meaning just three years of regular Latin. However, we did not escape Greek altogether. It was administered to the B's and C's as punishment during "jug".

All through my four years at Serra I remained in the B homeroom. It was the best place to be. In my sophomore year my faculty councilor, Father Williams, called me into his office, and with some pride told me my IQ test improved due to the great education I was being offered and partially absorbing. He said it was time for me to transfer to the A homeroom. I protested the test score as being a fluke; I protested leaving my B class friends; and I protested the prospect of more work than I could handle. Father Williams countered by saying my mother would be very proud of a son willing to work hard at the A class level. I pointed out that should I fail, she would be unhappy that I was pushed into the A class by my councilor. He agreed to let me stay in the B homeroom lest I do poorly in the advanced group, thereby tainting his heretofore impeccable counseling record. This political decision was one of thousands that eventually landed Father Williams a bishop's chair. I maintained a B average in the B group, just good enough to get into Berkeley, but not good enough to draw attention that would attract more work and cut into the growing up time I needed.

Immaturity plagued me all through high school, even though I suffered the disgrace of staying back in the 1st grade and therefore should have been, at least in years, relatively mature for my class. While I was of about average height, I didn't achieve my full height of 5"-11" until late in my Junior year. During most of high school I was a social blob and physically nondescript. These distinguishing attributes did not come without effort. I wore a flat-top hair-do; my mother cut the sides, kind of tapered so the side walls could be pasted back with the help of copious amounts of sticky Brilliantine. I cut the top flat with an electric clipper in front of the bathroom mirror. The idea was to start with a bald spot in the middle of the top of the head, then go straight out to the side walls, the flatter the better. I wore tan baggy pegged chino pants held up by a 1" blue suede belt. The tight cuffs increased the desirable impression of bagginess in the knees. A gray Serra varsity jacket with soiled gray leather sleeves, a required white shirt with collar, and suede desert boots, or my favorite, blue suede bluchers completed my sartorial statement. Add some acne, grease under the fingernails, and metal bands on my teeth, and I was groomed for action. No wonder I was a disaster with the opposite sex on those very rare occasions when I even had the courage to make contact with the Venetians. Sometimes it was almost forced. The Soph Hop, the Junior Prom, and the Senior Ball all required a date. My friends usually fixed me up with a nice girl from one of the Catholic girls' high schools in the area for an evening of embarrassment. The girls were always more mature than I was, but looking back, they were probably just as scared. The sight must have been a shock to many a parent when yours truly showed up to take their precious daughter out? I envied my sister who was very pretty, socially very desirable, and always "in". On Saturday nights she went on dates and to parties with boys in chopped down 1949 Fords or 1952 Mercury convertibles. My high school cars were all prewar. On Saturday nights my best friend, Bob, and I would go to movies or work on our old cars listening to bebop on the radio.

Immaturity also occasionally affected my academic performance. My second year history teacher, Father Ryan, a tough young disciplinarian priest called me to task in front of the whole class for speaking in class when he ordered silence. He said my misbehavior was becoming chronic. I wasn't sure what "chronic" meant, but it sounded like a personal affront. I decided right then not to study and invest my "valuable" time in Father Ryan's class, because he didn't like me. Did I get even with him! I earned a "D" in the class and came close to having to repeat the class with the same Father Ryan the next semester. I foolishly forgot that Father Ryan was not at Serra to make teenage friends.

Transportation was always a problem. Before I could drive I took the train. I rode to the Redwood City Southern Pacific station with Doc, our neighbor, in his rusty Pontiac station car. The wheezing steam train, the staple of Peninsula commuters to San Francisco, dropped me at San Mateo. There were usually 10 or 12 other Serra students on the train. On our first day an experienced sophomore train rider showed us newcomers how to replace the conductor's punch on the commute ticket for a free ride. The train Conductors each used a punch with their own special cut-out shape. After the Conductor punched a commute card, the little piece of punched out card would fall to the isle floor. When the Conductor moved onto the next car the student would look for the punch. The exact punch with the card's pattern had to be found among those strewn in the isle. By trial and error this could be done before the San Mateo station. When the punch fit the student would press it into the hole in the "commute" making it almost impossible to see the cut out marks. My freshman friend Earl, tried it. The next morning when the conductor made the new punch part of the old punch fell out. The conductor who was not new to this fraud, in a fit of temper, punched out a whole row (20 rides) as punishment.

From the San Mateo train station I hitchhiked or walked the remaining two miles to Serra. Once a nice lady naively stopped her 1948 four-door Dodge sedan for a big group of Serra hitch hikers. We were late. In our eagerness to all get in her car, the left rear door was ripped off. Father Maher, the Dean of Men, tracked down the offending students who were jugged (an extra hour of Latin or Greek after school for a week) and made to pay for the damages, plus a big bouquet of flowers. The lady was a Catholic. She never stopped again.

The 1 hour 15 minute one way commute made for a very long day. The regular school hours were 8:30 am to 3:30 pm. Sports and other extracurricular activities took place after 3:30. I left the house at 7:15 am and returned about 6:30 pm. This persisted until I could drive a car in my sophomore year. The week after my 16th birthday I passed the driving license test. Aunt Amanda's old '39 Hudson became the work- horse of the Barker Transportation Company. Unlike most public and private transportation companies, the old Hudson was always full.

Leaving Emerald Lake my passengers included my sister bound for Belmont, The Academy of Notre Dame, and my half brothers and sister, bound for Mount Carmel in Redwood City. After the Mount Carmel group was let off I picked up two Serra classmates in Redwood City refilling the car. My classmates each contributed 50 cents a day for a door to door round trip. At half the cost and half the time of the SP train commute, this was a real bargain! That $1.00 bought three gallons of gas from my favorite discount gas station. That was all the gas needed for the round trip.

Even with a car, transportation to private school remained time consuming, complicated, and expensive. I often thought my friends who went to public high school didn't appreciate the luxury of their free door to door bus service and short ride. They in turn let it be known that they envied the freedom and fun we had riding up and down El Camino Real five days a week, listening to Chuck Barry, Elvis, and Frankie Lyman in the "blue bomb". And it was fun! About once a week, or when our schedules coincided, we would drag race a municipal garbage truck headed for its bay dump at the stop light at El Camino and San Carlos Boulevard. For two years I tried to accelerate faster than that truck to the naively optimistic hooting and wailing's of my passengers. The garbage men hanging on the back of the truck took equal pleasure in the contest, literally dusting us time after time. The Hudson was surly the only car ever built that couldn't keep up with a fully loaded garbage truck! To save a little face in the certain knowledge of defeat, I installed a straight through muffler so that we might at least sound faster.

In my Junior year my friends convinced me to run for student body judge. My good friend, and Redwood City rider, Bill, was my campaign manager. Dan, my opponent was a popular top student in the A homeroom. He coveted the judgeship. The office was mostly honorary, since discipline was handled quite well by the Fathers who retained all power unto themselves. The Judge mostly advocated the student's interests in matters of jug. The office, like the other student body offices, existed primarily to provide an opportunity for students to develop civic skills, including campaigning and public speaking, neither of which I could do with any effect. When the pre-election assembly was held each candidate was given an opportunity to convince the audience of their merits for the office they were seeking. The teachers expected that the speeches would be quite well prepared and delivered; and they were, except mine. Several days before the speechmaking Bill let my opponent know that my speech would attack him as unfit for office. Bill also said we needed a gimmick. That's when the dummy idea came up. On the big day, Bill insisted that my opponent speak first since he was from the A homeroom and I was from the B homeroom. Dan attacked me first, fearing my attack later. He spoke very well. He convinced me that he was the better man. When I was called to speak I thanked Dan for his great speech and candidacy, and admitted he was the better man. Then I looked to the roof. Bill released a dummy from the catwalk. It was a Serra student hanging in effigy with the sign, "Don't get hung, vote for Barker". The assembly cheered for the surprise comic relief. The faculty was not amused by this trivialization of civic speechmaking. But, all the speeches, all the hallway posters, and all the political posturing were forgotten in the voting booth. I won in a landslide! In my Senior Yearbook, Dan wrote: "To a better vote getter". He went on to a Ph.D. in mathematics and a distinguished professorial career at Cal Tech. Bill went to West Point, eventually becoming a prominent lawyer on the San Francisco Peninsula. I never ran again.

In June of 1956, those motley fellows who were freshmen with me four short years earlier were now men. I was too! We graduated; and had some respect. Our driver's licenses and Selective Service "draft cards" created modest bulges of manhood in our slim wallets. The Fathers had done their work on us just as the good Sisters had done earlier. Mother was very proud. She and my sister attended the graduation ceremony in the school gym. The Student body officers, including the Judge, took prominent seats on the stage next to a temporary altar. Under my academic robe I wore a charcoal brown $18 flannel suit from Sears, purchased for the occasion. My treasured blue suede shoes and white crew socks anchored my majesty to the stage. Thinking back to my first assembly four years earlier seemed so very long ago, yet the years passed quickly. In four years I progressed backward, from the front of assembly to the coveted back senior rows. Now my last event at Serra had me back in front again, on the stage with the other student officers, where I would not be called upon to make remarks. None of the officers spoke except the Student Body President who was allowed to read the homily at mass and make kind remarks about the Serra experience, and the class Valedictorian who did his "cross roads in life" stitch.

The ceremonies started with a Mass. Father Maher gave the sermon, kind of a last shot at us before we were off. He spoke about our great academic achievements, our development physically and morally, and the crossroads in life ahead, steeling most of the thunder of the Valedictorian. Ignoring his words I looked him in the eyes as he spoke. I saw for the first time that Father Maher really did care for us and would miss us. This was heady stuff! Authority with a heart. Could it be? Well it was too late a revelation for our class anyway. When I was called to receive my diploma, as those before me, Father Maher cited my special accomplishments: member varsity track team, Student Body Judge, honor role from time to time, and driver of the "blue bomb". The last accolade drew a big laugh from my classmates. Father Maher never betrayed his sense of humor when we rolled in late in the Hudson because the radiator leaked so much we had to stop every few miles for water. Now he laughs! He didn't even smile as he handed out sentences of jug for tardiness. When my riders complained that they were mere victims of the old car, Father Maher observed that life was unfair, and increased the jug time to two hours to discourage further protest. Character building came easy to Father. During the reception following the graduation parents congratulated their sons and thanked the faculty. They especially thanked Father Maher for instilling a respect for authority and building character.

Mother seemed to be very happy that I was growing up. Standing there in my flannel suit, writing witty, but inane, comments in year book after year book being offered by my classmates, made me feel glad to be moving on. In one week I would be working as a firefighter in San Mateo County. I was surprised when mother tearfully embraced me and said she was sorry my father could not be there to see me in this moment of celebration. Cecil B. Barker died almost eight years earlier. Until then I thought she had forgotten all about my father. It seems that for just a fleeting second she flashed back to the rocky marriage she once had with my dad. There must have been some good times, probably when they were in show business together in San Francisco and in their early marriage in Bakersfield. Could the night I was conceived be as special for them as it was for me? Like looking back to the future at an old faded photo, was she fleetingly posing together with my dad in her imagination, just for that moment, the two of them standing there with a gowned son holding a high school diploma; some blurred recollection of long stilled embers of love, cold to the touch. She did not speak of my father again during her lifetime. None of us realized that mother herself had only 3 more years of life left. Sadly, neither the "Mr." or the "Mrs." of radio fame lived to see me really grow up.

CHAPTER X

AFTER WORD

The relatives, acquaintances, teachers, bosses, and friends, presented in story form on these pages interacted with my life to shape who I am. They in turn were shaped by folks of earlier times, and of course, great historical events, like The Great Depression and World War II. My views and values reflect more of the pre war values than does the generation born after the war, the Baby Boomers, who after all were raised in a radically changed post atomic bomb culture. Being the last of the Great Depression cohorts we were imbued with the older perspectives on hardship, rigid ethics, and life's instability. Who knows what the present crop of communication age children will have as inherited value systems. All I know for sure is that what I was given has served me well in my first 60 years.

"Growing up in California," ends in 1956; the year I completed high school. It covers the youthful, impressionable years. The three years after high school growing up continued in a steady predictable manner as I attended University. Then in November 1959 mother died after a long battle with cervical cancer that had spread throughout her body. I was 21 years old. My rate of growing up accelerated at unimaginable speed. At the time, she was legally separated from my step-father. He was remarkably absent and uninterested in his children. Suddenly I became the guardian of five minor children, four really. Helen, my sister, was quite mature and hardly a child at 20. Indeed, when mother was dying of cancer, she dropped out of college and tended her in our home in Saratoga, California, until the end. I also dropped classes at Berkeley to deal with family matters. The Aunts and Uncles in the preceding stories rallied. Their own large families did not impede their generosity in taking in the Hampton kids until I could arrange for permanent placement. The youngest was nine.

From the time mother died in 1959, to well into the 1960's, our family was in great turbulence. I placed the three Hampton boys in Saint Vincents, a Catholic boarding school for boys in Marin County. They were not happy in this situation, but it seemed the best available alternative at the time. At least they were together. After three years, two of them, over my protest in court, were reunited with their father who had remarried and asked for custody. This turned out to be an unhappy situation due to the alcohol addiction of Dave Hampton and his new wife. Had I or the court been aware of their alcohol dependency the boys might have stayed at Saint Vincents. Not wanting to keep Hilary, the most distraught by the family chaos, by himself at Saint Vincents, I placed him in a special home for disturbed boys in San Jose. A year later Grandmother Hobrecht, my mother's mother, invited Hilary to live with her and Uncle Ed in the old family house in San Francisco. This intergenerational arrangement worked surprisingly well. Loraine, the eldest and only Hampton daughter, stayed with childless Aunt Clare and Uncle Frank in San Francisco where she was accommodated immediately after mother's death. When it finally was all sorted out, three generations of Hobrechts and Barkers participated in making homes for the Hampton children in addition to their father.

My dear sister Helen, eventually graduated from San Jose State College; taught elementary school in San Francisco, and married a wealthy businessman, all the while doing exemplary family duty. I earned degrees in Architecture, and City and Regional Planning, from the University of California, Berkeley; married; and traveled to England for a professional opportunity in 1965. When I lived in England, Helen, selflessly took over many of my stewardship responsibilities. She typically hosted family dinners during the holidays that united the Hampton children several times a year. She never flagged in her devotion to the needs of the Hampton children even as she began having children of her own.

The Hampton children, to their credit, did "make something of themselves". Loraine graduated from Wayne State University. She taught elementary school in Detroit while her husband studied to become an orthodontist. They have two grown children and live prosperously in Marin County. The Hampton boys, in spite of all the family trauma, have done surprisingly well. David, the oldest, is a marine engineer. A bit of a recluse, he lives aboard a ship in Southeast Asia. Hilary, the second oldest, is an electronic technician in Silicone Valley, where he owns his own home. He has taken a very special interest in documenting family history on tape and film, making him very popular at family gatherings. Philip, the youngest, is a machinist in the San Francisco Bay Area. He has also started a small business making sports mirrors. On the side he composes pop music and plays guitar and harp in his own rock band.

THE END

ABOUT THE AUTHOR

Michael Barker grew up in California. He was born in Bakersfield in 1938 to former show business personalities. He spent his formative years in the San Francisco Bay Area. He attended high school in the "Fabulous 50's". He took degrees in Architecture and City and Regional Planning at the University of California, Berkeley, during the turbulent student rebellions of the 1960's.

His first book, "California Retirement Communities", was published in 1966. In 30 years of professional practice he has been published regularly on technical subjects. His publishers have included John Wiley & Sons, Pergamon Press, Her Majesty's Stationery Office, McGraw-Hill, and the University of California Press. "Growing Up" is his first non-technical work.

During his professional career Barker served as City Planning Director for Palo Alto, California; Project Director for the new town of Warrington, in England; Director of Urban and Environmental Programs for The American Institute of Architects, in Washington, DC; Principal of an architecture and planning firm in Vermont; and the Executive Director of the American Planning Association, in Washington, DC. He has represented the United States on behalf of the US National Academy of Sciences at international conferences on cities and the environment. Currently, he consults and writes.

Eighteen years of Barker's professional career were spent in Washington, DC, where he raised his two sons. Ironically, his sons who grew up in the East, are now both earning their livelihoods in Los Angeles, California; one in the motion picture business, the other a research engineer. Barker's non-professional interests include skiing, tennis, and sailboat racing. His Tartan 34, WINGDAM with sons

251

crewing, won many regattas on the Chesapeake Bay. He now races and cruises on Lake Champlain.

Printed in the United States
2407